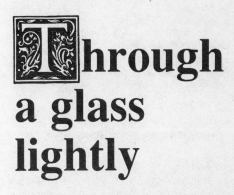

Through a glass lightly

JOHN J. TIMMERMAN

with a foreword by
Frederick Feikema Manfred

For Stuart & Thelma

with genuine affection
and the highest regard

Tim

WILLIAM B. EERDMANS PUBLISHING COMPANY
GRAND RAPIDS, MICHIGAN

Copyright © 1987 by Wm. B. Eerdmans Publishing Co.
255 Jefferson Ave. S.E., Grand Rapids, Mich. 49503
Printed in the United States of America

Library of Congress Cataloging-in-Publication Data

Timmerman, John J.
  Through a glass lightly.

  Includes index.
  1. Timmerman, John J.   2. United States — Biography.
3. Educators — United States — Biography.   I. Title.
CT275.T644A3   1987   973′.09′94   87-2977

ISBN 0-8028-0268-0

Dedication

To my beloved wife, Carolyn Jane
And to our children:

Lucarol Mathilde and Rodney John Mulder
John Hager and Patricia Lynne Timmerman
Miriam Shelley and Steven Robert Lilley
Luverne Carlyle and Velda Kay Timmerman

Contents

Foreword

This remarkable book is must reading for anyone who has ever been associated with Calvin College, as well as for those who are interested in American literature. It describes in a graceful and witty manner the odyssey of a man who was raised as a minister's son in the "bosom" of the Christian Reformed Church on the prairie, and who, after many adventures, becomes a respected and much admired professor of English in a ranking denominational college in a large city.

A doctor had almost given up on him when he was an infant in an orphanage in eastern Iowa. But a minister's wife felt sorry for the gaunt little fellow and with true womanly compassion decided to take him instead of a more lively boy who was also up for adoption. It was a wise choice. We don't find out in this book what happened to the livelier baby; but we do know, after reading this revealing autobiography, that the weaker infant became a strong and powerful voice for the good life.

The book is full of wonderful anecdotes, stories, brief incisive discussions on letters and religion, descriptions of various English departments in both denominational colleges and worldly universities, both in America and abroad, and humorous accounts of faculty meetings and impromptu bull sessions.

Timmerman has a novelist's eye for telling detail. He knows how to awaken the interest of the reader with a hint or two of foreshadowing, then builds up atmosphere, and finally gives us the arresting insight or climax. His figures of speech are always apt, right on the mark, and are of the kind that do not show off the author as a clever fellow, but are used so that they urge the reader along, "and then, and then." The reader often has to stop and go back to understand that a little bomb has burst in his brain as he was reading to help give him an ever widening understanding of the problem or the plot.

Timmerman knows his English literature and reflects it in his very style as well as in the substance of what he has to say. Chaucer has as much to do with the way he thinks and writes and lives as does Emily Dickinson. When Timmerman quotes Bacon or Pope, it is never to show off his learning, or to lean heavily on other minds to get his effects, but to illuminate his thesis or to bring more light to a scene. Presentation is all. And the presentation takes its jump from an astounding memory.

Timmerman also knows his American literature. His references to Faulkner and Hemingway and Tate are so penetrating that the reader is alerted he'd better pay close attention; and better yet, the reader finds himself hungry to look them up for further study. Timmerman's manner is infectious, lively, full of warm admiration, when he talks about a Dickinson or a De Vries. Timmerman may not always agree with the writer's religious attitude, or psychological findings, or philosophic conclusion, but he shows us that if we will look with even ordinary attention all authors have much to give us and help make our life more meaningful.

Timmerman has always had a good literary mind and has always written very well. I treasure some letters from him, written when I most needed them. They were witty letters, funny, deep. They told of books he was reading, of boredom when not conducting a class, of feeling lonesome for his family. Once he wrote me a letter telling of an excursion to a large city, writing it in the style of Samuel Pepys:

> *two shillings for a bus ticket*
> *two pence for coffee*
> *half-pence for a doughnut*
> *three ha'pence for a newspaper.*

The reason I needed those letters from him was to reassure myself that I belonged, possibly, in the company of fellows like him. He was one of my "mind heroes."

Reading this book, and his earlier books *Promises to Keep* and *Markings on a Long Journey,* I can't help but wonder what kind of novelist he might have been if he hadn't dedicated his life to the teaching of literature, to awaken sleeping minds to the beauties and visions and glimpses of a better life to be found in works of genius. Timmerman has always had the good ear for the telling comment and the lively dialogue of his day. He is always in control of his material and his selection is superb.

There is a lovely cadence in everything he writes. Even when he speaks there is a flowing cadence. And his laughter seems to have music in it. He writes that he has no ear for music, couldn't sing—but the truth is he has a natural musical bent in the way he uses words. He is one of the few men who uses polysyllabics in such a manner that the writing seems to be good, clear, Anglo-Saxon usage. It is because he thinks clearly, and he selects with exquisite judgment.

He says he had trouble parsing sentences. So did I. I still can't do it right. I have a theory about the problem: those who can parse can't write fiction or poetry or plays; those who can't parse might be able to write literature. Good writing is largely instinctive. Timmerman is a first-rate critic who doesn't write like a critic.

He became a great teacher and for that we should be thankful. There are so few of them. Without great teachers writers are lost, doomed to silence. And, we have Timmerman's three books—all of them worthy of being included in any study of literature, and especially American literature. Timmerman belongs in the company of other Calvin College writers: Meindert De Jong, David Cornel De Jong, Peter De Vries.

Here are some examples of what I mean by his selection and wit:

Reporting on what one preseminary student thought of Calvin dormitory food, Timmerman records: "Lord, we thank thee for this food. Some may enjoy it, but we do not know who they are."

"What I still marvel about is that a man who knew so much about a scintillatingly vibrant poet [Keats] could be so effortlessly dull."

"I once asked a girl in German class a question, and she replied saucily, 'Search me,' to which I replied, 'You don't want me to do that here, Miss.'"

"Aunt Jeanette . . . could sell mud at a profit."

"On one date her swain kept laughing loudly until midnight; finally I came downstairs and said, 'You get the hahaha out of here.'"

"There are also those for whom instilling grammar is like pounding a nail into stone."

"If, however, I was proved wrong, I didn't try to weasel out of it. We are all wrong at times. All that is, except theologians: they disagree but seldom admit error; they simply start another denomination."

"The long prayer is now written down and read to God."

I'd heard of John J. Timmerman before I'd met him. My mother Alice often told the story of how, when she worked as a maid for a Reverend Timmerman in Orange City, Iowa, a baby boy arrived at the Timmerman parsonage. The Timmermans had adopted the little boy and named him John. My mother spoke lovingly of him. Knowing her, I'm sure she often whispered gently down at him as she fed him the bottle. Remembering how my mother handled my younger brothers, I'm sure that when she dressed John in his baby clothes she always did it so that he'd look handsome. (I've been tempted sometimes to tease John that the reason I turned out so good was that my mother practiced baby care on him.)

I was eighteen when I finally met John. One September day in 1930, when I was in my room in the Calvin dorm, I heard through my open window the wonderful sound of a bat smacking a baseball, wood on horsehide. I was surprised. I'd heard that Calvin didn't have a baseball team. Baseball was my favorite sport; I'd played it for the Doon, Iowa, nine.

I got up from studying logic and looked out. Below on the lawn stood a slim fellow with broad shoulders, waiting for the ball to be thrown back to him. A half-dozen fellows were scattered over the far west side of the campus waiting for more fly balls to be hit to them. I watched the broad shouldered fellow catch the ball on the bounce, watched him set himself to hit another fly, tossing up the ball and then, swinging a heavy yellow taped-up bat, connecting and sending a prodigious high drive almost out to Benjamin Avenue. The way he got his shoulders and thighs into the swing, at the last second getting the powerful bulging of his muscles into it, told me there was a real ballplayer.

I was quite shy in those days. But when it came to playing baseball, that was different. All ballplayers are natural brothers. I hurried to my suitcase and dug out my old black glove and clattered down a flight of stairs and ran out to the fellow.

"Mind if I catch a few?"

The fellow looked me over. He had a wonderful head of curly brown hair and quick blue eyes. He looked at my six-foot-nine frame without a hint in it that he thought it out of line. Finally he smiled. "No, go ahead. Some of those fellows out there could use a model on how to catch a fly on the run."

I hurried out and took up a position almost on Benjamin, thinking that with his power he probably could get one over the street and then I could make a spectacular catch. I asked the nearest student with a base-ball glove, "Who's that bird hitting flies?"

"John Timmerman. Tim."

Aha. So that was the fellow my mother cared for when he was a boy. Here he was, one of the seniors living in the dorm.

I caught a few flies finally. One of them was headed for a lawn across Benjamin. The lady in the nearby house had been watching, and when she saw me pushing through some snowball bushes near her porch to catch the ball she shook her head at me disapprovingly.

A few weeks later old man Norden, the campus janitor, told us there had been complaints from the neighbors. He told us we could play catch on the campus grounds, but no more hitting flies. For a little while we then hit flies on the open ground between the dorm and the library, until one day a fly broke a window and landed on the librarian's desk. Again, no more hitting flies on the campus. After that we all went over to Franklin Park. Among those catching flies were Herman DeJong, Calvin Youngs, and several preseminarians whose names I've forgotten. Except for basketball, Calvin at that time wasn't too interested in a sports pro-gram. It has always been one of my regrets that Calvin then hadn't supported a baseball team. We had many good players during the early thirties and could have fielded a slick team.

At the end of my freshman year, when John was about to graduate, he let me know that I could write. I'd finally handed in a poem, "Breath of Neumenon," to the editors of the *Chimes*. John was on the *Chimes* staff at the time. When it was published, I was razzed about it in the dorm—what, a big fellow like me, basketball player, write poems? It didn't fit. But John, along with Henry Zylstra, told me to ignore the gibes and keep it up.

In those days John and Henry were my campus heroes. They were my intellectual stars. When I wrote it was them I wanted to please. For some reason, I had a higher regard for them as literary people than I did for Peter De Vries, who later became a famous American novelist. I wasn't always sure I could earn the praise of a John or a Henry, but I was sure going to try.

It was at the end of my junior year at Calvin, in late August 1933, that I finally felt I might have a chance of belonging to their august company. Henry and John both needed rides to Iowa where they were to begin teaching. Henry learned that I'd been asked to drive a Chevy, whose engine had been overhauled, from Grand Rapids to Doon, Iowa, my home town. A man in Grand Rapids owed Mace Klomp of Doon some money, and he finally agreed to give up his car for the debt. Mace wrote to ask if I'd drive it home for him since he'd heard I was planning to hitchhike home for a week to see my five brothers. Mace told me I wasn't to drive faster than twenty-five miles an hour with the overhauled engine the first two hundred miles. Mace also sent along a set of license plates taken from his own car in Doon. (I still wince when I think about the license plates. It was illegal. But all the boys from Iowa—Siouxland— did this in those days. We were too broke to buy temporary legitimate plates.)

I was to pick up Henry on Virginia Street where he was having a last rendezvous with Mildred Reitsema (whom he later married). When he finally bungled out to the Chevy, he said brusquely, "Move over. I'm driving! I've got to drive or I'll go nuts. Man, man, it's so hard to leave her. Now I won't see her until Christmas. Man, man!" I was a mite startled. I didn't know what kind of driver Henry was. He was born and raised in South Dakota, and South Dakotans were known to drive as if there were no stop signs or fences or city limits. I was sure that Mace Klomp wouldn't like the arrangement should he hear about it. And I want to say right here that that ride from Mildred's house to where Timmerman was staying was one of the wildest I ever experienced. I don't know how many cars we missed, or missed us, since all the way over I rode mostly with my eyes closed.

Well, when we picked up John, I somehow saw to it that I got behind the wheel, John got in back with boxes of Henry's books and clothes, and Henry settled in the passenger seat. Then we set out. It took a half day for various sphincters in my body to relax. Look—besides the wild ride, I was also responsible for the safety of what I thought at the time were the supreme brains of Calvin College.

We stopped in Benton Harbor for some coffee. That was almost a mistake. When I tried to start up that stiff motor, it wouldn't start. I hadn't driven it far enough to break it in after the overhauling. We sat a while to let it cool. I went over to a filling station to get some advice. The attendant told me I was doing the right thing. Let the motor cool off and then the expansion from the heat would contract. It was then that Henry's surging emotional nature cooled too, and we began having some wonderful conversation. But finally, when I tried to start the motor and stepped on the starter, it still wouldn't go. Henry soon spotted the trouble. That second time trying to start it, I'd forgotten, because of the wonderful talk, to turn on the ignition.

Later, toward morning, as we drove past Chicago, we'd finally driven the required two hundred miles. The motor began to purr as smooth as a sewing machine, and we relaxed even more, and took apart Aristotle and declared our love for Plato, and wondered how Bavinck would do with Socrates. Henry and John discussed various literary problems like a couple of Sam Johnsons. The two of them were gentle with me, and tried very hard to have the same tolerance for my stammering remarks that Sam Johnson had for James Boswell's irreverent sallies.

We first took Henry to Iowa City to pick up some more of his possessions, then turned northwest to Grundy Center where John was going to teach in the Grundy Center College. And after we'd deposited Timmerman in the college building, where he said he'd sleep on some chairs until morning, Henry and I rolled on to Hull, Iowa, where Henry was to teach at Western Academy. I saw Henry settled in.

Immediately lonesome, I drove on alone to Doon, where I turned in the Chevy in first-class broken-in shape to Mace Klomp, along with the illegal license plates.

That trip was one of the big turning points in my life. For the moment I'd belonged in great company. I was special. I might be able to "make" something of myself after all, create something of lasting value some day. At that.

Though I must finally confess that there are times when I wonder, when I look back at what I've "wrought" and when I consider what John and Henry have made of their lives, if I've measured up to what they expected of me. I still have a ways to go.

FREDERICK FEIKEMA MANFRED

Roundwind

Preface

William Wordsworth wrote a long poem, *The Prelude,* on the making of his mind. This book is a postlude to what happened to mine. It is a semiautobiographical story, an informal account of growing up and serving in the Christian Reformed Church, a packet of interesting persons, glimpses of vanished lifestyles, bits of history, many scenes from many places, complimentary and uncomplimentary comments, books, magazines, writers, and a host of little stories. I write little stories because, unlike my son John, I cannot write long ones. There is legitimate homesickness in the book.

I wish to thank William B. Eerdmans, Jr., for inviting me to write this book, as well as for many other kindnesses; and Jon Pott for his enthusiastic endorsement of the invitation and all the fine things he has done for me over the years. I thank *The Reformed Journal* for permission to reprint three poems, two articles, and a part of a third. I thank *Origins* for permission to reprint "Growing Up in New Jersey." I wish also to thank the relatives and friends who encouraged me to do so when I am well into the shadow line. I especially thank my wife, Carolyn, for her meticulous typing of a poor script (even after I endured boring years of practicing the Palmer method of writing), for her many helpful suggestions, and for interrupting her preoccupation with well-doing to do it.

Part I

Embers of the Past

Chapter 1

From Germany to German Valley

During the last decades of the nineteenth century millions of Europeans immigrated to the United States in pursuit of freedom, security, and religious independence. For some the dream proved a temporary nightmare in the sweat shops of New York and New England; in the ghoulish colors of big fires in the steel mills of Pennsylvania; in breaking the tough grasses of the great prairies and plains. Some died in the bleak blizzards of the West; and some, wild with loneliness in the eerie silence of great spaces, killed themselves. Yet millions of them could echo the simple words of a Michigan immigrant:

> Penniless, I entered this country 25 years ago with three small boys. Now I have a 100 acre farm all paid for and my three sons have graduated from MSU and have good jobs. All that cost me was a lot of real hard work and will power.

Millions of immigrants and millions of visions and dreams: a mother with four little children hoping for land and life; civilized, artistic Bohemians destined to sow and reap the wheat on the great farms of Nebraska and Kansas, which changed the power structure of nations; Dutchmen inured to the quiet contours of low, flat fields chopping down endless trees in Michigan; Italians from rural Sicily smarting from the acrid smells in the Paterson silk mills. Millions of individual dreams and millions of individual destinies—but all united in one dream: a richer, freer life for them and their children, a dream that this country made possible and one from which many of us here profited. Whatever was and is wrong with our country, for this opportunity we owe her great gratitude.

In 1871, in Neermoor, East Friesland, my father, Jan Timmerman, a little boy of six, was indelibly impressed by the big guns being rushed on railroad cars to the battle against France. He grew up under Bismarck, with his policy of blood and iron and the glorification of military might. His father was a carpenter of lowly estate, since he enjoyed no union benefits. His stepmother was a harsh woman who saved and savored her

3

grievances during the day until her husband, fretted by the day's work, came home, and she coerced him into severe punishment of the offending children. From his sixth to his fourteenth year, my father attended the village school, which, though publicly supported, was taught by a devout and pious Christian. I still have his diploma from that school, which proves that he was both a good student and a good boy. Apparently destined for the carpenter's trade in Germany, providence nonetheless led him to become a builder in the church in America.

The Timmerman family immigrated with its three sons, Jan, Ralph, and Henry, to the United States in 1882. Unlike most immigrants, they disembarked at the port of Baltimore. Then came the long, slow ride on the Baltimore and Ohio. The coaches clacked for many hours over the picturesque terrain of wooded and mountainous Pennsylvania, finally arriving at the feverish, smoke-filled station at Chicago. There the family boarded an Illinois Central coach to Freeport, Illinois, in the heart of the great prairies. None of them knew any English, but they had friends and relatives who lived in or near German Valley. They joined the Silver Creek Reformed church, a country church whose churchyard we once visited to find my grandfather's grave, but the lettering was so worn that it was not to be found. We did, however, notice that many graves had the legend "Der Herr Kennet Die Seinen" ("The Lord knows his own"), a truth that formed the bedrock of my father's faith.

My father's pilgrimage into the ministry was long and arduous. Already as a boy he had had intimations of this calling, but doubts about his own salvation troubled his aspirations. He was successful in his farm work, which consisted of hauling cans of milk from early morning until late in the day from isolated farms to Freeport. It was hard work, driving heavily loaded wagons over inferior roads, rutted in winter, muddy in spring, and clouded with dust in summer. He learned the rudiments of English in a little country school, a man among little boys and girls. But he had an insatiable passion for learning and a linguistic gift that later enabled him to preach in three languages, including English without the trace of an accent. In 1887 he was memorably converted, and he always considered it a remarkable coincidence that he professed his faith under Dr. N. M. Steffans, who had baptized him in Germany decades before.

In 1887, at the age of twenty-two, my father felt called to the ministry. Throughout his life he had strong convictions about that calling, and once when I talked to him about it, he said, "Don't enter the ministry unless you feel you absolutely have to." At that time, preparation for the ministry involved graduation from a four-year literary course, plus three years of seminary training (no high school was required). Since he belonged to the German Reformed Church, he enrolled in Mission House College in Franklin, Wisconsin. But he felt theologically ill at ease there; and a professor with whom he was discussing his problems snobbishly said to him, "Die Reformierte Kirche kann sich ihretwegen nicht aenderen" ("The Reformed Church cannot change itself for your sake").

The next year he enrolled at the Theological School of the Christian Reformed Church, where he was influenced for the rest of his life by Dr. Geerhardus Vos, a brilliant scholar who later became a professor at Princeton Theological School. He worked his way through those years of training by selling Bibles, books, ornate calendars, and magazines to church members in Illinois and Iowa, traveling by horse and buggy from farm to farm and village to village.

During the seminary years, after he had been granted licensure, he preached in many churches and spent the weekends at the often humble homes of the parishioners. (Once, when he preached in South Dakota, he slept in a small space partitioned off by a curtain, which the little children tugged out to peep at the preacher). In the seminary he belonged to Krans, a student organization that listened to and criticized sermons preached by fellow members. The criticism was often unsparing but nutritious. The seminary training relied heavily on memory. Dr. Vos would mimeograph his lectures, and the students would practically memorize them word for word. My father kept them all his life, and when he died, a professor from the University of Potchefstroom in South Africa was eager to buy them. It was a rigorous course, dissimilar in content and method to that of today. One had to be a B student to survive it, and I still believe that one ought to be a B student to be admitted to the seminary.

My father was graduated from the Calvin Theological School in 1895, and he accepted a call to Cincinnati, Ohio. However, he remained but a year because he felt called to the church in Wellsburg, Iowa. The Wellsburg church held services in both Dutch and German, a fact that made securing a preacher difficult and also aroused tensions between the partisans of each language. One man, who wished Dutch to be used exclusively, was elected as elder but refused to serve. My father, a mild and tactful man, simply let him sit out a year in the pew, during which conversation and conscience moved him to assume his duties.

My father was not a great orator, but he was a gifted sermonizer, pastor, and teacher. Dr. Henry Beets wrote in *The Banner* that he was a "wonderful exegete," and William Spoelhof, in an interview in the same magazine, called him "a scholar preacher." Both are accurate statements. In his youth he did a great deal of writing for *Der Reformierte Bote*. His study was his castle, the Bible the light that never fails, and Jesus Christ the great Joshua of our earthly journey. He carefully crafted his sermons and delivered them in a clear voice that reached the corners of large churches without electronic aids. He was an intellectual and a mystic who was fascinated by the numerology of Scripture. And he consistently preached the most inspiring pre-Communion services I have ever heard.

My mother's father was for some years in the German merchant marine before he became a farmer in German Valley, Illinois, where my mother was born. I saw him only once. He was a tall, mild man given to few words, an apt listener to his keen little wife, who was given to many. We once visited the small home where they retired, and I have a picture in which he towers over his tiny wife.

Unable to have children, my mother and father adopted two. My sister, Mathilda, who was twelve years older than I, they adopted as a pretty girl of five. Our difference in age and her early marriage to a Presbyterian clergyman prevented a very close relationship between us. My grandmother lived in our home almost as long as Mathilda did, and she was interested in everything—whether it was her business or not.

My mother was a noble lady, a giver not a taker. Though able to converse in three languages, an inveterate reader, and a superb minister's wife, she was clothed in humility and almost enshrined in self-sacrifice. I never saw her commit an unkind act or speak a mean word. She could, however, become angry. I remember being whipped for walloping a dog and making a nuisance of myself in church, which I had to attend three times every Sunday. Never very strong physically, she spent herself serving the church, its societies, and the sick. She assuaged the occasional sternness of my father. In the depths of the Depression, when the family was short on means, she squirreled away dollars in order to give me some spending money. She never lost her love for her adopted daughter, who would at times wait a month between writing.

Before she was fifty, mother suffered a debilitating stroke from which she never fully recovered; but she never complained. In 1938 she was suddenly stricken and died within an hour—when I was 850 miles from home. I will never forget that train ride from Paterson to Grand Rapids: images of her goodness kept me awake all night. She was buried in the New Jersey sand beside her mother. One of the boys on the baseball team I coached at Eastern Academy said to me after the funeral, "It is a good thing we know where they are." It is also a good thing that I know where that boy is, since he died in World War II.

They are all there now—father, mother, sister, and grandmother—in the true country.

Chapter 2

A Hard Way to Join a Family

Six weeks after I was born in the University Hospital in Iowa City, I was consigned to the unloving care of the Iowa Children's Home in Des Moines by Grace, my biological mother—whether with relief or regret, I do not know. What I do know is that, through the boundless grace of God, that abandonment brought me into a wonderful Christian home. There were two baby boys available for adoption when I was nine months old, a healthy boy and I, who was wasting away and looked like a starving famine victim. The doctor told my parents, "Don't take that one; he is going to die anyway." But they spent the night in a hotel thinking it over. Later, my true mother told me that she was haunted by the look in my eyes and filled with pity. They adopted me the next morning and took me on the long train ride to Orange City.

I had to be fed with great caution and very sparingly. When we arrived in my new home, they took me to their family physician, Dr. Stadt, who told them, "That kid's going to be all right; he's got a good head on him." At first I needed constant care, and the young girl who helped provide that care later became the mother of Frederick Manfred, a fact he frequently mentioned and something that has established a special rapport between us to this day. I am happy that in his superb novel *Green Earth* he gave us such a marvelous picture of this Christian saint. I am still overwhelmed by the providence of God and gratitude to the dear people who took a dying baby home and gave him unfailing love until they died.

Orange City, Iowa, in 1909 was a little town almost lost in the endless prairies. Most of the members of my father's church were survivors, sturdy people of great faith and superior intelligence who had refused to be conquered by successive waves of crop-devouring grasshoppers. In the ensuing years they became prosperous farmers and merchants, one evidence of which was the splendid parsonage they built as our home. Orange City was in Sioux County, and although the Sioux were long gone, evidences of their way of life were often found, and memories of their dominance were alive in stories. In Germany my father had read

"Indianergeschichte"; now he was on the terrain where their paints had galloped freely. The land was rankly fertile, as I often saw as I rode in a buggy over dirt roads hemmed in by corn when my father visited the sick. It was a land of larks, sunshine, and always a breeze—something rustling the crops and sometimes bending them severely. It was also a land of awesome storms, hail, and an occasional tornado. Among the devastating tornado effects I saw there were a dead horse impaled on the limb of a tree and a schoolhouse ripped to shreds. At the edge of town was the Chicago and Northwestern Railroad station, at that time the way to distant places.

The city, as it called itself, was to a large extent a Dutch town. Dutch was spoken in the stores, on the porches, in sermons and catechism classes; even the horses understood some of it. The city paper, *Volksvriend,* was a Dutch paper. It was a very civilized city: I don't remember if it even had a jail; and I never saw a drunk. The congregation was, as my father often said, well above the average in intelligence and reading habits, and some of them read Kuyper and Bavinck instead of merely displaying their works. Religion was at the core.

As a little boy, I had no awareness that our church was a citadel of conservative and exclusivistic religion. From the perspective of a boy, we were, as a church and individuals, in the infallible hands of the Lord. God's eye was upon us, especially during the three Sunday services, devotions at every meal, and evening prayers—but everywhere else also. I remember my mother saying, when some children were missing in a storm, "De Heere Jesus zal de kinderen wel bewaren" ("the Lord Jesus will surely care for the children"). Life in those days was often harsh: childhood diseases were less curable; pitiful accidents occurred on the farms; great storms ravaged the land; hail wiped out crops. Tornadoes were eerie and devastating. However, nothing—nothing at all—was outside the pattern of the Lord. Religion was a comfort in life and death, and the grave a resting place before glory.

This was the spiritual milieu as I remember it. However, for a little boy, many of the religious experiences were an exercise in tedium. Sunday was a long, long day: there were three services of an hour and a half each, and however edifying to those who understood them, they were a bore to a child who bore the additional burden of being an example. I once said to my mother, "Ik wou dat ik de kerk omschoppen kon" ("I wish I could kick the church over"). There were few interesting distractions: a howling baby appeased by breast-feeding, counting the pipes of the organ, and seeing my father shake his finger and saying "Jongens!" to restive young men in the gallery. Sometimes there was welcome news, as Mrs. R. L. Haan relates in *Centennial Year*. She reports that if threatening weather was on the horizon during the afternoon service, my father would go over to the window and remark, "It is not appropriate for us to meet this evening," and thus cancel the service.

During the school year I attended a frame building with a cupola that contained a tolling bell, which called us to school. I have only pleasant memories of the school. I liked my teacher, Miss Zoerinck, very much, and I enjoyed the company of my classmates, although I sometimes fought them, especially when someone made a brutal remark about my biological origin. I used the school pump more than once to wipe away the blood. We had Dutch lessons one day a week, and we were effortlessly bilingual. Sports were unknown in the school. All was strictly business under the principalship of Mr. Aue.

The attitude toward adopted children in 1909 differed markedly from our attitude today. Adopted children, which were few in number, were often the object of waspish remarks by the young cherubs of the church, who, when angry, were explicitly vicious. Baptism of adopted children was supposed to be delayed, according to the majority opinion, until their confession of faith, which youths usually made at the age of eighteen. But my father had enough clout and support in his church to baptize me shortly after the adoption. In fact, I remember my mother's telling me that I was the first adopted infant to be baptized in the Christian Reformed Church. For twenty-five years my father carried on a long struggle to legitimate this procedure in the church. I remember reading his thoughtfully composed and convincing overture in favor of baptizing adopted infants, which was adopted by Classis Hudson in 1928 and passed by Synod the same year. Now the baptism of adopted infants and children is commonplace, and we rejoice as we vow to promote their Christian nurture, "so help us God."

Isolated scenes from that distant past linger in my mind. One of the prominent elders of the church was a very fat man. One day he sat in a delicate reed chair in our living room, and he went through the seat onto the floor, with the chair wrapped about his middle. My father, my mother, and his wife tugged and strained to release him. I could not help bursting out into uproarious laughter. After his release, I was hurried to another room and duly informed that funny things are not always fun. One day several friends and I were playing Sioux Indians, whooping about the parsonage. My father opened the window and called, "Don't be an idiot." I understood the word to be "Indian" and was proud to be called an idiot.

Childhood images linger long: the large grove where we celebrated Fourth of July with plenty of ice cream and plenty of speeches; the black hobbyhorse my father brought home from Synod; hanging by one leg in a tree until rescued; digging deep in my sandbox and hitting the remains of a dead cat; the swirling smoke of cigars when the consistory was invited to the manse; the ripe grapes in Van Osterhout's yard; the big ice-cream

cones from Eerkes' store; trips to Sioux City and Rochester in a fancy
Pullman car. It was a world with little worry, a time without fear. It was
over in a few years, and nothing like it ever recurred.

In 1916 my father was faced with one of the most crucial dilemmas of his
life, the poignancy of divided loyalties. World War I had eliminated the
importation of German-speaking clergymen to minister to the German-
speaking churches of our denomination. Through the tireless efforts of
Dr. W. Bode, Classis Ostfriesland sought to establish preparatory
courses and a seminary to train pastors to serve this classis. My father was
asked to teach in this institution. I have letters he wrote to his friend Dr.
Henry Beets, who heartily supported this endeavor, in which my father
expressed his doubts about the viability of the institution and his competence to serve there. He faced not only a loyal congregation reluctant to
see him leave, but also a drastic reduction in salary and fringe benefits
such as free housing, and the end of work that he thoroughly enjoyed. To
move into a dubious future meant sacrifice and extremely hard work. In
one of his letters he wrote: "I do not know what to do. Pray for me that
God will make His purposes clear." Finally, after an extension of time
for consideration, he accepted the call, though his salary was to be cut 25
percent, he had to borrow money to buy a home, and there was no
certainty that the institution would survive—which it did not.
    I remember clearly the large crowd of parishioners at the little
yellow depot. As we boarded the train, the congregation was singing,
"Dat 's Heeren zegen op U daal" ("May the Lord's blessing descend
upon you"). Then the wheels of the engine slipped, took fast hold, and
the train whistle echoed over the fields as it sped away. My father spent
the next four years watching a noble dream turn into a lost cause.

Chapter 3

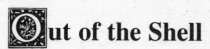

ut of the Shell

Most small Iowa towns are physically almost indistinguishable. Surrounded by cornfields on some of the most fertile soil in the world, edged on the one side by the railroad tracks and on another by the cemetery, geometrically plotted in a rectangle, irregular at the edges, bisected by a Main Street, dominated by the courthouse, streets radiating in straight lines into the country—small Iowa towns look as if one man planned them all. The big difference between Orange City and Grundy Center lay in ethnic origins. The inhabitants of Grundy Center were almost wholly of Scotch, English, and Scotch-Irish ancestry (the name Grundy is taken from a county in Scotland). There were few Germans living in the town and even fewer Dutch; the Germans who established the school lived in the countryside and other smaller towns in the vicinity. It was a distinctly American town. Dutch was used in few places outside the college church services. It was a new world for me, and I was not very brave about it.

We moved into a large and attractive house on Depot Street, which crossed a small creek—in which I once saw Prof. Diedrich Kromminga skinny-dipping early in the morning—over the Rock Island tracks and into the fields. On one side of us lived George and Vernie Canfield, who became good friends. George was a White Sox fan in the days when they were impressively good, and I am still happy when they win. On the other side lived the Biebisheimer family, distant and unapproachable. Across the street lived Isabella Dalglish, a banker's daughter and a supreme snob, whose idea of humor was to induce hiccups in class. Years later I walked past the insignificant frame house she had emerged from in all her glory, and I wondered what she had had to be snobbish about. At the corner was Main Street, like every other Main Street in the Midwest.

I enrolled in the third grade, and the teacher, Miss Graham, was one of only two of my teachers I detested. Gaunt and lanky, with a horse-like face and the temperament of a mustang, she ruled the class with tyrannical fervor, modified in queenly fashion for a few children of small-town bigwigs. My mother finally went to visit the class because she was disturbed by my jeering comments. She tried to tell the teacher that I was ill at ease as an alien surrounded by unfamiliar names, faces, and practices. Miss Graham replied that I was spoiled, a bit of manifest baloney to anyone who knew my father. I was greatly relieved, then, when the year was over, only to fall into the jaws of one even more formidable, Miss Kerr, a pretty, smallish self-appointed goddess who had no patience with imagination. I needed only to wiggle to be sent out into the hall. I spent a great deal of time in that hall thinking unChristian thoughts about Miss Kerr. And I think she passed me to get rid of me. Imagine my enduring delight, then, when in the fifth grade I had Edyth Khyl as my teacher, one of the best I ever had, a lady who led by attraction, sympathy, and imagination. She changed my report card so drastically that there was joy on Depot Street. After all these years, this shining lady touches me still.

A child's disillusionments often seem trivial to adults, but two incidents occurred in my eighth year that affected me for life. It was customary for third graders to give valentines to each other on Valentine's Day. Even at that age I had a cynical eye for such unmitigated tripe, but I wanted badly to belong; so mother and I bought and prepared some thirty valentines. I sent them to Eels, Hummel, Willoughby, and even Dalglish. The children handed their cards to Miss Graham, and she handed them out in a flurry of pseudo-affection. When the results were in, I had one card—from pretty Sarah Slosky, the daughter of a ragpicker who trundled his carts through the streets shouting, "Rags, paper, tinfoil to buy!" Sarah received one card also—from me. There we were, the German and the Jew, rejected by the small-town WASPs. That any teacher should have omitted some preparatory word about elementary fairness amazes me still. I suppose it never entered the solidified torpor of Miss Graham's mind that children could be scarred by rejection. One thing I resolved never to do when I became a teacher was to show open favoritism, even if I felt it.

The second incident occurred in a drugstore where two young men were drinking sodas. I found a five-dollar bill on the floor and, responding to my training rather than inclination, I brought it to the druggist. One of the two boys drinking soda immediately claimed to have dropped the bill. I knew he was lying, they knew he was, and I think the druggist knew; but he gave them the bill anyway. They went out laughing. The incident toned down my trust in people at an early age.

In 1917 my father bought his first and only car for $800—a Chevrolet. He was a gifted man, but driving a car was not his forte. Not that he didn't prepare: he would don driving coat and hat, goggles, gauntlets. I also doubt whether a car was ever better groomed. He drove at a slow, steady pace, peering through the windshield as though he were Captain Ahab looking for whales. Occasionally he would drive it to a preaching engagement. A trip to Holland, four miles away, consumed about twenty minutes. One time the car stopped dead a mile from town, and he sent me for help. I got it: I went to three garages, and three rescue crews descended upon him.

A drive to Marshalltown, some thirty miles distant, became a major experience. What really finished my father off, though, was the drive to Wright, Iowa, where he was to serve for the summer. Rounding a little bend in the road, he ran squarely into a herd of cows. Since he drove slowly and applied his brakes vigorously, the damage was slight. But my future brother-in-law had to drive us home at the end of the summer. During that summer my mother thought that she could learn to drive it, and she decided to rehearse in the large pasture where we kept the cow that had been donated for our use. Mother took the wheel, with my brother-in-law beside her and my sister and I in the rear seat. Father watched from the fence gate. Cows are curious, and this cow began to approach the car. Mother, as though mesmerized, drove straight toward the cow, who went loping off—with the car in pursuit and my sister and I in gales of laughter in the back. Finally my brother-in-law stopped the car. My mother had had it. After we returned, my father sold the car. For the balance of his career he walked, took the bus, or used paid help to visit the sick.

I lived in little towns surrounded by farms for thirteen years, and I later worked on a little truck farm in New Jersey, but I only lived in the country for three months. In the summer of 1918 my father served a country church, where the nearest house was almost a mile away. It was an ideal summer. I was allowed to run barefoot, and the only fear I had was of stepping into a nest of garter snakes. The parishioners gave us dozens of chickens and some amorous roosters, half of which were killed or maimed one day by a car in a cloud of dust and feathers. We spent the next day canning them, and I had to pluck the steamy feathers. The church people also gave us a friendly little pig, which I found one morning flat on his back with his four legs in the air. I buried him with regret. My brother-in-law climbed into the cupola of the church to fetch some young pigeons, which I had to part with later.

I went to the neighboring farms to watch the old-fashioned threshing machines, which were run by steam and raised clouds of particles that found their way under shirts and hats. Threshing was bone-wrenching work as the sun poured down on an open field; but it was a bountiful summer, and the farmers were prosperous. I remember a farmer showing off his car to us, saying, "Mooie car, huh?" Of course, I was a kind of genteel spectator rather than a participant in farm life. I did not have to sit beside a cow in early morning, work in the fields the whole day, and return to the cow in the evening. I was a tourist on good pay, for these Ostfrisians were most kind to us.

My last year in Grundy Center, from June 1919 to August 1920, was an enormous improvement on the previous years. The war was over, and so was the petty persecution in school, the suspicion attached to Germans, and the burdensome repetitions of German sermons in English ordered by the governor. Since the demise of the seminary—maneuvered by the Calvin Board of Trustees and necessitated by World War I—was set for June 1920, my father realized that he would need a call elsewhere, because he had no interest in the high school or the junior college. He sold our house on Depot Street at a profit, and we moved into a house with five acres of land at the opposite edge of town. The large pasture supported a Jersey cow, which my father milked. In the spring the cow produced a calf, which became a pet. In the middle of the pasture was a large apple tree that bore tasty green apples before we left. The house had no indoor toilet, and I shall never forget the penetrating chill of visiting the outside accommodations at twenty below zero.

Best of all, this was a street with friendly families: the Cheneys, Ericks, Moores, and Morrisons, each with a quiverful of children. After three years of an almost friendless existence, I had many friends. Finally, in the sixth grade, which was taught by a big-hearted lady, I began to play baseball at the school, and there are few things more likely to impress your peers than a good fastball or the ability to hit one. My last summer in the town was a great one. I remember running across the empty field opposite our house after the Sunday afternoon service, looking forward to a week instead of dreading it.

The Grundy Center library was a good one for a town of its size, especially in two respects: an abundance of children's book and a gracious, unforgettable librarian, Mrs. Holden. She knew books boys would like, and in my world at least, fortunately unfamiliar with radio and television, books were the frigate to take me lands away. I fought the Indians in Altsheler's fine boys' books, the British redcoats in Tomlinson's stories, lived in the woods with E. T. Seton's superb *Rolfe in the Woods* and *The Young Savages,* had fun with *Penrod and Sam* by Tarkington, and, best of all, romped with *Tom Sawyer* and *Huckleberry Finn.* My parents also gave me books, the *Rover Boys* series, one after the other. These books and the excellent boys' magazines of the time, *St. Nicholas Magazine,* which was not a Christmas magazine, *Boy's Life,* and *The American Boy,* brought a stir of adventure into my boyhood, where games, a rare fire, a runaway horse, or the drama of disease and death were about the only excitement around. These were magazines of high quality and published stories by gifted authors, some of them famous in American literature. The stories were rooted in human experience and human history, from drama in a small town to adventures in the forest, the frontier, the windswept coast, the buffeted ships, and the endless plains. The central characters were usually youngsters who dramatized virtues such as honesty, courage, loyalty, generosity, and simple decency in a harsh world. They were moral without sentimental stuffing and pompous lessons. They were healthy books. When I think of the sexually sick world that I, as well as many little children, now see on the television screen, I am enraged at what our culture has done to the innocence a child deserves and needs.

Grundy Center in the years 1916-1920 was a religious town, but it was not dominated by religion as Orange City had been. No church held three services on Sunday; even the college church had only two, one in Dutch and one in German. Nor could the ACLU have found any fault with the school: we had no prayers, silent or vocal, and no Bible study or Bible clubs. Dancing was taught, and in the spring the students danced around a maypole holding a ribbon. I escaped this piece of silliness as a conscientious objector, as I did the dancing. The Presbyterian church served the elite, the Baptist the conservatives, the Methodists the emotional, the German Presbyterian church the Germans in the countryside, and the Catholic church the very few Catholics around. The college church was largely comprised of students, professors, and their families, and a few local residents. I enjoyed the preaching more than I had in Orange City, not because of the density of the sermons but because of the variety of homiletical styles. I attended a little catechism class taught by William Masselink, who was a student at the seminary and whom I will describe in another chapter. He was such a kindly gentleman that some of the warmth infiltrated the catechism book. There may have been a tinge of ecumenicity in the town, though we shared little of it. The only other church I was ever in was the German Presbyterian church, where I attended Sunday school classes for a time, and where I lost a good sister to a good brother-in-law.

My father accepted a call to the Fourth Christian Reformed Church of Paterson, New Jersey in the summer of 1920. Almost all our possessions were packed on a freight car, whose journey to Paterson took an entire month. During that month we borrowed furniture and beds from the college dormitory. When the time came, Dr. W. Bode drove us to Parkersburg to board the Illinois Central to Galena, where my sister lived. On the following Monday we left for Paterson in Pullman accommodations fit for pastors. We had left a town of 1600 for a city of over 100,000—seventeen miles from the largest city in the country.

*　*　*

In 1982, on a meandering trip through Iowa for a speaking engagement, my wife and I took a detour to see Grundy Center once again. We drove up Depot Street across the Rock Island tracks, where no passengers wait. The house where Sarah Slosky lived was still there, shrunken and weathered. Farther up the street stood our old home, sharp and sturdy as ever. Carpenters in those days nailed board on board instead of uniting prefabricated sections during the night, as they do on neighboring Saginaw Avenue in Grand Rapids today. Isabella Dalglish's home was a shabby remnant from an undistinguished past. The college building had been razed, preempted by fashionable homes that were mounted by television aerials. The dormitory was a dilapidated wreck, full of broken windows through which pigeons flew; but the girls' dormitory still looked livable. Main Street looked the same, except for a Greek restaurant, which served delicious food. The public school had been replaced by modern buildings, and the fields I had played in were full of dwellings. We visited the library, looked into some old books, and found my name still on some of the cards. There were new homes in the town and new graves in the cemetery; but little towns don't really grow—they persist.

On our return from Grundy Center, we noticed signs advertising a bazaar at the Lincoln Center Christian Reformed church. I had spent a weekend there with Rev. John Schuurman and his family in the early 1930s, enjoying the fine hospitality of his wife and the excellent sermons of her husband, one of the last of our clergymen who could preach in three languages. It was fifty years since I had been there, so we asked for directions. After following them for some time, we found ourselves in a little town called Lincoln, but without the church, which I knew was in the cornfields. We were reluctantly returning to Grundy Center when my wife spied a sign lying in the ditch that said "Lincoln Center Christian Reformed Church," with an arrow pointing east, "Three Miles." We found the churchyard packed with automobiles. I told my wife that these people were Ostfrisians, reserved and shy, nothing Rotarian about them, but warm-hearted and friendly if they knew you.

Every inch of the basement was filled with tables for lunch, stands for homemade artistry, and counters with a superb variety of foods. The place, buzzing with talk as we came in, became muted suddenly as they saw us strangers. We were greeted with the reserved welcome so characteristic of Christian Reformed churches. No one was actually hostile, but some of them looked as if we had dropped in from outer space. We bought some articles, filled our plates with food, and sat down next to a man with a gift for silence. My wife, who is easily friendly, tried to talk to him, but his answering grunts put us in mind of the farmer in Grant Woods' painting, and we felt like complete intruders.

In the midst of our exile, the pastor's wife, Mrs. Hannink, one of my former students, spotted me. She greeted us with exceptional cordiality, and we could immediately feel the change in the atmosphere. She said, "I'll get my husband." The latter came decked in his best, with a sprightly bowtie chirping beneath his friendly face. He was greeted by the church members as if he were a splendid gift from the Lord, which he doubtless was. Some of the women patted him on the back; some put an arm around him. He filled his plate and sat next to us. The surly German came alive, all smiles. I was asked to go to the counter to greet another former student. Everything was changed. I have never seen such ministerial charisma: we were changed from suspect strangers to angels visiting them unawares. When we left, everybody was smiling and waving good-bye. When we got into the car, I said, "This is what the Ostfrisians are really like; all you need is a good introduction."

Chapter 4

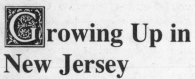rowing Up in New Jersey

The Roaring Twenties did not roar very loudly in Paterson. Although New York City, with its sheiks and shebas, jazzmen, follies, art colonies, and all that "Ain't We Got Fun," was only seventeen miles south of Paterson, it had little impact on the latter's citizens. Fitzgerald's world of Gatsby was as foreign as Arabia. A silkworker making fifty-six cents an hour had little money for razzle-dazzle. The seven Christian Reformed churches in Paterson and Prospect Park, with their solid homes, conservative churches, and Christian schools, solidified the isolation. The mercantile savvy of the Dutch profited from the transitory prosperity of the decade, and Hollanders were growing comfortable through success in real estate, insurance, business construction, and prominent positions in the mills. But their strong religious commitments eschewed worldly amusements, and their most desperate moral struggle was over the propriety of bobbed hair.

The fabulous, semimythical, flaming twenties across the Hudson were not exported to Paterson, and to write as if I were involved in a dramatic clash of moralities would be fake. What strikes me now, over sixty years later, is the astounding innocence of our generation. I never saw a movie until I was a sophomore at Calvin College, when in the company of a preseminary student I saw *Uncle Tom's Cabin*, and that was forbidden! The one feature of the 1920s that was real and decisive was the wound of the Great Depression at the end of the decade, which with its loss and fear changed permanently the relationship between the governed and the government.

I first saw Paterson from the Lackawanna Railroad station in August of 1920. On one side was the withering splendor of Lambert Castle; on the other side, in the valley, lay the compact city of Paterson, crossed and partially looped by the Passaic River, which two centuries ago, as W. C. Williams said,

Comes plunging in above the city
And crashes from the edge of the gorge
In a recoil of spray and rainbow mists.

In 1920, however, the river wound sluggishly around the city, growing increasingly murky with the varied dyes that polluted it. Gone were the big bass and giant sturgeon. It was a slow river, and I lived within four blocks of it for fourteen years, crossing it thousands of times, but never on ice. Throwing a stone across it was the mark of a strong arm. To an eleven-year-old boy who came from a small town almost lost in the endless openness of Iowa, the city had a foreign, almost exotic look. It turned out to be a city of many languages, one of which was Dutch.

In 1920, Paterson numbered about 100,000 citizens, of which 9,448 were of Dutch origin or descent. Although it was densely populated with two-story flats, it still abounded in empty lots, sandlots, and baseball diamonds—or "ovals," as we called them—on which young boys and men played baseball with taped balls and bats and new Spaulding balls and Louisville sluggers. One heard only the sharp, solid sound of wooden bats then, rather than the tinny diminuendo of aluminum bats one hears today. The streets were narrow, some poorly paved, often crowded and without traffic lights. As traffic approached the congested center of town, it was directed by policemen. The city had an extraordinarily effective system of buses crisscrossing town: from my home I could board eight bus lines to the center of town and seldom waited more than a few minutes. The city was also served by three railroads: the Erie; the New York, Susquehanna and Western, a big name with a short run to Scranton; and the Lackawanna, which ran at the edge of town. Walking to work and church was, however, as common as riding there, and our parking lot in the early twenties included horse-drawn vehicles. Our butcher, vegetable man, and milkman served us from wagons; the meat wagon was refrigerated but still well acquainted with flies. A few miles from home, in Hawthorne, Ridgewood, and Fairlawn, were numerous ten- to twelve-acre truck farms that were plowed by the same horses that transported fruit and vegetables to Market Street in the early hours of the day. In the city and suburbs lived a polyglot population who were taught English in English.

Our family—father, mother, grandmother, and I—were greeted by two elders, who took us to the parsonage in two Model T Fords. When we arrived, our new home was a prize exhibit of ministerial perks: newly painted walls, beds made, furniture in place, larder equipped. The house was large and roomy, and I could still find my way in it today in the dark. It was flanked by two lawns: one devoted to green grass and a bed of roses my father tended and from which Tony Damato would beg me to pluck him a red rose for a date (which was a risky business because my father had a phenomenal memory); the lawn on the other side was devoted to croquet and guinea pigs, which mowed it, to the janitor's chagrin. The back of the lawn was fenced in. A large peach tree that was owned by a Swiss neighbor extended a branch into our yard. The peaches were large and luscious, and I took some from time to time, until the neighbor cut the branch off. Pasquali lived next door, and every fall he would tread grapes with his bare feet; every Christmas he gave us a bottle of powerful elixir. Across the street Jimmy D'Orio practiced piano and directed a jazz band, which on summer evenings would pour the marches and waltzes of Jean Paul through our windows late in the night. Across on the other side was a large empty lot devoted to games and small fires at twilight, enlivened by mouth organs and song.

When I ventured out the first morning after our arrival, all I heard was Italian—in the neighbor's yard and on the street. Parents ordered their children around in Italian. They were tough disciplinarians: if Tony disobeyed, the father ripped off his belt and beat him in public. In our home such discipline was almost unheard of. The Italian people I saw and heard were volatile, gesticulative, given to laughter, quick temper, generosity on scant resources, and music.

My new playmates were dark-haired, dark-eyed tough little guys; I had to manufacture respect. Since they didn't know Iowa from Ohio, they readily believed that the Sioux were still riding their pintos bareback and raiding settlements, so that the horses in our church barns in western Iowa still had to be guarded by two of the fastest guns west of the Missouri, Cupido and Wiersma. Furthermore, as we played baseball, they realized the retributive power of a fastball. We became friends. I learned to admire them and their parents, and they mine. When my father was ill, some of them visited him in the hospital; when my mother was ill, there was real concern. I respected their pluck, industry, family loyalties, openness, and gift of song. In the 1940s, when my wife and I visited Paterson, we went to Santo's store, where I had bought so much lemon ice. To my wife's utter amazement, Mr. Santo not only shook my hand but kissed me on both cheeks. Growing up in Paterson owed much to my Italian connection: I saw what it meant to live on the edge of poverty with grace and good humor. I never knew a whining Italian.

Growing up in a parsonage with our family had significant advantages and disadvantages. Father, mother, and grandmother spoke Dutch, German, and English fluently. My father was a fount of German proverbs that he constantly quoted and applied. The house was filled with books, and all of us read them. But no minister lives free of worry, and the tensions of his work sometimes made my father curt and irritable. He was caught in a tangle of sermonizing, house visiting, the ill and dying, the wayward, and even the hostile. I remember that one of the Hollanders I was working with in the silk mill commented on the indolent lifestyle of the clergy, working one day a week and stealing sermons out of books.

One crusty old man who belonged to our congregation said, "Our minister doesn't do that; he makes them up himself." As a preacher's child, one had to further endure the annoyance of the alleged necessity of setting an example, with pressures from inside and outside the home. I grew so weary of being set up as a stuffed shirt yearning to don the mail of Sir Galahad that I proved my humanity by getting Cs in deportment.

The church was served by a half-cocked janitor who detested my seventy-five guinea pigs and approached hysteria when, for my father's relaxation, the consistory built him a superb chicken coop and populated it with gorgeous Rhode Island Reds, master cluckers and crowers. Now he had to put up with the detritus of two foul species. I enjoyed bouncing a ball against the step of the garage in a game called "Points." Once, when the ball crashed through a pane of the colored-glass window, he told me I was bound for the penitentiary. Church members pointed out my lapses with unfailing devotion. On the other hand, some members of the church always helped me get a summer job, and many others were unusually kind.

A minister has many tasks, some of which have curious results. Once my father had to preach at Goffle Hill Sanitarium, where one old lady ate an apple during the service and then threw the core at him. Every fall he spent six straight weeks engaged in house visitation. After he had rebuked one errant husband, the wife arose, shook her fist in his face, and said, "You leave my man alone." He had to feign appreciation at the Ladies Aid banquets, where some sweet singer of Israel always read a long poem in doggerel. He had to endure one elder who was strongly and vocally opposed to Christian education in a church almost unanimously for it; it always puzzled him that such a man could have been elected. Those were also the days when a minister paid for his own coal, lights, and telephone. Once, when everybody in the house was ill but me, I had to stoke the furnace, with the result that every radiator was steaming.

Ever since he had driven into that herd of cows in Iowa, my father dared not drive a car. During my college years I owned a Model T Ford, so during the summer I often drove father to the city hospitals. I can still see him in immaculate elegance, hat firmly held on his head by his hand, sitting in the front seat as if he were in peril—which he probably was. He was not proud of that car, and when I wanted to park it on the street for a few weeks because my brother-in-law's car would be in the garage, he insisted that I rent D'Orio's garage for that time. Unfortunately, in backing out of the garage, I chipped D'Orio's door; the latter went into Italian anger, which is something volcanic. We repaired the damage.

Between March 1926 and June 1927, my father and mother lay for eighteen weeks in the Paterson General Hospital. Grandmother died in the same hospital during mother's hospitalization, but mother was unaware of it because of her delirium. For eighteen weeks I visited that hospital every day, vacillating between fear, despair, and hope. It was a time of prayer and testing. My mother had had a cold that developed into pneumonia; that was followed by a stroke, which left her partially lame for the rest of her life. She bore that with amazing grace and without complaint, "charging within the cavalry of woe." In the delirium of her illness, she was grievously hurt that I did not bring the four kittens of her beloved cat to the hospital. It was a tragicomedy, painful to father and me. My father needed gall bladder surgery, and he was attended by one of the best surgeons in town; but he still had to spend four weeks there in preparation for the operation and three in recovery. It is inconceivable today.

My grandmother died of pneumonia. The last time I visited her, she said with a shining face, "Ich höre die Engelen singen" ("I hear the angels singing"). Her funeral was on the same afternoon I was scheduled to pitch against Eastside High School. I will never forget the munificent charity of the congregation: Mrs. H. Schultz, who walked to our house every day for three weeks until my sister arrived to make meals and help with housework; and the D. A. Kuiken family for their special kindnesses. Despite all the financial help and much lower medical costs than today, the illnesses deferred my going to college for a year, but that was as nothing compared to the survival of my parents.

In the fall of 1920, when I was eleven, I was enrolled in the Riverside Christian School, located on the lower floor of a house on Third Avenue in Paterson, backed up by a barn and usually flanked by muddy water and less savory substances. Back of that was a large field, on which we played baseball, and a hill, on which we used our sleds a few times. After having gone to school in Grundy Center with Eels, Hummel, Dalglish, and Willoughby, it was a shock to be surrounded by Tilstra, Hutting, Kuiken, and Hulsebos. Educationally, the adjustment was not easy. At Riverside the teachers were zealously committed to elaborate diagramming of sentences, and the blackboards were regularly filled with intricate patterns. I had no idea where to place a participle or gerund even if I had known what they were. The only thing that saved me from complete embarrassment was the fact that the teacher read some of my compositions as examples of good writing, innocent as they were of grammatical learning and the mystery of diagramming.

This school also believed in paddling. Some boys who threw a neatly dressed boy into the water by the barn were called to the front of class, told to bend forward, and were soundly paddled in an awestruck silence. What I appreciated in the teachers was that they read every day from an exciting story. What I squirmed under was the recurrent singing of "There Is a Green Hill Far Away," during which I moved my lips. We also had regular Bible study, at which I was expected to be more meritorious than most. I was graduated without honors in 1922.

During the following summer I worked on a small truck farm

picking cherries, tomatoes, and beans. The farmer had half a dozen acres of beans, and he paid twenty cents a bushel for picking them, a back-wrenching ordeal if one met the quota of ten bushels a day. The farmer's son did the plowing, and he would take his frustrations out on the horse, which he would beat and vituperate in two languages. Images of beaten horses still arouse painful memories in me. I have seen four horses pull wagons up the steep incline of Madison Avenue while they were whipped without pity. The land I worked on became increasingly valuable, and a friend told me recently that lots in that area now sell for $80,000 apiece, more than that farmer saw in his lifetime, although he worked from dawn until dusk and once a week went to the city market at 2 A.M. in addition.

Eastern Academy (now Eastern Christian High School), in which I was enrolled in the fall of 1922, had opened in 1920. Anyone who has read Cornelius Bontekoe's account of the first twenty-five years of its existence, *An Historical Review of Eastern Academy,* must have been poignantly moved by the initiative, courage, and generosity of its founders and early supporters. Page after page of his well-written book document the struggle and the desperate need for funds. Christian higher education in that commercial milieu had to be fought for. Its beginnings were meager: in 1923 it numbered only forty-eight students; it was housed in cramped quarters on the third floor of the North Fourth Street grammar school, and there were four teachers and a principal. The principal, who served both the high school and the grammar school, was a rigid disciplinarian, short on temper and long on misunderstanding high school students. The grammar school students marched from class to class as if they were in a military youth corps. He had a ruler and used it. He was also a self-appointed linguist who maintained that "food" should rhyme with "good" and pronounced "food" that way in the Lord's Prayer. He expelled Frank Holwerda and me for a week for throwing at and catching a golf ball from the front steps. Frank was not a pliable student. Once the principal attempted to hit him, and he said, "You do that again and I'll nail you." We spent two years there with its playground crowded with little children. There was nothing in the way of extracurricular activities.

All this changed in 1924 with the appointment of W. G. Roozeboom as principal and the shift to a remodeled house on North Seventh Street. Roozeboom had an extraordinarily winning personality, uncommon ability as a teacher, outstanding musical talent, and the ability to attract students and charm their parents. He transformed indifference into esprit de corps and made the school a happy place and an indelible memory. He made history live: I remember his saying, "I could paint the colonies black," and then doing it with fervor and imagination. I remember with gratitude three of the other teachers. Miss Bell taught us Latin and English; she was a gentle, competent lady who suffered us philistines with a smile and good humor. High school English teachers generally did not then have the excellent textbooks they do now. Halleck's *History of*

English Literature was exactly that—a red book with a lively style, good quotations, and a biographical emphasis that sparked in me a lifelong interest in literature.

John James Ahasuerus Ploos Van Amstel came from distinguished Dutch forebears. He taught English, German, algebra, geometry, and whatever else necessity demanded. He was a sprightly teacher with homiletical tendencies. But he could get angry, and he once said to an incessant whisperer in our third-floor quarters, "Shut up or I'll throw you out of the window." I took a year of biology with Mr. E. Kuizema. I remember two things: memorizing endless lists of the Latin names for insects, and the ringing laughter when he began an illustration by saying, "Take a pea, for example." In my senior year I more or less wandered into an elective that he taught, commercial law. I still remember that course with real pleasure: it taught me accuracy and logical thinking.

We had chapel every day, including one I will never forget. One of our clergymen had the habit of asking rhetorical questions and then waiting and waiting for the congregation to ponder it. He waited so long on this occasion that several boys burst out laughing. He walked down from the platform and resoundingly slapped one of them and returned to the platform as if it were a part of the talk. It is a better school now, but it remains in my experience an age of innocence: no alcohol, drugs, pregnant girls, dancing, or even movies. The wildest worldly entertainment was beamed from WOR featuring the Happiness Boys, Ernie Jones, and Billie Hare. It was a world within a world, where baseball was our greatest diversion.

By the time I was graduated, Eastern Academy had almost tripled in size. The student body was well above average academically, since those who disdained further education procured "working papers" at the age of fourteen and went into the mills and commercial pursuits. Among the ablest students was Floyd Fortuin, who clamored for Virgil, whereas most of us were relieved to escape Caesar. He had a phenomenal memory and an inquiring, original mind. He came from a distinguished and idiosyncratic family in whose presence dullness was nonexistent. At one dinner when I was there, the father trending into prolonged prayer was interrupted by "time's up!" Once I accompanied Father Fortuin and his partner, Mr. Van Goor, to Brooklyn. The back seat caught fire from my pipe. We stopped in the tunnel and stamped the fire out, and Mr. Fortuin said, "Never mind, it's covered by insurance." We played gin rummy on many occasions, once through a whole night. Floyd's brother Henry and I took many long walks together.

The Paterson silk mills were strikingly different from the well-appointed factories of today. They were simply buildings to work in, wholly functional and correspondingly dreary. I spent three summers and a period of almost a year working in these mills. I saw and felt the world of unskilled labor with its monotony, hazards, and low pay. There were no unions, no medical insurance, no unemployment compensation—and no way to escape the tyranny of the boss, if that was his nature. I worked for an Italian with a flaming temper, which sometimes resulted in cuffing, and I saw an elder of our church kick a slow workman in the rump. One of my jobs was to pull the ends of ninety feet of silk out of a steaming tub and feed it into a bag—over and over from six to six—beside a murky window along which the greasy water of the Passaic River inched by.

For almost a year I worked for a Christian gentleman in a clean, well-lighted room sewing together pieces of silk destined for the print shop, where the aristocrats of the silk industry worked. Some of these pieces were worth six dollars a yard, so the printing had to be meticulously accurate. Ahead of me worked Jimmy Iandoli, a born singer, who would sing long arias of Italian operas while he worked. The workers there made between $.46 and $.56 an hour. During one month we worked from 7:30 A.M. to 9 P.M., with a free lunch and a dollar a day bonus. The vast majority of workers were immigrants, and they had it better in these silk mills than in Sicily or the Netherlands. But they were being rooked, and they were impotent. The prosperity of the 1920s never trickled down to them, and the Great Depression plunged them into fear and misery.

Religion did not dominate Paterson as it did Orange City, Iowa, but it dominated the lives of the Christian Reformed churches in Paterson and neighboring areas. A remarkable consensus of faith and practice prevailed at that time: There were no liberals to fight, no bitter controversies; even the gradual transition from Dutch to English in the churches where this occurred was peacefully accomplished. Sunday services were rigidly structured and the sermons metronomically similar in a tripartite division. The church was a place of worship and instruction; every activity reinforced the nature of the heavenly country and its imperatives for living in ours. There was one notable difference between their church services and ours today: the absence of loudspeakers. A clergyman had to have lung power and clear enunciation. Furthermore, the preachers were not riveted to electronic devices, and this permitted the exercise of some of their more dramatic instincts. Ministers of that day had more authority and less salary than they do now, and they were allowed less vacation. Parishioners were expected at both services and warned and visited if they did not come. Sermons were more minatory than they are today—and more daring in criticism.

The seven churches in Paterson and Prospect Park numbered 4,210 souls in 1929; by 1985 the number of churches was down to six, and the number of souls was down to 1,683. Churches and their members had moved to other suburbs; many of them moved to faraway places, and the homogeneity of these churches diminished. In the 1920s all seven churches were within walking distance of each other, and since for a large portion of that decade my father's church had no evening services, I visited all of those who did have services. There was no television, few radios, only rook players, and relatively few readers. So young people from our church often attended other churches at night, not necessarily for spiritual growth but out of curiosity and the hope of meeting new acquaintances in the parade of young people on Haledon Avenue and the streets of the borough. I was always expected to report on the text; the problems arose with remembering the exegesis, which was sometimes murky—at least to me. If one walked a young lady home, one was never invited in. When one was invited in, the acquaintance assumed serious dimensions. Surprisingly, I remember visiting a non-Christian Reformed church only once, not because it was forbidden but because it was simply never contemplated. We were a genuinely adhesive group: these evening services were well attended not only by the bald and greying but also by naturally blonde and brunette. A church of one hundred families then would draw a much larger crowd than one of three hundred does today. *Optima dies—prima fugit.*

Baseball and boxing were the national sports in the Roaring Twenties. The sandlots were used from March to late September, and the teams were numerous: junior teams, uniformed church teams, independent teams, teams supported by business enterprises, and two professional teams of uncommon competence—the Peerless Plush and the Paterson Silk Sox. At about fourteen I played with the Parkways. Eastern Academy had its first team in 1925, and the uniforms were furnished by Lambert Steen, whose family will always be associated with baseball for me. I pitched to Peter Steen, who died an early and tragic death; John Steen was our coach in my senior year; I played on a team with Herman Steen; and Barney Steen played first base for the team I coached in 1938. John Steen organized a team he called the College Allstars (at least we were all college students). We played the Midland Park Rangers, whose pitcher, Johnny Vander Meer, went on to become the only major-league pitcher ever to pitch successive no-hit games. He was a fearsome pitcher: he was fast and he was wild. You were not only afraid of being struck out but of being struck, and the latter fear often caused the former. The games were largely financed by passing the hat, and the crowds at many games were sizable.

Baseball was not only a fascination in itself; it also widened my associations with society outside our exclusivistic Dutch community. Without it, I would never have had friends with diverse ethnic backgrounds and names like Schillinger, Wentink, Terry, Brewer, Granito, "Yankee" Renzo, "Porky" DeLucio, and the like. I once played with a team that was almost wholly Italian. The game was umpired by a member of our church. He made a distressing call, and almost the whole team went for him—and he went for Fairlawn. Baseball taught us the values of loyalty, sacrifice, and endurance. It is saddening to see professional baseball caving in to greed and substance abuse.

As one grows older and less engrossed by contemporary pressures, images of the past—often with startling clarity—flash through the mind. Time collapses, and I am pumping up the long, hard slope of Haledon Avenue on my heavy Ranger bicycle, walking in the picturesque woodland beside Squawbrook Creek, standing outside Courthouse Square watching the posting of the World Series scores. I remember hurrying home from a twelve-hour day in the mill and then pitching for seven innings:

> *What cared this body for wind and weather*
> *When youth and I lived in it together.*

I see and hear the sadness caused by the death of little three-year-old Luigi, a favorite of the block. Mr. Giminetti rushes from the house, while Mrs. Giminetti pours a bucket of soapy water over him. There he lies still, the drunken oculist whom Bill Spoelhof and I carried home on Fifth Avenue. His wife gave us each a half a dollar, and we looked for him again and again.

The home we lived in was moved, the church burned down, my parents lie in Fairlawn cemetery; but the ties to them all are unbroken. In that home and church and in those schools I lived in two countries, both real today. George Bernard Shaw once said that it is too bad that youth is wasted on the young, but it wasn't wasted on me. As far as a minister's son can have a hometown, mine was Paterson. In a stanza from Housman lie my sentiments for that city:

> *That is the land of lost content.*
> *I see it shining plain.*
> *The happy highways where I went*
> *and cannot come again.*

Chapter 5

olden Branch
among the Shadows"

In the early decades of this century my father went frequently to Grand
Rapids as a curator of the board of the Theological School. He meticulously recorded the expenses he incurred on these trips in a little red
booklet I still have. The trip from Orange City to Chicago cost $12.25; a
tip to the porter, .25; travel from the Chicago & Northwestern Station to
the Pere Marquette, .50; from Chicago to Grand Rapids, $3.55; parlor car
and diner, $1.65; cab to his host's house, .50; streetcar fares, .60; cigar,
.10; paper .05. On a later trip, the fare from Orange City to Chicago had
risen to $14.50; a hotel in Chicago was $4.05, and the trip to Grand
Rapids $4.55. While in Grand Rapids he spent $42.00 on paper, which I
think was for the booklets in which he wrote his sermons. In the fall of
1927, when I rode from Paterson to Grand Rapids, the train fare for
approximately the same mileage as Orange City to Grand Rapids was
$27.63, which held steady for many years.

The Theological School was then located on the corner of Franklin
and Madison. It was later renovated and added to by Grand Rapids
Christian High; it is now rubble somewhere, and its place is occupied by
the city's Social Services. In 1927 the college provided a milieu with a
distinct cultural and spiritual atmosphere, born of two traditions rooted in
the Old World—maintained, expanded, challenged, and modified in the
New.

In 1876 a small, poor, and humble people in a strange land established a theological school, and then successively an academy, a junior
college, and in 1920 a college. They were in many ways attached to the
culture of their old homeland; but they were citizens of an often bewilder-
ing new land, and they profoundly believed themselves to be citizens of
the kingdom of God. Between this kingdom and the secular world there
was a profound antithesis, which demanded a form of education on all
levels that would be uniquely designed to meet the demands of both
kingdoms. One group, the descendants of the *Afscheiding* in the Netherlands, viewed education essentially as a caretaking operation, devoted to
an unaltered transmission of the Reformed faith with minimal dilution by

28

worldly culture, and unfortunately sometimes tending to identify the antithesis with ancestral habits. The other group, the *Doleantie,* also believed in the antithesis; but they saw education not as flight but as conquest, not safety but bold appropriation of the fruits of common grace, which when properly mediated by the believer required him to modify or conquer the culture around him. These two impulses for many years lived in uneasy alliance, even at times in opposition, but until the 1930s no word was more pervasively influential at Calvin College, whether in bold prominence or quiet remembrance, than *antithesis.*

The pervasive emphasis on the antithesis did not diminish the appreciation for learning or produce an index of forbidden books or a cowering from challenge. In the classroom it resulted in the search for truth from alien sources and a critical appraisal of fundamental religious options. Some teachers did this brilliantly, some rather feebly, but they all did it. Calvin College then, as afterwards, emphasized the best that had been thought and written. Although only six of the eighteen professors held doctorates, all but two of the rest had master's degrees or their equivalent. The teachers were well acquainted with scholarly habits, and almost all insisted on rigorous work. One of those who did not compensated for it in illumination. Calvin graduates were admirably prepared for university studies beyond Calvin, and many of them enhanced its academic reputation. I think most of the students would have agreed that they were well prepared in their majors, confronted by the deep questions, nurtured in the Reformed faith, and given a genuine liberal education. There were, of course, real or self-appointed geniuses who would dispute that, but I think I state correctly the attitude of the vast majority of students.

The emphasis on the antithesis was also apparent in the insistence on chapel attendance. There was little surveillance in those days. Prof. Rooks wandered around occasionally, checking likely retreats; but in actuality there was little disciplinary action. There always were inveterate skippers, but chapel was generally well attended. A far greater proportion of the whole student body attended than do today. In fact, in actual numbers there were often more students attending daily chapel at Calvin then than there are today in a college ten times its size.

Chapel services varied. Occasionally, clergymen and celebrities were invited to speak, but most of the sessions were conducted by faculty members. Those humble enough to recognize their ineptitude at public speech regularly devoted the session to song, Scripture reading, and prayer. Others, however, spoke frequently. I remember a fascinating series of talks by Prof. Johannes Broene on the personalities of the apostles. Prof. Vanden Bosch always spoke. He was a meticulous man, almost fussily neat. Annoyed at the litter dropped in the building, he once spoke on the text "Let him that is filthy be filthy still." Dr. Peter Hoekstra often illuminated Scripture passages with historical data. Prof. Rooks gave his talks in the Oxford accent he had acquired in Graafschap. Dr. Ralph Stob spoke on the same topic for quite a while, and he always assumed that the students remembered the content of the preceding speech. Prof. Nieuwdorp, a fine mathematician, gave several talks on the "Stahrs."

In those days each preseminary student had to give a chapel talk. One of them gave a very funny talk on the "dead languages," in which he inveighed against their disinterment. One brilliant presem relied on extemporaneous inspiration: he spoke on "pioneering," but he floundered in the tall grasses. He was later scolded by Dr. Jellema, whose talks were models of preparation and meaning. At its best, chapel was spiritual refreshment; at the lowest level it was a rendezvous, a brief date, a study period, or a time for sleep. For most it was an activity to participate in, not something to escape. It was a boon not a bore. Students did not often skip chapel; and neither did the professors.

The antithesis failed in the matter of amusements. Many leaders of the church demanded abstinence from movies, card-playing, and dancing. These are dead chestnuts today; but in the 1920s these prohibitions, questionable in theory and unenforceable in practice, were on the books. I never saw either card-playing or dancing at Calvin, though I heard about the latter. Movie attendance was another matter. Often somebody in the dormitory would holler, "Who's going to the Wealthy [theater]?" and a group would gather. The fact is that many Christian students saw no evil in attending a good motion picture. In 1928 there were movies you could take your mother to. The students broke the rule as a silly one; some faculty members felt the same way but observed it. This rule triggered more dissimulation than did anything else at Calvin.

The first movie I ever saw was *Uncle Tom's Cabin* in 1928. I went to see it on the invitation of a preseminary student, a gentleman who has since served our church with devotion for a lifetime. The theater was a place some went to nonchalantly and some with guilt attenuating or intensifying their enjoyment; some sneaked in, and some bought their tickets defiantly. For some time, students had to sign pledges not to attend. Were it not for the profound convictions of the church leaders, rooted in their idea of loyalty to the Lord, the insistence on the rule would now seem to have been much ado about nothing. In the 1920s, the defense of movie attendance cost Prof. B. K. Kuiper his seminary post.

As a freshman, I took board and room at the home of Mrs. Kuiper, the mother of Rev. H. J. Kuiper. She rented out two rooms, one to me and the other to Hero Bratt. It was the best room I ever rented as a student. She also had a sort of dog called Sport, but the latter did not appreciate the sport we had with him. She was a very frank old lady. The first time I washed my hair, she noticed that it retained its prior appearance and said, "I thought you curled it." Hero and I enjoyed each other's company, and we walked many miles back and forth to the public library. That year the library offered a series of lectures by distinguished scholars, among them the famous Mark Wenley of the University of Michigan. I have never seen a better demolition job than he did on a cocky question by a Calvin Seminary student.

The next year I roomed with a tight old lady who had belonged to one of my father's churches. Sometimes she served hot dogs for my Sabbath dinner; and when I went to the library, she would shut off the heat in the room. She also had very small light bulbs in the sockets. I bought an electric heater and larger bulbs, which I secreted into my room to use when I studied there. I left at the end of the semester to room at the home of Mrs. Wheeler, an Irish Catholic, the soul of kindness. She left little dishes of fruit on my desk all fall. I got my meals at the dormitory for $4.50 a week.

The last year I roomed at the dormitory. Fortunately, I was teaching a section of Freshman German, so I could afford a single room. I wanted to be a part of that beehive for one year at least. The Calvin dormitory was a home away from home for about eighty students. Except for their common religious background, they were as piquantly varied in personality, capabilities, and attitudes as any group I have ever associated with. They were almost all Dutch, but the Dutch are not noted for monotonous unanimity. They ranged from the outstandingly brilliant and pertinaciously studious to bonvivants and those who knew how to waste an hour well. There were the ultrapious who seemed already poised in the prestige of the pulpit, and there were the bed-wreckers, the room-dishevelers, and pranksters. And, of course, there were the stolid mediocrities who faithfully attended every class and managed to maintain a C average.

One preseminary student imported little bombs the size of golf balls, and another presem dropped them from the third floor to the first, where they erupted like thunder. All ate the food, but one offered this concluding prayer: "Lord we thank Thee for this food. Some may enjoy it, but we do not know who they are." There were the boasters, one of whom was pushed under a shower and forced to take off his suit, which was then hung high on the tree near the door to freeze. Telephone pranksters had fun calling up strangers: one called up a Pole on the west side and told him he had a hundred sheep to take to the market and offered the man a job. Two students went to a naive gentleman and told him they were collecting money for the victims of the moth inundation of Vladivostok. He gave them a quarter. Bull sessions abounded, some solid sense and others mostly bull. It was a place where good students got their work done, and malingerers had a good time.

Pranks on the campus ranged from amazing ingenuity to the edge of cruelty. Prior to one chapel session, some students planted carefully timed alarm clocks; as the speaker began his address, they went off a few minutes apart from various places in the chapel. The statue of Moses at the door of the chapel was an irresistible target. Sometimes he wore a cap, then scarves and vests; and sometimes a hat and a cigar stuck in his mouth. Coats were thrown on him as students hurried into chapel. The most outrageous prank was played on a young man with a brilliant mind, one on whom flattery could be laid with a trowel. He was almost a prodigy in Greek and Latin. He also thought he was a singer: he had a high tenor voice, and he sang songs to Briz Hiemstra's syncopated beat. We convinced him that he should sing over the radio and that the song should be "There's A Wee Hous 'Mong the Heather." He practiced it in his room and in the empty chapel. He was told that arrangements had been made with WOOD radio to broadcast from the chapel, and the appropriate electronic gear was brought in surreptitiously. The time of performance was set, but the dean heard about it and canceled all arrangements. Fortunately, the student believed another explanation for the cancellation.

One student called up Rev. H. J. Kuiper and arranged an interview with him to discuss the heavy doubts he had about his faith. Rev. Kuiper consented, and the student came to his study under an assumed but real name. Later he felt remorse about it and apologized to Rev. Kuiper. He was forgiven in a gracious Christian manner. President Ralph Stob was wont on occasion to visit dormitorians unannounced. By some sly means, some students found out where he intended to go on one of these visits, and they rigged up a bucket of water. It fell and drenched the president as he entered the room. This event was an extracurricular project of a preseminarian. One student who had a taste for good cigars but could not afford them invented recurring doubts about his faith, which brought him to the home of Dr. Meeter; he was always sent on his way rejoicing, puffing on a good one.

In 1927 seventeen professors taught 320 students in a college almost wholly supported by the Christian Reformed Church. Tuition was $100 a year for students from Grand Rapids, $75 for those from Paterson, and even less for those from more distant places. There were no scholarships, and student aid came in the form of pay for serving in the kitchen, sweeping floors, and shoveling coal. There were a few names like Yared, Washington, and Uhl, but the student body was overwhelmingly Dutch.

Professors taught fifteen hours a week. There were two professorial offices, usually unoccupied, and counseling was nonexistent except when asked for. Professors prepared their studies at home, filled their briefcases with the results, emptied the contents out in class, and hurried back. The only professor's home I was ever in was President R. B. Kuiper's. He had a sense of humor; he invited some students who had pilfered apples in the dormitory over on a Sunday evening and gave them apples. Professors were much more distant then than they are now, and the only really approachable professors I had were Dr. W. H. Jellema and Prof. H. J. VanAndel. The rest were not unfriendly; they were just aloof. On the whole, they practiced what Prof. Johannes Broene preached when he said, "The faculty is the heart of the college." It did indeed move the institution, but it did not move about with its students.

During my college years I took courses taught by eleven of the seventeen teachers. All of them taught me something, though in one case it was very little; some of them taught me so much that they enriched and inspired me not for a semester but for a lifetime. Dr. Jellema, with his winning personality, acute mind, and inimitable skill as a teacher, acquainted me not only with the great minds but also developed in me a mind to think with in order to assess other minds. Dr. Ralph Stob was a superb teacher of Greek who individualized his teaching by bearing down on the mistakes of his students until they were corrected. He also taught a fine course in Greek culture attended by just Lewis Grotenhuis, John Verbrugge, and me; he prepared for it and taught it as though there were fifty of us. One day, when the Depression was deepening and whom you knew counted for as much as what you knew, he said, "If at first you don't succeed, suck, suck, suck, till you do succeed." Pitched in his high nasal voice, it was a truth I never forgot.

Prof. VanAndel was man of many talents: historian, art teacher, musician, and Dutch teacher when he did not pursue his amusing digressions. Late in life he became enamored of the *Wetsidee* philosophy of Dooyeweerd and Vollenhoven, and when he came toward me, I knew that the sixteen categories of sphere sovereignty were not far behind. Prof. Johannes Broene, a soft-spoken man with the polish of an Oxford don, illuminated the history of education in language notable for its precision and color. From him I learned the allurements of biography. Dr. Peter Hoekstra, stern until you knew him, taught history in detail; from him I learned how to master detail as well as how to interpret it. Dr. Hoekstra almost always sat down while lecturing, and Prof. A. E. Broene always sat down. When he had to write on the blackboard, he leaned backward to do it—in imminent peril of tumbling. I took five courses in German literature with him, and that stimulated my permanent interest in the subject. His lectures were models of organization; I wish some of them had been in German. Only one of the courses was easy, and all of them prepared me well for graduate study.

Prof. J. G. Vanden Bosch taught me in more courses than any two other professors—eleven in all, two of them in the year I was forced by the Depression to obtain a teacher's certificate. He was the one man on the faculty who could be called a "character"—independent, unpredictable, aloof yet kindly, quirky, impassioned, often intolerant and even hypercritical of small mistakes, reserved yet hospitable. His chapel talks emanated a touching piety; his witness to his Lord was loud and clear, as was his hostility toward views he alleged another faculty member was disseminating. He was a friend of my father and once visited us at our home in Grand Rapids, where he inveighed against the teachings of this professor, whom I admired. He was the best reader of poetry I ever had as a teacher. I think he was torn between aestheticism and Puritanism—and reacted in terms of the latter. He was an abrupt man who could walk away in the middle of a conversation. Sometimes he would call me up and, when he had learned what he wanted, simply hang up. Yet when I was accidentally hit by a baseball bat at a ballgame, he was one of the first to visit me. When I was about to leave for the Netherlands, he called to express his wish that I not go, and he wrote me several long letters while I was there. He gave me high grades, but he never encouraged me to go on to graduate school. When I was nervous and nonplused about giving my first chapel talk at Calvin, I went to him for a suggestion. I wondered whether it would be fitting to relate some of the life of John Keats to a text. He said no and walked away. One day he flabbergasted me by saying, "John, you are too popular." Prof. Vanden Bosch was an enigma to me to the end, when my wife and I visited him in the loneliness of the nursing home. He taught me a great deal, especially in a splendid course called "Principles of Literature," and also, surprisingly enough, in a course on the Romantic poets. I cherish the memory of this unique man, who carried an intolerable number of courses with competence and a memorable, if sometimes intrusive, Christian emphasis.

Calvin was a very clubby college. There were nineteen organized and sponsored clubs in 1931. There were also clubs that arose by spontaneous combustion, among them the Conblos and the Friggers, described in the *Prism* by somebody, probably Peter De Vries, as:

> A contrivance by which a grain of intelligence is amplified into a bushel of nonsense. Low on batteries, yet plenty of volume.

However, most of the clubs were serious, diligent, and genuinely educational. Almost every discipline had a club. There were two clubs for philosophy, one for men and one for women, both sponsored by Dr. Jellema. The clubs included a Literary Club, a Dutch Club, International Relations Club, Biology and Chemistry clubs. There was the K.K.Q. (Kalvin Kulture Questors), composed of a dozen girls who said, "Every now and then we throw a jolly party." Nil Nisi Verum (nothing but the truth) must have been a difficult club to gain admission to and contribute to. The Knickerbocker Club was founded to perpetuate Dutch "tradition and heritages," and it humbly announced that "it has far surpassed the hopes of its founders." The Pre-Sem Club was interested in "excellent speeches and good fellowship." It congratulated itself on good speakers, "fairly good attendance, and excellent doughnuts." Then there was a club called Prattones Didaskomen, which, according to a learned note I received from Dr. Robert Otten, literally means "Doing we teach." The members asserted that through their activities they "have been truly bound to one another." There was also the Men's Glee Club, which represented Calvin "in a most commendable manner," and a Ladies' Glee Club, which had "memorable experiences that are destined to become rosy legends." The Chemistry Club bound its members "to nature and anatomy," and the Knicker Club had "another brilliant year."

I devote a separate paragraph to the Neo-Pickwickians, who met in bizarre places to read papers on the writers whose names they assumed as club members. The members of the club were thus St. Francis, Izaak Walton, Rabelais, Tolstoi, Turgenev, Aristophanes, Sophocles, Boccaccio, Dickens, Omar Khayyam, Villon, and Confucius. We met in the cupola of the college, the restroom of the Morton Hotel, the Union Station, a consistory room, and other odd quarters. Seven of the members later became college teachers—at Calvin, the University of Arizona, the University of California, and the University of Michigan; one became a professor at Calvin Seminary; two became clergymen—one in the Christian Reformed, the other in the Orthodox Presbyterian Church; one became an editor; one became highly successful in sugar; one became a judge; one died while a student at Westminster Seminary; and the last member became a successful and vocal right-wing Republican. Our sponsor was Dr. Ryskamp, whose geniality, wisdom, and graciousness maintained order and intellectual results. In the spirit of scribes I have quoted above, "'Twas a great club, and all the papers were first-rate."

An activity I greatly missed at Calvin was baseball. For a time we played on the field bordering the dormitory, but the broken windows on Benjamin Avenue obliterated that. Then we played on the empty field between the dormitory and the library. When I hit a ball that broke through a window and bounced over the head of the librarian, President Kuiper had had enough. "Kid" Venhuizen, who was a superb basketball player, organized a sort of team and we played a few games. Fred Feikema (now known as Frederick Manfred) was also on that team; he was a good player, as was George Stob, and our makeshift team was not wholly ineffective.

Though it was never advertised as an ideal or objective, many of the students and their parents hoped that the college would provide suitable in-laws. My good friend Abel Poel arranged several dates—all blind for me. He had connections and maneuvered a double date to take two girls from the southwest side of town to Bethel Christian Reformed church and then home for coffee and lunch. The girls were Zena and Trena Piet, but I don't remember which Piet I escorted. Lewis Grotenhuis set up such a date with two Polish girls from the west side who were showpieces of stupidity and swallowed the wildest nonsense with blank faces. I told them that Calvin students were so studious that they wore a path from the administration building to the library into the sidewalk so deep that only their heads showed above the bordering grass. I also informed them that Calvin students never wasted time. If they were thirsty in the library, they would press a button and a cup of cold water would come to their seat on a line suspended above the table. Abel Poel was a one-man dating bureau, and I, of course, had pleasant dates at Calvin; but they are married now and so am I.

The *Chimes* in the 1920s was a monthly that featured outdated news, stately editorials, now dated humor, satire, and protests. The editorials had titles like "Aim Straight," "Fatness of Soul," and "Preface to an Unwritten Book." The editor was elected by the student body, and the magazine was supported by advertisements and student subscriptions at $1.50 a year. When I was editor, I appointed Mildred Reitsma, George Stob, Henry Zylstra, and Bill Frankena as assistant editors. During that year Dr. Hepp, a short, pudgy professor from the Vrije Universiteit, gave a Stone Lecture entitled "Calvinism and the Astronomical Conception of the Universe." Bill Frankena wrote a blisteringly satirical review of that address: Hepp in some cases, he asserted, "says nothing new," in others "proves nothing and is merely amusing." Further on he said, "Hepp does not verify any hypothesis that Calvinism might make; hence he brings us no further." Sometimes Hepp seemed to be getting somewhere, "but after all only seems to." Hepp promised in his title to present "the world image of the Calvinist"; but this, says Frankena, "we have not yet learned from Dr. Hepp." I include this because I vividly recall the lordly attitude of the man and the appropriateness of the recoil. Our sponsor was Prof. Vanden Bosch, and, except for pointing out a comma fault in my first editorial, he said nothing about the paper during the rest of the year. We treated innocuous subjects uninnocuously.

All this changed in the fall of 1930, when Peter De Vries became editor. He brought journalism to Calvin College: he made *Chimes* a weekly, jazzed up the contents, and took on everybody, beginning with the Board of Trustees. Probably for the first time, people other than the contributors would anticipate publication of the next issue. At the end of the first semester, however, De Vries resigned, ostensibly on account of ill health. It was regrettable because he was doubtless one of the ablest editors of *Chimes,* and he later became the most famous. He expunged the general stodginess, electrified some of the prose besides his own, and in addition was a most colorful person to work with. Except for the late sixties, *Chimes* never achieved such brashness, competence, and readability.

I think it would be difficult for Calvin students today to even imagine the college chapel jammed to hear either an intercollegiate debate or an oratorical contest, but that was the case in the 1920s. The only debate I attended at Calvin while I *taught* there was held in a classroom with about twenty people in attendance. In the twenties Calvin debated prestigious college teams and often won. Such debaters as Bill Frankena, Henry Zylstra, Henry Stob, and Vernon Roelofs were sharp and eloquent. In oratory, Peter De Vries was singularly successful: he

won the state extempore contest at Michigan State, the state peace oratorical contest three times in a row, and he took third place in the
Michigan Colleges Oratorical contest before a record-breaking crowd at
Calvin's chapel. It was a contest whose results were swathed in humor. I
was at that contest, and it was clear to me and the rest of the audience that
Peter had won it. We later heard through a leak from one of the judges that
all the judges but one had given Peter first place. We could only guess at
the identity of the dissenting judge. I admired and envied the talents of the
men and women who enhanced Calvin's reputation, and I am sorry that
these activities have become so minor at the college today.

Prism has had a long history and undergone drastic changes. The
college is now over ten times the size it was in my student days, and
intimacy, picturesque comment, literary selections, and dedication to
faculty members is impossible. In the 1920s, the photographs were
devoted to college personnel and scenes. In later years they came to
include shots of visiting celebrities, street scenes, birds on wires, foreign
faces, and many pictures published for photographic skill rather than for
memorial interest. The *Prism* of my day printed beside the portraits
quotations designed to encapsulate the nature of the graduate. Here are a
few of them: for a tenor, "Lo, the peep of day"; for a recluse, "And
singular am I"; for an over-eater, "Better fed than taught"; for a girl
chaser, "A Man of all Hours"; and for a wise guy, "The wit we long for
spoils the wit we have." On the other hand, and more affirmatively, "A
scholar and a ripe and good one"; "Thy modesty is a candle to thy merit";
"Where he falls short, it is nature's fault only"; "She is all so slight/so
tender and white/as a May morning." One of the most striking: "Let no
man write my epitaph; no man can write my epitaph." But the prize was
printed beside the name of an egoist: "Hence ye profane, I hate ye all."
Let no one think that selecting all these quotations was a tiny task.

Calvin College years were a golden time, and one of the reasons
they proved to be so was my acquisition of a Model T Ford for transportation to and from the college. The Model T was not a thing of beauty, nor
did it last forever; but it was a tough car until it literally fell apart. It was
little more than an oblong box with seats, covered by a roof and flanked
by running boards for entrance and luggage. Curtains shielded the passengers from rain and a little of the cold and the wind. The hood opened
from the sides. It was economical on gas and easily repaired. Its $350
price was within the average man's income, and the introduction of
installment buying made sales zoom. Ungainly and uncomfortable, it
changed the economy and the face of the country.

Sinclair Lewis wrote: "To George F. Babbitt, and to most of the
prosperous citizens of Zenith, his motor car was poetry and tragedy, love
and heroism"—a fitting accolade to the mind of George F. Babbitt. The
motor car, whether a humble Ford or a Pierce Arrow, provided a new
freedom and a new work force; it put a sneer on the faces of the affluent

and longing in the eyes of the poor; it filled with delight those accustomed to the pace and sight of the rear end of a horse; it sprouted suburbs, enlarged the highway system, and doomed the passenger trains. The automobile was a major status symbol: if you earned $1,500 a year, you bought a Ford; if you made a little more, a Chevrolet; then as your income waxed, a Dodge, a Reo, and finally, a Packard Twin Six. Imports were as scarce then as American-made motorcycles are now.

In 1928, I bought a 1924 Model T for $40. Its original price was around $350, and it had a lot more than $40 worth of car in it. It was sturdy, efficient, and as aesthetically appealing and as functional as a pitchfork. It was open to wind and weather, though curtains could be fastened to mitigate both, and it had a horn that was much more powerful than that of the car I now own. It was started by cranking, a risky business that could and sometimes did break arms with its backspin; and unless one had someone inside to monitor the gas flow, it was at times difficult to start. Its average speed on level ground was about forty miles per hour, although if one allowed it to coast down a long hill *and* shut the engine off, one might end up with insufficient braking power. Mine was not a car one took on a date; for that I relied on the superior vehicles of friends like John Hamersma or Joe Memmelaar.

What astounds and even frightens me today is that I drove that car without a driver's license or insurance through Toledo, Cleveland, Buffalo, and New York City. A driver's license was unnecessary at that time in Michigan; and I confess I never thought about insurance. Fortunately, I was involved in only one minor accident. Coming around a sharp bend on a Pennsylvania road, I saw almost directly before me a long freight train. There were no stop signs on the road, and I had heard no whistle—and in those days of steam trains one could hear whistles far away. There was one old jalopy waiting for the train to pass. I had the choice of ramming the train or the jalopy. So I skidded into the jalopy and bent the fender. The driver, a grizzled, calm man, got out and looked at the damage. I asked him, "How much do I owe you?" He replied, "Two bucks," which I gladly gave him.

In the twenties, except near and through large cities, all the highways had but two lanes. On the level we could easily be passed, but on steep grades faster cars found us a nuisance. On U.S. 6 two lanes presented a real problem: that route's winding up what seemed mountainous slopes to us, but to a westerner mere hills, caused the radiator to boil and finally erupt with steam that encircled the car. We would have to stop and wait until the engine cooled off. Worst of all was being preceded by a groaning truck. The car could not move quickly enough to pass; so again we would have to wait for the steam to subside. On one long hill the low gear weakened, and we turned the car around and backed up the hill—to the toots and jeers of other cars. U.S. 6 is now a slow, almost a side road; but the dense forests it cut through in the twenties and the stunning views it provided from the tops of high hills were scenes I have not forgotten.

Abel Poel bought my second-hand Model T for me, and I had my first driving lesson bringing it back to Grand Rapids from Grand Haven. That was my driver's training course, and Poel gave me a B. He accompanied me on my first trip from Grand Rapids to Paterson, and he did all the difficult driving straight through the big cities. In those days U.S. 20—now U.S. 80—was paved with brick, a most enduring way to build roads (at least by the example of Wealthy Street in Grand Rapids, which carries perpetually heavy traffic on the same bricks it used in the twenties). Driving through large cities not only meant maneuvering for position but an endless succession of traffic lights, a time-consuming business. We slept in the car, in a hayfield, and once in a haystack in Vermont, whose owner charged us a dollar. From Vermont we rolled into New York, and as we neared Central Park, the radiator boiled over. We parked. In those days, there were no underwater sprinkling systems; Central Park was watered by a hose that drew its water from a large water wagon. After the radiator cooled, the driver of the wagon kindly drove over and filled our radiator. Abel drove down to the old Chambers Street ferry, and the Ford rested in the bowels of that huge boat.

The next fall I drove back to Grand Rapids with Leonard Haan, for whom I called at an early hour in Midland Park. Rev. R. L. Haan was up and about also, and we retired to his study for admonition and prayer. On the way, the large cars would always pass us, and Leonard would say, "Don't let it bother you, they stop for a long lunch."

The car, as I said, was not a satisfactory vehicle for a date, but I was pressured into using it. During the winter I lived near a student who had a wooden leg. He was an interesting chap with illusions of philosophical aptitude. On stormy days or in the case of icy streets I would help him walk to school. He was always trying to express his gratitude by arranging a date for me with his beautiful sister, whose intellectual endowments, however, did not match her physical pulchritude. Finally he succeeded. I had a double date with Henry Zylstra, who took out the daughter of the president of the college. With today's three programs a day, access with untainted conscience to all kinds of films, and evidently enough money to attend them, such a date would hardly be a problem. Henry, however, was the president of our class, and the young lady was the daughter of the man who had written a book entitled *On Being Reformed*, which was in deadly earnest against worldliness. We decided to take our dates to Lowell for coffee, sundaes, and conversation. It sounds "chintzy" today, but there was little money, and merely going to the Deluxe Cafe seemed too penurious. The ladies were the best of sports about what was probably the least impressive car either had ever ridden in.

My friend with the wooden leg always had money, and he used to say that he had an "angle" in Chicago, whatever that was. But before summer vacation that year, he borrowed twenty dollars from me. Nothing came until late in August, when I received an envelope with a blank piece of paper in it and a twenty-dollar bill.

During the same spring, Lewis Grotenhuis and I took the car out for a test. Lewis, a medium-sized young man who wore a moustache and sometimes a monocle, was accustomed to moving through the dormitory halls saying, "Gangway, gangway, here comes Lewie." And when Lewie came, one was in the best of company. We drove along the dirt roads winding through the woods bordering Reeds Lake, which were wet with sizable puddles of water. Then we came to a hollow where the water was at least three feet deep. We turned the car around with real skill. As we were about to move away, a car came toward us from the opposite side of the large pool. The driver, evidently thinking we had just gone through, drove without undue haste straight into the water and was immobilized there, with water reaching his windows. There he was, marooned in a bit of tragicomedy so grotesquely funny that we nearly burst with laughing. He could not get out without being soaked to the waist with muddy water, and there was no way to help him. Help had to be obtained eventually from the outside in the form of proper equipment.

Students have told me that in the years before the 55-mile-an-hour speed limit they could drive to Paterson in sixteen hours. I doubt whether they can now—not if they go through Pennsylvania. In the twenties this was completely impossible. The fastest time I ever made on that trip was thirty-six hours, with only necessary, brief stops. We regarded it as something of a feat.

On the final trip, we took what was then Route 17, a gloriously picturesque ride and a memorable trip. I had four passengers: Bill Spoelhof, later president of Calvin College; his gifted brother and a good friend of mine, Henry; Carl Becker; and William "Briz" Hiemstra. Briz was a razzle-dazzle jazzman, a kind of Calvin Liberace who would play by ear as long as the demand lasted. He was a desultory student with unimpressive results, but one forgot that when he hit the keys. I often wondered what happened to him in life, until one day when I was teaching at Calvin, a taxi stopped in front of our house and Briz came in. He stayed for an hour while the taxi meter ticked away. He had become a salesman for Rath Packing Company; selling was obviously more lucrative than teaching "Follow the Gleam."

On this final trip in the car, we enjoyed dinner and beds at the home of the Bruinsma family in Rochester, New York, and "Briz" provided the entertainment. When one is young, one takes such generous hospitality somewhat for granted; as one grows old, one realizes how few times in a long life such hospitality was proffered and enjoyed.

The long drive from Rochester to Grand Rapids was largely on level ground, and we averaged about forty miles an hour. It was fortunate that we did, for the car developed signs of failure as evening approached.

The battery was dying: the horn was a bare squeak, and the lights were hardly discernible. We arrived at the dormitory, where the failing brakes scarcely brought us to a stop just before dark. I had no further use for the car, but Henry Stob, philosopher and preseminary student at that time, did. He was working his way through college by hauling ashes to the dump on Saturdays. I sold the car to him for $5, and he repaired the ailments. Then it performed a noble service until it too joined that waste heap.

Today Calvin's old campus is in other hands—good hands. The faculty members who taught us there are no longer living, but they have left us an enduring legacy of illumination and inspiration. Although some peripheral loyalties have vanished, the essential loyalties remain both in most of its alumni and their successors. Learning was leavened with Christian perspectives and at times with moving piety. I never ride by the old campus without a surge of reminiscence. I see the old familiar faces, I hear the sound of many voices, and I relive the unfathomably precious tone of youth. One of the last songs we sang in chapel just prior to graduation was "God Be with You till We Meet Again"—here or in a better country. He has been with us, and he always will be.

Chapter 6

Maize and Blue

On a dismal Friday in October 1929, the Stock Market collapsed. Millionaires found themselves poor, and the poor were plunged into peril. A quarter of the American work force was unemployed by 1931, and farmers received eight cents a bushel for corn, which they often burned for fuel with stricken conscience. Long lines of forlorn men and women waited for great periods at soup kitchens. There was no welfare system, and individuals, churches, and private agencies exhausted their means. Millions of formerly hardworking Americans were immobilized in corroding idleness. A few made money during these years, but they were rare. Factories stood silent, cottages were boarded up in summer, and teachers were often paid in food and services. The same dresses and trousers were worn to shreds. The roads and the railroads were full of wanderers seeking rides to possible work or just to keep moving. America was in one of its darkest hours.

When I entered the graduate school of the University of Michigan, the Depression was actually a year away for me. I was not a greatly concerned spectator. Though my father had taken a voluntary cut of 20 percent in pay and had lost much of his savings, we were far from poor. Furthermore, my fellowship at Michigan paid my tuition and $42.50 a month. Although it sounds unbelievable today, on that stipend one could rent a private room, buy meals and books, and still have a little left. Many students were poor, however, subsisting on meager food and peanuts. Jobs for students were almost unobtainable; typists received fifty cents an hour, and the one time I had a paper typed with many German quotations, the typist produced such a wretched product that I typed the other papers myself. What surprised me was that the football stadium was always packed.

In 1931, Ann Arbor was a city of about 20,000 inhabitants dominated by the university, then as now, more widely known as a football power than as one of our best universities. Already at that time Calvin graduates enjoyed an enviable reputation at the university, and there were quite a number in the professional schools and the graduate school when I

42

enrolled. A part of Calvin formed an island in the sea of students. I obtained a room on North Ingalls, now razed in favor of a university building. On the first floor four Calvin alumni roomed together. Among them was Bill Frankena, whom I knew as a brilliant student at Calvin, and whose powers of concentration astonished me here. He could work at his desk for long hours despite the activities surrounding him. That he later became chairman of the University of Michigan Philosophy Department was no surprise to me. Jack Van Vessem, a former Calvin basketball star, lived there also—an ebullient, campus-wise history major who would write out the questions expected on the final examination and almost always hit the mark. He was a good friend with a keen sense of humor. The University was for him a way of outwitting the Depression rather than a way to learned monographs. Jack was one of three people in my life who voluntarily offered to loan me money when I needed it. Among the girls he dated was a drawling Southern girl with big glasses who loved "Moonlight and Watah." Vernon Roelofs, an excellent history student, also lived there. They all added much to the congeniality of life. In that respect, the year I spent at Michigan was totally different from the years I spent at Northwestern.

I had five teachers at Michigan, none better than the best at Calvin and one considerably poorer. They were all admirable scholars, and several had written important books. Prof. Parker, whose year-long course in aesthetics I found fascinating, was the most accomplished lecturer I ever had. His lectures were precise, gracefully phrased, lucid, and delivered from a few cards that he rarely consulted. The class was very large, and I was sorry that its size made personal contact almost impossible. But since Parker was the embodiment of courtesy, I made bold to make an appointment with him in his office just to know him a little better. His basic definition of art was "an imaginative satisfaction of desire," which, though often fitting, is also often unfitting. I preserved the notes I took in his class until I retired and lost the use of a large attic, which housed so many things I wish I could have kept.

The course for which I did by far the most work was a seminar in Rhetoric and Literary Criticism. It was taught by Prof. Roy Cowden, a middle-sized man with a round face, which he would twist oddly while lecturing. He was the director of the prestigious Hopwood Awards for original writing, sponsored and inspired the splendid historical novel *The Loon Feather* by Iola Fuller, and had been host and friend of Robert Frost during his year as resident poet at the University of Michigan. In our first semester each student had to present an extensive paper on some aspect of literary criticism. The final examination consisted of one question: "How would you organize a course in literary criticism and why?" The class was composed of very able people, from Giovani Giovaninni to Katherine Swift, and peer pressure kept one working hard.

In the second semester of this course our papers compared the stated or implied critical theories of writers with the original manuscripts of published works. I read most of the novels of Thomas Hardy and all the poems and prefaces. The book I used to illustrate Hardy's practice in the light of stated or implied theories was *Tess of the D'Urbervilles*. Hardy actually made few alterations in his manuscripts and hardly wavered from his theories. Shelley, on the other hand, wrote twelve versions of "To a Skylark," which in reading appears as effortless as a bird song. My paper ran to seventy-five pages, and among the things I learned in writing it and handing it in for assessment was one dramatic lesson. Prof. Cowden misplaced the entire paper, and I had made no carbon copy. When I was writing my dissertation at Northwestern, Dr. Faverty lost a chapter. He was profusely apologetic, but I was delighted to have made another copy. I also understood the consummate agony Carlyle must have experienced when the family maid carelessly burned his huge manuscript of *The History of the French Revolution*. I marvel yet at the indomitable spirit that enabled him to rewrite it. No wonder he suffered from dyspepsia.

Chaucer is a fountain of humor, wit, wisdom, narrative skill, characterization, troublesome doubt, irony, medieval lore, and Christian insight. Prof. Reinhard, a very able man, was my teacher in two courses on Chaucer. He was a little man with a formidable moustache, a bent back, a gruff voice and manner, and an intimidating style of teaching. He was a linguist and an etymologist par excellence: he traced words as far as possible—to the point of pedantry. He seldom talked about Chaucer's art or the medieval perspective that pervades the work; he had learning but lacked poetic sensibility. The first semester's class had forty students, the second eight. During the entire year we did not even complete the *Canterbury Tales*. He never gave compliments; he limited them to good grades. The apex of Reinhard's friendliness was when he said, "Hello, Timmerman" to me when I met him. He was a somewhat surly old bachelor who immured himself against loneliness by unfriendliness. He was a distinguished scholar, but the gentleman was in his learning.

Prof. Thorpe, with whom I took a seminar in Romantic criticism, was an authority on John Keats. What I still marvel about is that a man who knew so much about such a scintillatingly vibrant poet could be so effortlessly dull. It almost seemed as though he worked at it: his lectures were readings from his book on Keats. And he was much given to satirical asides on other Keats scholars, the one ray of life in his presentation. During one discussion on a student paper he said, "If you don't believe me, read my book." It was a colorless seminar. When a professor exudes dullness, the papers seem to be infected by it. Furthermore, he was as tough as a marine sergeant: for the final examination, a take-home test, we had to comment on a host of passages taken from assigned readings. It was the hardest test I was ever given, and I took about a week to prepare it. His meticulous exactitude appeared in the mark I received: B++. Why not A–? Ironically, this man was the only professor who invited the entire seminar of about fifteen students to his home, where he proved to be a most genial and generous host. Unlike Reinhard, he was a scholar and a gentleman.

I found myself in a bizarre situation during the period of examinations. A student by the name of Worfel roomed next door to me. He was taking a German course, a language for which he had a lamentable ineptitude, and I would help him from time to time. During his final examination the ineptitude confronted him. He burst into my room with a bruised, taped, and still bleeding nose. He had deliberately punished himself in the nose, been excused, and then rushed to my room for German aid. How could I refuse? Later, in his gratitude, Worfel offered to arrange a date with a Wilma Morrison, whom he described as a beauty. Since his own girl's picture showed extremely good taste, I agreed. The date was arranged, and Wilma turned out to be rotund everywhere, with tightly curled hair and big glasses—a blind date for the blind. This was the last blind date I ever agreed to. Worfel had opened my eyes and rooked me.

The year at Michigan was a memorably enriching one: some great teachers, a superb library, good companions in an interesting town. What I missed most was religious commitment and perspective in the classroom and the communion of our church. The Christian Reformed Church did not then have a flourishing church with a stimulating pastor in Ann Arbor. Once a month a Christian Reformed minister came to preach at the student union. But I found the other churches in Ann Arbor disappointing, so I was largely thrown on my own personal devotions. In later years I have often reflected on the risk of sending freshmen from our churches to the great neutral and impersonal institutions of learning when fine Christian colleges are available. Extraliterary judgments were totally absent, and I encountered some wrenching spiritual problems. For a time I was much influenced by I. A. Richards' *Principles of Literary Criticism,* a thoroughly naturalistic perspective. Furthermore, being immersed for weeks in the somber pessimism of books like Hardy's *Jude the Obscure* and *The Dynasts* created a mood not easily exorcised. However, I valued the experience and am in debt to a magnificent institution, the University of Michigan.

Chapter 7

Brother, Can You Spare a Dime?"

It is difficult to write about the Great Depression, because everyone who has experienced it thinks he has had a tougher time than you did. Since fellowships were very scarce in 1932, I accepted a position at Grundy Junior College, which Mrs. Rutgers, wife of the president of the college, once rightly called "a school that isn't a school." We had sixty students and six teachers, and that ratio was the only respect in which we resembled Harvard. The school had no library. I thought that after fourteen years it would have had a respectable number of books, that it would have inherited at least a library or two from deceased ministers. In the first year there was not even a table for the *Des Moines Register* or the *Grundy Republican*. The attractive building contained six large classrooms and a small office with a tattered chair and an empty safe. The building was heated by an old furnace, which on cold days shook the building. The dormitory was disintegrating, and the gymnasium floor billowed up and down. The college was well shaded, with a campus that was large enough for baseball but featured a cow instead. It was flanked by dirt roads, where eddies of dust lingered after passing cars. It was little more than Hopkins' log school without Hopkins—the final flicker of a dying dream.

After living in metropolitan areas for thirteen years, I was struck by the quiet of the place. About once an hour a car rattled past my window. There was not a student who owned a car, and only two faculty members did. During my second year there, the college owned a cow, which supplied milk for the meals served in the college basement. Grundy Center was a decent, respectable town with six churches and a good library for a town of its size, managed by an affable, knowledgeable lady who helped our students in their search for materials for term papers. Except for the Depression, there was little to worry about: Hoover was in the White House, and everybody expected Landon to be there next; there were no commies in the cornfields and no menace from the skies. There were no troublesome minorities, no junkies, no drugs, not even a visible town drunk. The major leagues in baseball were still functioning.

I taught seventeen hours a week, but the small size of some of the classes made that less of a burden. I had to teach a year of philosophy, but I had the aid of excellent notes and two excellent texts. One of them was Stace's *History of Greek Philosophy,* which for lucidity I have never seen surpassed in a text. More than half of the students were non-Dutch and non-German, with names like Stark, Brockway, Cheney, and Rayburn. There were about a dozen Baptists, who impressed me permanently with their abilities and confessional openness. They were honestly pious with enthusiasm. Except for a few local loudmouths, who left after the first semester, the students worked hard for and at their education. They were attractive people—modest, industrious, and appreciative. I had none of the superlatively gifted students I later had at Calvin College, no jaunty sophisticates, soulful artists, or philosophical "whizzes." But I taught them in one of the most pleasant classrooms I have ever enjoyed: the morning sun poured into four large windows, and there was never the need for perpetual lighting or a submergence into sunless rooms in the basement of a building.

My most difficult book to teach was the text in Freshman English. I had no hand in choosing it, and no time or power for burning it. I wish now that I had a copy left to illustrate its inadequacies. It tried to teach graceful writing by means of a soporific and wooden style. It was intended to be used a year, but whatever good one could acquire from it would have been consumed in a month. I was forced to invent a supplementary text. Furthermore, there was no book of helpful readings and no money to buy one. I think I assigned and corrected more compositions in that class than I ever did later in my career. It was a hard year. Fortunately, I had excellent texts in both first- and second-year German.

Since the school was so small—it dwindled to forty students the second semester and never exceeded forty-five the second year—I remember many of the students. I once asked a girl in German class a question, and she replied saucily, "Search me," to which I replied, "You don't want me to do that here, Miss _____." Wilson Cheney was a cheerful, chunky redhead who simply could not learn to pronounce certain German sounds. Anne Hook was a hefty peroxide blonde who could play boogie-woogie with the best of them. Ed Tiesma was a good pitcher, so good that he was later drafted by the Chicago White Sox, who buried him in the minor leagues. Duane Griesy looked and acted like his name. There were also gifted students like Nancy DeBruyn, the Schelling sisters, and Chester Brockway, who became an excellent Baptist clergyman.

The times were out of joint and money almost out of sight. As the western winter approached, some friends donated sixty tons of coal to the college. The poor filled a bushel here and a bushel there; but filled coal cars were not immune to theft, and we could spare none of it. We were determined to keep that coal; so Jack Heerema and I sat on the back seat of his father's car playing gin rummy until 4 A.M. with a loaded shotgun on the floor. The next day the coal was delivered to the homes of the college president, two of the teachers, and to the college; Jack and I received money instead. When the college had a campaign for funds in the town, they raised $50. To make matters worse, at the opening of the school year the Austinville bank grabbed $450 to pay a debt. When President Roosevelt declared a bank holiday, I received $13 for a month's work. Bill Kingma, who had a wife and a child, was in even more dire circumstances. I would draw money out of my Paterson bank account to help him with his rent until he was paid again. The whole year cost me $75 of my own money, earned at Cramer and King Silk Company.

Even at that, my experiences were not as trying as those of the young ladies with two years of college and no teacher training courses; they taught in the rural schoolhouses for $30 a month. One teacher who had an A.B. from Calvin College was hired for $30 a month, but his contract was canceled in favor of one who would teach for $29. These people taught all eight grades, hoping the little ones would learn to read and that the eighth graders would pass the state examination. They came early through snow, rain, and sleet to build a coal fire in a stove that warmed the center of the room but hardly the edges. They ate lunch out of a dinner pail. They kept the room clean and the naughty quiet—or tried to. They worked hard and did so with a smile. After all these years I admire their spunk and dedication.

Grundy Center would have been impossible if I had not been able to get out of it once a week, and the only way to a change of scene was hitchhiking. The roads in the early thirties contained all kinds: college students, the homeless poor, the aventuresome, even families. Everywhere was the doggerel of Burma Shave to cheer a hiker:

> *Does your husband misbehave*
> *Grunt and grumble, rant and rave*
> *Shoot the brute some Burma Shave.*

Sometimes there were a dozen hands beckoning at a city's edge. Little America, Young America, and even Senior America were on the pick-up trail. Times were friendlier then, sympathy more general, hoodlums scarce, and trust common. Professor Rooks once picked me up and then dropped me off at a berry patch, which cars passed at sixty miles an hour. After a long wait, a car stopped with four ladies in it. They put me between two sizable ones in the back seat. They were a jolly, generous lot: they shared their lunches with me and dropped me off at the Loop in Chicago. I have hitchhiked thousands of miles: I once got a ride from Elkhart, Indiana to Towanda, Pennsylvania; a man from Oklahoma picked me up and said, "I want to sleep, you drive the car." I sat next to one driver who carried a large pistol in the inside pocket of a jacket; I rode with a man who turned out to be a drunk, and when he saw a statue of George Washington in a town said "Good old Georgie," and drove for it while I grabbed the wheel. I once received a ride of fourteen miles at eighty miles an hour during an entire day and I waited until evening when I joined two Westminster College students in catching a freight to Wheeling, West Virginia. One time I had to walk seventeen miles to my sister's home through falling snow.

In all my hitchhiking I never saw a hobo. They traveled on freight cars: above them, between them, in them, and under them. Their disheveled appearance and ramshackle clothes intimidated people. They were free spirits or hounded spirits, always on the move. We had them at our door more than once, even in Grand Rapids when we lived near the Grand Trunk tracks. They would tip their caps to my wife and get some sandwiches. When our address became known to them, they came more frequently. They were a seedy but picturesque group of men dedicated to a life of roaming, a breed disappearing when freights travel at eighty miles an hour.

I suppose there are many who, like me, feel guilt when we whiz by hitchhikers today. We have enjoyed so many free rides. I remember how many boys used to hitchhike to Grand Rapids from Ann Arbor for the weekend. Love drew them there, and kindness provided the way. I have passed hitchhikers waiting in lonely places in Wyoming, beckoning at the edge of cities, and in the city of Grand Rapids. Unless I knew them, I did not pick them up. Our fears overcome our gratitude. The trust of the thirties and forties has eroded, and we pass them by with sadness and discomfort.

Grundy Center, a good place to be, had to be escaped from at times. Walking through Grundy Center was only exercise. Since I had no money to buy books, the only places I could get the books I wanted to read were the two good libraries of Waterloo, Iowa, thirty miles away. I hitchhiked there almost every Saturday. Some of the delightful books I borrowed I still remember: *Gallion's Reach* and *All Our Yesterdays* by H. M. Tomlinson, a distinguished writer now largely forgotten, and the enthralling *Good Companions* by J. B. Priestly. There I discovered and read all the plays Eugene O'Neill had then written. I read Maugham, Galsworthy, Chesterton, and many others. I owe much to those libraries.

At the end of the summer I became acquainted with a Model A Ford that belonged to a friend of Frederick Manfred, who had secured an illegitimate license plate to drive it from Grand Rapids to Hull, Iowa. Fred had arranged passage for Henry Zylstra on his way to a teaching position in Western Academy, and for me to return to idyllic Grundy Center. By the time Fred and Henry picked me up near midnight, the car was already sagging with luggage. Fred was six-nine, Henry six-four, and I six feet. Henry and Fred were jammed into the front seat, and I squeezed into the back, which was already well packed—as were the running boards. Conversation and storytelling were so brisk that by the time we reached Benton Harbor, we needed coffee and doughnuts. When

Fred tried to start the car again, the starter ground and ground but to no avail. Since it was now about four in the morning, we tried to take a nap. In the morning Fred hitchhiked for help, but his intimidating height made for slow service. Finally the trouble was solved.

Fred drove the car through the heavy traffic on the crowded highway around Chicago. Then we rode through the endless cornfields of Illinois, miles upon miles of huge fields. I was so cramped in the back seat that I put my legs out of the window. It was late twilight when we reached Iowa City, where we had to take on additional luggage for Henry. If we had been in a boat, we would have had to bail out water. But Fred drove on in the blackness of night, on through more cornfields and small towns until we reached Grundy Center at about 4 A.M. I pried open a window in the college and slept on the floor until daylight.

As Henry told me later, Fred drove all the way to Hull, Iowa, another two hundred miles—talking, laughing, and smoking. Fred drove every inch of the way—some thirty-six hours of driving. This is characteristic of the giantism of his physique, person, and perseverance. The one thing Fred never did was quit: discouragement, critical illness, and a very slow rise to prominence could not block his way to his present corpus of twenty-three books. He is still writing books and planning others, and he has the vitality to speak on numerous occasions at considerable distance. There is something of the majesty of the oak about his person and work.

In the spring of 1933, Dr. Rutgers accepted a call to Chicago, and the board appointed Bill Kingma as acting president for one year. He and the faculty did everything they could to assure the survival of the school, but the Depression was deepening, and that spring was ungracious from the beginning. Huge clouds of dust from the Dakotas swirled over the town, at times becoming so thick that cars had their lights on in broad daylight. Mounds of dust lay in gulleys, and the corn drooped and withered under a burning sky. Drought and dust extinguished the school. Though it opened in the fall, only fifteen students enrolled; the teachers who were still there—which did not include me—worked for the government at fifteen dollars a week.

The college building ended with a bang that spring of 1934, when a severe storm blew the chimney and half the roof off. Bill Kingma was to give the commencement speech, but his wife gave birth to a child, and he was unable to. In one of the strange twists of fate, I spoke in his stead at Grundy College's last commencement—in the same chapel where my father had given an address at its beginning.

The next day Verda Mae Wilson, a student, drove me and my trunk to Parkersburg, Iowa to board the Illinois Central to Chicago, the same station and railroad our family had deported and traveled on twelve years before. I waited on the platform of that little station for the whistle one could hear for miles in the still night air and for the slithering, steam-enveloped stop of the engine. I was leaving an unforgettable past for an unknown future.

* * *

When I left Grundy College, I had about fifty dollars in cash and $800 in worthless bonds. There was no place to go but home, where, as Frost says, "When you have to go there, they have to take you in." Fortunately, my parents, who had retired there in 1933, welcomed me with love and sympathy. During that summer I sought work at all the school systems in Grand Rapids and its suburbs. Through the clout of a board member of the Grand Rapids public school system, I got an interview with its superintendent. He had just finished lunch and was engulfed in the aroma of Blue Ribbon beer. During the interview his head began to nod, and he fell asleep. What was I to do? Jolt him awake, silently sneak away, or wait until a bad dream woke him up? He finally awoke, embarrassed and sulky. The interview came to nothing; every interview came to nothing.

I soon perceived that I would have to procure a Michigan certificate to teach. So after three years of teaching, I reenrolled at Calvin College to get a teaching certificate. Through the good offices of Professors Vanden Bosch and Jellema, as well as the favorable impression I had made on President Stob while taking his courses, I was offered free tuition and $200 for teaching a course in freshman English. And through the generosity of Vanden Bosch, the class included the students with the highest grades on an achievement test. I am still grateful for that class. They were all good, but I especially remember James Prins, who later taught at Hope College, William Vander Ploeg, our family physician for many years, John VanAndel, Clazina Baker, and Miss Edwards (where she came from and whither she went I do not know, but she was one first-rate scholar). To augment my income I taught two catechism classes, a job tough enough to test the mettle of Socrates; and I marked papers for Miss Timmer, who was a little irritated by the comments I wrote on some of the papers.

I had attended catechism classes for many years, and I had seen an assistant to my father shake a boy up with impeccable vigor, but I was not prepared for the lion's den I was to brave. The class was large and was quite literally everywhere. Some boys had crawled under the seats, and one had managed to ascend the hot water pipes; there was a tornado of babble. I felt like walking out, but I needed the two dollars a session, so I began hauling and pulling until everyone was seated. Then I opened with prayer and tried to teach. My predecessor, I was later told, managed the class by hollering louder than anyone else. Finally, I thought, forget the consequences, and I cuffed one of the boys and hurried him out of the room. When I told this to Carolyn, my future wife, she said: "Don't

worry about it; if his parents find out, he will be hit a lot harder at home."
The fact was that the boys were showing off, the subject matter was
obtusely formulated, and I realized that methods that had worked in my
father's church would not work here. I offered to teach the boys and girls
in separate classes, and I changed my methods. After that, the class was
still no island of joy on a Saturday morning, but the work got done—
though these classes were the low point of my teaching experience. I did
not have rapport with these boys and girls of twelve to fourteen. Some
years later I taught a class of high school seniors and a few college
students, with whom I had a most enjoyable experience. Ever since then,
I have admired a minister who can preach a good sermon and a good
children's sermon, for I could never have done both.

Among the education courses I had to take was "Observation and
Practice Teaching," taught by an opinionated man who often confused
animation and inspiration. During the first semester we had to observe
teachers in action and write reports on their teaching. For some reason,
my assignments were limited to public schools and Catholic Junior College. I don't know whether the teachers were paid for these intrusions,
but they were all hospitable and helpful. Some of them were excellent,
especially a nun at the Catholic Junior College. Some were frankly mediocre, and I am glad that the necessarily acidulous reports, which the
professor called "striking," were not revealed to them. During the second semester we had to fashion lesson plans, far-fetched exercises in an
imaginary series of questions and anticipated answers, a mechanical,
wooden artifact that any imaginative teacher would find stultifying.
These imaginary dialogues had to be preceded by a long-winded preface
of objectives. If actual teachers carried on this way in real life, they would
be writing largely irrelevant lessons all night. I am sure they do this better
today.

I rode to the college with four other students from the west side. On
one trip a young lady practiced her talk on George Washington on the rest
of us. Her beginning line was "Now class, today I am going to tell you
about George Washington." If she said this once, she said it six times.
All the people who were in the car were also in the class. Later, when she
said the same words to the class, she burst out laughing. Any humane
teacher would have sensed her embarrassment and laughed with the
class. This professor, however, had little sense of humor; he seemed to
regard it as treason and turned red with anger. The Dutch schoolmaster in
him had had his feathers ruffled, and he ordered her out of the class. It
was insensitive and petty.

During the year I availed myself of the opportunity to enjoy three
fine courses: "Modern Philosophy," "The Romantic Poets," and "Abnormal Psychology," which should have been called "The Psychology
of Abnormal People." The first illuminated modernity, the second was

an experience of great poetry, and the third convinced me that we are all a little nutty.

In the spring of 1935 I received a fellowship to Northwestern University that amounted to $600, $200 of which consisted of tuition. This dramatizes the stupendous inflation in the last fifty years. Evanston was an expensive city, part of the north Chicago "Gold Coast." Today tuition for the graduate school is $9,000, and the total cost of a year's study tops $15,000. In the teens and twenties of this century, a silk worker in Paterson—through uncommon thrift, of course—could manage to own a home on $.50 to $.60 an hour, which averages out, with overtime and layoffs thrown in, to less than $25 a week.

The school year 1934-1935, which had begun in frustration, was changed into new hope by excellent teachers, the education in Plato Club, and meeting my future wife.

Chapter 8

Purple and Gold

Northwestern University, like so many private colleges, was founded to mediate learning and the Christian faith. Ardent Methodists sought to preserve the faith of John Wesley. By the time I enrolled in the graduate school in 1935, however, faith had been delegated to the churches and learning to the university. Its faculty and student body adhered to many faiths or none at all. The city of Evanston had elegant churches and one nationally known clergyman, but they were all silent on Sunday evening. There were two Swedish Lutheran churches, one for the affluent and one for blue-collar workers—both equally unfriendly. Their services were heavily liturgical, with a good deal of singing by the pastor whose back faced the congregation; the sermons were brief and not nearly as good as Luther's *Table Talks*. Churches in Chicago were difficult to attend: miles to travel to and hard to find. But the University library was closed, and Sunday was a lonely day. There was no nucleus of Calvin graduates to lighten the day. Even though I went regularly to the blue-collar church for the school year, the response of the church was icy; one had to be a superb infiltrator to become a member of the little hive. In neither Swedish Lutheran church were visitors ever welcomed from the pulpit, and I often felt like a spy rather than a member of the body of Christ. Doubtless they were the body, but the body was not warm; they professed the communion of saints every Sunday, but they were the saints.

Evanston was an alluring city, bounded on the east by the variegated splendor of Lake Michigan, especially when lightning flashed over the water, and on the south by the city of Chicago, with its splendid cultural resources. Among these were the Cubs, whom I watched lose some games, and the White Sox on the South Side, whom I went to see because they had two magnificent players—Ted Lyons and Luke Appling—on an otherwise mediocre team. (It didn't make much difference to shortstop Appling, but in the case of Lyons, pitching for the Yankees instead of the White Sox would have made him a superstar.) Evanston was a city of marked contrasts: the luxurious homes on streets shaded by towering elms and the deluxe downtown stores on the east side and the slummy west side inhabited by blacks and other poor people. Once on a Sunday afternoon I wandered into that area, and an angry black man accosted me. He thought I was an employee of a collection agency; after I told him I was only a student, we had an amiable conversation. In the western part of town the "Magnificent 400" of the Chicago Northwestern drew me when I was bored to watch it thundering past at ninety miles an hour. For a semester and a summer session I lived on Sheridan Road, and the rest of the time on Sherman Avenue. Sheridan deserved a magnificent street; Sherman, a gifted commander but a malicious exterminator of Indians, got what was coming to him. Toward the north, the rich area of Evanston bordered elite suburbs.

Northwestern's Evanston campus, at the time partially erected on Lake Michigan, was a delightful place. A large grass meadow fronted a superb library, and great trees were scattered around the campus with the names of former professors engraved on stones at their bases. There were numerous shrubs and flowers and an exquisite Shakespearean garden. The sciences and technology occupied the finest buildings, while the English Department was housed in one of the oldest and creakiest, a fit place to teach Anglo-Saxon, Old Irish, and Chaucer. I spent half a year in a student dormitory; but those exuberant, wealthy boys, who owned cars and were satisfied with a gentleman's grade of C, irritated me. Their Methodist benefactors would not have appreciated the call in the corridors, "Who's going to Howard Street?"—a red-light district at the edge of Chicago. They engaged in water fights and listened to loud music. I spent most of my time in the library, and during the second semester I moved to Sherman Street, to the home of a woman chiropractor. Once, when I had a bad cold, she decided I needed chiropractic attention; I was never so shook up in my life. Half a block away ran the elevated railroad, which I did not notice after a few days. The second year I moved to another house on the same street, which was a good place because the lady had a little baby and enforced quiet.

During my first weeks at Northwestern, as well as throughout my studies there, I was impressed by the cordiality of the professors. At Michigan it seemed as though one should be ecstatically pleased to be admitted; at Northwestern I felt that the professors were pleased you had been admitted. Northwestern had one of the best and best-paid faculties in the Big Ten, but no professor there addressed students in the aloof, magisterial manner that Dr. Rice of the English department at Michigan employed in his lectures on bibliography. The professors I had were all learned in their subjects and gracious in manner, and they were approachable and concerned. As a matter of fact, with a few exceptions, they were more democratic and affable than were the professors I had at Calvin.

The English department was chaired by a Southerner named William Frank Bryan, who had left the University of Chicago to become chairman of the department. He was a courtly gentleman with rigid standards and an awesome mastery of his subject matter, Old English, which I took from him, as well as History of the English Language. Old English demanded a mastery of the language and a reading of the best poems and prose of that era. *Beowulf* was a delightful and difficult study, at which I spent many hours in translation and which we examined line by line in class. There were no formal lectures, but we got inside that poem through the translation and professorial comments. We relived the poem's mythical exploits of a saintly man wavering between the ultimate control of Wyrd (fate) and providence, a strong blend of paganism and Christianity. Matthew Arnold once derisively applied the phrase "the slow and steady Saxon" to the Germanic peoples; those people were steady but never slow. Prof. Case taught a year-long course in eighteenth-century literature, which met at the unseasonable hour of 1 P.M. He was one of the best lecturers I ever had—even if he sat on a chair—lively, informative, and erudite without pedantry. He became one of my models in teaching. The course was superbly organized: we had a bluebook every other week on material about to be discussed. I enjoyed all of it immensely, except for *Pamela* by Richardson. This novel, for me at least, raises boredom to an art. It is a story about an attempted seduction, which drags on for hundreds of pages in the form of letters, but never occurs.

Of all the impossible pleasures one dreams about, one for me would be to hear Coleridge, with "glittering eye," read the perfect poem, "The Rime of the Ancient Mariner," which he composed in seven parts. The man behind this poem was one of the most complex and gifted of men: poet, philosopher, literary critic, editorialist, and conversationalist with few peers. I was fortunate to take two seminars in Coleridge and Wordsworth with Prof. George G. Fox, a man talented in both abstract thinking and thinking through images. I wrote a long paper on Coleridge, which involved reading all his published letters. Letters are not the most magnetic reading for me, although they are indispensable to a biographer; but Coleridge's letters were electrifying, and often funny as well as wise. During the second semester the class read and discussed Wordsworth's *The Prelude,* line by line, a long poem that describes, sometimes vividly and sometimes dully, the making of a mind. Wordsworth had a mind that could write the wonderful poem "It is a Beauteous Evening" and the disaster "Peter Bell" with the same monumental seriousness. He could pen, with grace and power, "thoughts that do often lie too deep for tears"; but he could also tell us, "And at the Hoop we landed, famous Inn."

Prof. Fox was a highly gifted scholar and conducted a most interesting class. The class contained two feisty women, neither young, who were both compulsive talkers. One did her talking outside the classroom, while Mrs. Starbird chirped at inappropriate times in it, until finally Fox did what I only saw done once in graduate school—he ordered her out of the class. There were only about a dozen of us in the class, and the event was memorably dramatic. It was also in that class that I first witnessed the power of Catholic censorship: a young lady was prohibited from writing on Rousseau. Instead, she wrote a paper on the imagery in a selection of Wordsworth's poems. The acuteness of the teacher and the congeniality of that class made it an illuminating and appealing course.

In my second year I discovered the charm of Old French literature, especially the *Song of Roland*. Prof. Brown taught *Gawain and the Green Knight*, line by line, a course I should have liked to teach that way myself but could only find time to assign it in modernized English as outside reading. Brown was approaching senility rather early: he was a learned man, but he gave preposterous assignments. He assigned me the topic "The Church in the Middle Ages"; authors have written volumes on selected aspects of the subject. I whittled it down to "Chaucer and the Church," but even that was gargantuan. Brown, who was in his late sixties, was a bicyclist; he was killed a few years later near Joliet while riding his bicycle.

Sometimes students append compliments to their final bluebooks, but I was not accustomed to doing that. Later I sometimes wished I had. In the case of Prof. Virgil Heltzel, I did it because the *Northwestern Daily*, which printed evaluations of professors for a time, wrote what I considered a lampoon rather than an evaluation of a fine scholar and most gracious man. He was publicly slain by the jawbone of an ass. So I wrote an appreciative note on my final examination. The students also published an evaluation of the nationally famous author of the textbook we had used in *Abnormal Psychology* at Calvin. I sent a copy to Prof. J. Broene, who replied by saying that he would have been utterly demolished by such a judgment. I thought the whole practice unjustifiable. If a teacher is a failure, fire him, but don't torture him first in public.

Unimaginable as it seems today, Northwestern University was a prime football power in the Big Ten in the mid-1930s. They ended Minnesota's winning streak of twenty-six games by a 6-0 score, a game that I saw battled out in squalls and mud. In the final game at Notre Dame, they won 14-0, and the next day (Monday) was a holiday. As late as 1947, when I was completing my dissertation there, Northwestern won the Rose Bowl. In the thirties college football teams had only one squad for both offense and defense, and that enabled Northwestern to compete with the much larger schools in the Big Ten. They could field twenty-five good players but not fifty; some players played the entire sixty minutes. Those Saturday afternoons were about the only recreation I had, in the days when football was still a sport and not a national mania.

In high school teaching, a Ph.D. degree may become an encumbrance; in college teaching, it is the only way to the plum tree unless one is George Lyman Kittredge or a poet of importance. Northwestern was gracious to me in allowing me to complete my work in 1946, after eight years' absence. I was also very fortunate to have Prof. Frederic E. Faverty as my teacher and research director. In the summer of 1946 I took two courses with him in a nine-week quarter session: Victorian poetry and a seminar in Matthew Arnold and Thomas Carlyle. A genial gentleman who believed in rigorous demands, Faverty was learned, witty, and lucid. He had the rare ability of a scholar who can write in an enriching popular fashion. He wrote a fresh series of short pieces for the *Chicago Tribune* on some of the world's literary masterpieces, which brought the classics to the masses. He also wrote an erudite book entitled *Matthew Arnold as an Ethnologist,* which shows how one of the sanest of men could embrace some of the wildest ideas on racial differences. It is a little-known book, but written with charm and wit.

For the seminar and later for my dissertation, I had to consult materials in the richly endowed, handsomely equipped, and abundantly stocked Newberry Library in Chicago. The neighborhood around the splendid building was turning into a slum, where unsavory characters wandered around by day and pimps and prostitutes by night. After dark there was menace in the air, and I always returned to Evanston before dark. Chicago itself had become a darker city in the interim years between my studies at Northwestern. I was always uneasy when I walked from the Loop to the Grand Central Station to take the 11:30 P.M. "milk train" to Grand Rapids on the Pere Marquette. One bitterly cold night I saw a drunk lying in the gutter with his suitcoat open and his trousers half off. There was no one near, so I pulled up his trousers and wrapped his coat around him and walked on. I hoped the police would find him before he froze.

The trains were always crowded, and one had to have a number to obtain a seat in the coaches. Blacks coming from or returning to the South chattered all night. If one were just dozing off, the conductor would shout "Bangor" and then a little later "Fennville," and the train would grind to a stop for the milk cans to be unloaded or a lone passenger to get off. After spending Saturday and Sunday at home in Grand Rapids, I would return to Chicago at 11:30 Sunday night and rejoice in a similar experience. During those long nine weeks, my wife did yeoman's work, caring for two busy bodies, mowing the lawn, caring for the house, and managing to subsist on little so that I could be at school. I could come home only a few times during the summer quarter.

I was extremely fortunate in the subject of my dissertation: Leslie Stephen as a biographer. Stephen was steeped in eighteenth-century thought and its literary polish. He wrote not only analyses of that thought but also superb book-length biographies and hundreds of incisive biographical sketches for the *Dictionary of National Biography,* of which he was the first editor. The subjects of his succinct sketches ranged from the indisputably great like Swift and Pope to "intolerable bores who are the salt of the earth," from first-rate philosophers like John Stuart Mill to

Douglas Steward, who was "too much a professor of the philosophical department." His style is astringent and often sardonic. Stephen's avocation was mountaineering, his domestic behavior a combination of encouragement and complaint. He married a daughter of Thackeray and was the father of a genius, Virginia Woolf, as well as Vanessa, her brilliant sister. There were few dull pages either in his life or his letters.

I am still grateful for a dissertation topic that interested me, for the accumulation of materials I could use for many years, a professor whom I admired, and especially for my wife, who typed a thesis of 300 pages with many intricate bibliographical entries. She had to type four carbon copies plus the original on an old-fashioned typewriter, an act that involved genuine physical exertion. I appreciated that so much that she, her mother, and our two children received round-trip tickets to Baltimore via Pullman to a sister-in-law's home as a down payment of appreciation.

As has become abundantly clear, I owe much to my years at Michigan and Northwestern. The professors, all of them, were genuine scholars engaged in their profession out of consuming interest and a passion for truth. I never knew from their teaching what any of them believed on the deepest issues of life. Whatever their religious commitments were, they kept them private, but for one conversation in which Prof. William Frank Bryan said to me, "I wish I could believe as you do, so that I could join my mother there." The ACLU had no need for a firebell: the Bible was literature in the classroom, not a standard for truth and morality. The great options were not presented and personal choice among them never emphasized. Learning was one thing and religious commitment another, and not one of them tried to integrate them. If one is deeply committed to Christianity and feels impelled to reveal it, the place where one can most freely do so is a Christian college. I say this without any diminution of respect and high regard for my professors, some of whom may well have been Christians.

Chapter 9

Paterson and Eastern Academy

When our family had arrived at the Lackawanna station in Paterson in 1920, we were greeted by two elders and two cars and quickly whisked to a splendid congregational dinner in the church basement. When I arrived at the same station seventeen years later to teach at Eastern Academy, I was confronted by an empty platform and a few trunks. I lugged my heavy suitcase to the bus line and spent the night at the Y.M.C.A. I wondered if I had chosen the wrong profession. The next day, instead of settling comfortably into a newly decorated home, I sought a place for room and board. I found both at the home of John De Vries and his genial wife. I then walked over to the high school, where a new brick building had been added to the old frame house. Husselman's barber shop, through whose large window I had once batted a baseball while the principal reclined in a chair getting a shave, was still there. So was the ice-cream store to which Milo Velzen had gone to buy an ice-cream cone after jumping out of the open window of the session room. This session room was a muted circus in which at times the whole class would burst out singing "I've Been Working on the Railroad." The teacher was an admirable man destined for another vocation—which he entered the next year. The tailor shop, where the kindly tailor had sewed up my trousers ripped open in the rear, was still on North Eighth Street. I went back through the school, down the steep stone steps facing North Seventh Street, and walked two blocks down a street I had so often pedaled up laboriously on my heavy Ranger bike (which some Sicilian had snatched out of our garage in my senior year). I was now close to school in a good home.

Paterson had changed little since 1931. But the Depression had left its marks on the city. From the Lackawanna station to Hawthorne and Prospect Park and Fairlawn everything seemed the same. The river flowed murkily under the bridge, and River Street was packed with little shops. All my old Italian friends were still living around the church and the parsonage. The Pasqualis invited me to dinner with undiminished hospitality. Yoke's meat market was across the street, and Mr. Hommes

60

occupied the home where the delightful Jaarsma children once played, directly across Nineteenth Street. Santo's still sold lemon ice on Third Street, and the Peerless Oval, where I had watched and played many baseball games, was still in use. One day I retraced what had been my daily walk for about a year to Cramer and King, crossing Lyons Oval, where I had played with the Parkways and some other good teams managed by Robert Walter. I walked past the store of the proprietor who served customers by pushing a chair on wheels, to which he was confined; and then I walked up the hill past the small elevated park where I often played as a boy. I returned down Nineteenth Street, a magnificent hill for sledding when there is snow. I suppose that today Lyon's Oval is occupied by buildings; the church and parsonage are gone, and most of my Italian neighbors have died.

I joined the Fourth Church and walked twice to church on Sunday over the same sidewalks I had walked to Eastern Academy. The church had been remodeled, and I sat in the back instead of marching in from the front with my mother to occupy the ministerial pew. Eastern Academy was a notable example of profound commitment and vision in a day when the community expected and was accustomed to see fourteen-year-old boys and girls enter the work force of the city. The mercantile-minded members of the community saw little necessity for secondary education. They did see the value of commercial subjects, and during the years I attended they were annually increased, reaching their peak in 1941, when graduates from the commercial courses outnumbered all the others. In 1950, twenty-five years after I was graduated, college preparatory graduates numbered sixteen students, general high school students numbered ten, and the commerical students thirteen. In this respect, Eastern Academy differed substantially from some of our other Christian high schools: it had been peculiarly sensitive to the needs of the community and met them by teaching *all* subjects in a context of Christian perspectives.

When motorists speed effortlessly through Ohio today on U.S. 80, they seldom if ever think that most of the terrain they hasten through was once largely dense woods, in places almost sunless. Conrad Richter's novel *The Trees* gives a vivid picture of these magnificent forests. Before they became fertile fields, the trees had to be hewn, uprooted, and burned. So we often forget the tireless spadework that produced our Christian schools. Indifference had to be uprooted, hostility burned out, and the new seeds of faith and vision sown. The sacrificial and unstinting labor of board members and others who sought to establish Eastern Academy was obvious. Though often pressed to the edge of anxiety, they never deprived the teachers of an adequate wage, a good deal of which came out of their own pockets. As I read over the list of board members, some names appear again and again. D. H. Kuiken served eleven years, the longest tenure on the list. Other names that keep recurring are Lambert Steen, Peter Damsma, and John Van Buiten. Rev. J. J. Hiemenga,

Calvin College's first president, served the board as president for some
years. Toward the end of the quarter century, John Hamersma's name
begins to appear. John was a master storyteller and an unforgettable
companion when I was growing up in Paterson. He served the cause with
manifest devotion until he was tragically stricken by a heart attack at a
Christian School Association meeting. Later on, gifted board members
such as Robert Walter, Henry Fortuin, and of course many others served
admirably. Anyone who has seen the splendid new quarters of the school
in its picturesque setting would agree that their labors were not in vain.
Together with a competent staff and the blessing of the Lord, they
brought into being a school every graduate and supporter can admire.

Except possibly for a course in church history, about which I knew
little and the students less, I taught only college preparatory students. I
did become acquainted with the general student body of 167 in chapel and
in session periods. They were a memorably pleasant group of young
people. The only disciplinary problem I had was in a physical education
class I was drafted to teach to junior and senior girls. I liked sports, but
this stomping about, raising and lowering arms, squatting down and up
was a minor trauma. During one session, the prettiest girl in the class
simply sat down and refused to participate. Here was a problem: should I
order her to leave? Should I carry her out? I simply let her sit there while
the class gyrated around her.

I had one embarrassing experience. I had given a Latin final examination during the hour before lunch. I put the papers in a desk drawer,
intending to correct them during the next test. When I returned after
lunch, all the papers were gone! Some failing student had wanted another
chance. At any rate, all the students had to be called up and informed that
the examination was to be given again, and that meant writing a new set
of questions as well as needless travel and trouble for thirty students. I
never found out who the culprit was.

I taught Latin and German as I had been taught them; today's
electronic support system was as yet unknown. I had taken two years of
high school German and two and a half of German literature; in the latter,
to my disappointment, the professor had given only one lecture in German. Conversational German was not taught in the schools I attended. I
tried a little of it—with disappointing results. When I was in the Netherlands years later, I was amazed that the Dutch schools achieved such
impressive results with the same old-fashioned methods; walking by
classrooms, I could hear the whole class conjugating verbs and repeating
sentences. I also used no projects to divert the students: no construction of
catapults, sewing of togas, preparation of a meal with sauerkraut and
wienerschnitzel, or fashioning the uniform of an officer in the Luftwaffe.
(In later years I had a colleague who had students fashion replicas of
"Feathertop" in one of Hawthorne's minor stories instead of reading
more of the superb stories!) In Latin class the students mastered conjuga-

tions and declensions and translated the exciting Latin sentences. We bored our way through a good deal of Caesar's *Gallic Wars,* and I am sure that students remember this classic with nostalgia. In the second-year German class we studied some great poems, stories, and several novelettes. Since they were bound for college, I never heard the dismal question I often heard later in teaching English grammar in high school, "What do we have to study this stuff for?" They were good students, a few exceptional, and I remember them with pleasure.

I was fully aware of my distinguished predecessors in language teaching, who had established a tradition of excellence in the classics at Eastern. In the seven years preceding my tenure, these subjects had been taught by William Radius, a superlative classical scholar and teacher who spent most of his life teaching classical languages at Calvin; and by Bastian Kruithof, fascinating preacher, elegant writer, humorist, and later teacher of Bible at Hope College for many years. Dr. Kruithof has written significant books on Christianity and learning, *Christ of the Cosmic Road* and *In God's Milieu,* as well as two other excellent books, *The High Points of Calvinism* and *Instead of a Thorn,* the latter a compelling and authentic novel on the early Dutch pioneers in western Michigan (now unfortunately out of print). As a couple, Bert and Marie Kruithof enriched not only Eastern Academy but the lives of many others through their unusually generous hospitality and entertaining companionship and talents. (One New Year's Eve, the Kruithofs helped us usher in the New Year. It was an evening of delight and sleet. When they were about to leave, however, Bert's car was encased in sleet. He could not insert the key. For a long time we poured kettle after kettle of hot water on the car. Finally, Bert's dander was up, and he asked for my hammer with which to break the window. We offered them a bed for the night; but he was determined, and the hammer was delivered. Going out to execute the break-in, we suddenly discovered that we had been working on a little red Volkswagen that was exactly like his but was not his. I still tremble to imagine the publicity had he hammered in the window of another person's car. We slept that night interrupted by laughter.) In later years, H. Evan Runner, whose gifts as a philosopher have been widely recognized, also taught languages at Eastern Academy for some time. If one adds the name of Dr. C. Van Zwoll, who also taught languages there and later at Calvin and Alma colleges, Eastern Academy had an exceptional tradition in the teaching of Latin and German.

When I was a sophomore at Eastern Academy in 1923 and the school numbered about 120 students, I had organized an unsponsored baseball team. Since we were in no condition to battle giants like Central and Eastside high schools or even the coached Catholic teams, I went to the principals of four elementary schools and asked if some of their boys would like to play our team, suggesting that we would prove to be less than formidable opponents. We beat them all. The next year, however,

William Roozeboom coached our team, and we played nine games against a bizarre assortment of teams. We played our home games in the open field facing the quarry in Prospect Park. We won most of these games also, playing in uniforms donated by Mr. Lambert Steen.

Things had changed by the time I taught at Eastern. In the spring of 1938, I coached a well-equipped team that was composed of players who were eager and faithful but not very good at baseball. We had a schedule of ten games and lost them with monotonous regularity. We achieved one tie by courtesy of the weather. The minute it began to rain, I asked the umpire to call the game, hurried the players into the cars, and rejoiced at our triumphal nondefeat. There were three good players on the team: Barney Steen, first baseman, George Holwerda, catcher, and Herb Soodsma, an indisputably coming southpaw who was beaten only because our team lacked hitting power. I heard later that Soodsma arrived the next spring and the team had a winning season. At a chapel session near the end of the season, the players were awarded letters for effort. Effort is a good quality and a pleasure every coach can count on.

During the early fall I witnessed a student activity I have never seen before or since. About a half hour every school day was allotted for the entire student body of 167 to practice the sacred cantata "The Woman of Endor," which they later sang at the autumn festival. I marveled at it then, and I still do now. Surely there must have been some in that student body whose voices rival mine in deficiency. I am no singer; I move my lips in church to please my wife. When I was a student at Eastern Academy, Mr. Roozeboom, who praised me as a baseball player and history student, suggested that he test my voice for singing. I said, "Voice is what I don't have." But he insisted, and so one evening in the school chapel, he played a Stephen Foster song for me to sing. After a stanza Mr. Roozeboom said, in his always affirmative way, "Well, one can't have everything." I had the honor and the talent to raise and lower the curtain between numbers.

My year at Eastern Academy was pleasant because of the civility of the student body, the quality and friendliness of the faculty, and the efficient, almost too meticulous administration of Mr. J. R. Bos, who had the gift of hearty laughter among other engaging traits. When he was really amused, he would slap his right knee with zest. I deeply appreciated the extraordinary hospitality I enjoyed at the homes of friends, mostly from the Fourth Church but also from Prospect Park, Clifton, Hawthorne, and Midland Park. I was often invited for Sunday dinner and the rest of the day; I think I spent half my Sundays there at the homes of friends. Old, familiar ties were reinforced and new ones were made. I was also enriched by being invited to join two clubs, a literary club that discussed current books and the Alethian Club, which was composed of a group of professional members who discussed everything. Years later, with the hearty cooperation of my wife, I tried to repay some of this generosity by inviting students from Eastern Academy at Calvin for Sunday dinner—a time for reminiscence and fellowship.

My four years as a student at Eastern Academy had been the most carefree in my life. Compared to today's world, it was an idyll in innocence. Substance abuse, broken homes, leaving children in a maelstrom of indirection, bitterness, worry, and divided loyalties were unknown there; the disturbing spiritual disintegration of the twenties never penetrated our sheltered lives. Unemployment was almost nonexistent, and the horrendous apocalypse of aerial doom did not hover on the horizon. One of the days I should like to relive if it were possible would be a spring day with a class under William Roozeboom and a baseball game after school—when my right arm still had power. The latter was so unimportant, but it was so much fun. To paraphrase a familiar saying, "You can take a boy out of New Jersey, but you can't take New Jersey out of the boy."

Chapter 10

Lackawanna Limited

One of the forbidden pleasures of my childhood consisted of sneaking off to the little yellow railroad station in Orange City, Iowa to wait for the passenger train to arrive. It was wonderland in a town of familiar horses and drab wagons. A few passengers and greeters stood on the platform, while the waiting room contained elderly men puffing corncob pipes. The bluish rails stretched into the interminable prairie, and as you walked on one of them, you heard the insistent humming of the telegraph wires and the songs of larks. Finally, a distant whistle burst into the emptiness, and if you put an ear to the rail, you would hear a faint throb. Then the ground began to tremble, and black smoke and white steam swirled into the fields. Puffing and panting, the engine slid to a stop with a slow, rhythmic breathing. In a few moments the baggage was disposed of and the passengers were aboard; the big wheels slipped and slowly spun into action, and the train moved rapidly into the empty prairie. The only sound was the ticking of the telegraph—and sometimes, unfortunately, my mother's voice, which meant a humiliating journey home. During the night I would sometimes hear that lonesome, unforgettable, and unduplicable whistle echoing over the great plains and causing me to reflect, as Edna Millay wrote:

> There isn't a train I wouldn't take
> No matter where it's going.

Years later, during graduate school in Evanston, when I was utterly weary of tracing sound changes in the English language and even weary of translating the exploits of Beowulf, I would walk to the edge of town to watch the thunderous passage of one of the nation's great trains. The Chicago and Northwestern 400, which gulped up the 400 miles from Chicago to Minneapolis in 400 minutes. One could already hear that train whistle from ten miles away in Chicago, and it grew steadily louder as the 400 raced clangorously by—a splendid, gleaming train of twenty passenger cars hurtling along at ninety miles an hour. One had to keep a safe distance to avoid being sucked into the cars, and the houses trembled blocks away. Beowulf and his warriors, mail-clad, walked on the sea-plain and rowed the sea-lanes; on this train ordinary men and women drank ale at spotless tables where roses in tall glasses hardly moved.

A few summers ago the Chessie system ran a special excursion steam train from Grand Rapids to Detroit. Its coming was heralded by a whistle heard all over town. When I saw it bursting from under the viaduct, it was already passing sixty, a glittering twelve-passenger-car train, the last gasp of a dying splendor. That train was the coda to the long, greedy, and raucous history of the iron horse. It is a picturesque story dramatically recorded by the now defunct *Railroad Magazine* in exciting stories of collision, flooded bridges, deep snows, courage, and rescue. The railroads were built by hunkies, Irish, Magyars, Italians, and Chinese—immigrants, as MacLeish says, "not born to be buried in this earth" by the railroad bed. They built the roads but seldom traveled on them. The American railroads were paid for four times over by the American people as Morgan, Hill, Stanford, Huntington, and Vanderbilt manipulated railroads to build great fortunes. Frank Norris's great novel *The Octopus* shows how the Southern Pacific, for example, raped the ranchers. The Irish and Chinese were buried in nameless meadows in unmarked graves, while Stanford breezed through the tunnels they hewed out and gave his name and a lot of his money to a great university.

No one who rode on or heard of the great steam trains of the twenties and thirties will ever forget them. They were splendid, dramatic, and a thrill to see. Passengers boarded the *Airway Limited* in the old Pennsylvania Station in New York, transferred to the *Atchison, Topeka and Santa Fe* in Oklahoma, and arrived in Los Angeles forty-eight hours later. The wagon trains made ten miles on a good day, and the deep ruts of the Mormon trail are still visible in Nebraska. Today the great planes cruise the country in five hours, but on an overcast day the passengers see only each other, a murky movie, and the *United Airlines* magazine.

There were cannonball freights as well as passenger trains. The biggest engine I ever saw towed over a hundred loaded cars on the now defunct Big Four railroad. One of the most spectacular sights in railroad-ing was seeing a hundred-and-twenty-car freight train struggling up the Laramie grade pulled by three locomotives, and then coming to a long bend, where the men in the caboose could see the engines far ahead.

An affinity for trains was not without risks. The Delaware, Lack-awanna, & Western Railroad crossed the Passaic River on a long trestle fifty feet above the dye-stained water. One evening three of us decided to walk across it. Halfway across, we heard the whistle and the dim roar of a train coming around a hidden bend. Reaching land on either side was impossible; so the three of us crouched around a water barrel on a small platform as the long freight clicked over the old-fashioned rails. The platform seemed to undulate the whole time above the lethal grasp of the dark water. As the red lights of the caboose died away, we crawled to land.

During the dark Depression, when young men had to hitchhike or board freight cars if they wished to escape the monotony of immobility, thousands upon thousands rode the rails. I once saw at least fifty men in a boxcar; and on another occasion I winced at the sight of a man's leg that was deeply gashed, his pants matted into the blood.

During one spring vacation I wanted to visit my sister. My friend Olsen knew the ropes, so we squeezed between two passenger cars on the Wabash line from Detroit to Fort Wayne. When we disembarked at that city, two railroad officials were there to greet us—with amazing courtesy. After we assured them that we were only students at the University of Michigan, they told us to leave town, which we later did via a Wabash freight car. I got off that car at Hannibal, Missouri, where Huck Finn once swung a dead cat down Main Street. Sometimes slightly ethical questions may even arise on trains. Once I sat beside a lush on the *Twilight Limited*. He would look out the window and say again and again, "Where there's smoke there's fire." When I was leaving, he opened his wallet and said, "I've got lots of money, here's a twenty." Something in my catechetical training made me refuse. Later I wondered whether that twenty might not have been better spent on books than on more Jack Daniels. Shortly after World War II, travel on the *Pere Marquette* was so heavy that one had to have numbered tickets for coach seats. When I came to mine, a tigerish lady had my window seat and refused to surrender it. I went to find another seat rather than risking a showdown with this early edition of Bella Abzug.

The great steam trains are gone now, and many of the depots where they arrived in hissing steam and splendor have been dismantled or put to other uses. The huge smoke-filled Grand Rapids trainshed of my college days, which Calvin College, quixotically, once tried to buy, is now gone. The large, ornate station with porters, restaurants, newsstands with *good* magazines on them, convenient taxis, and an uninterrupted bustle is only a memory. Now however, there are stirrings of new life in railroad service: Amtrak offers a train to and from Chicago once a day, and the ridership has been sizable. Though a far cry from the thirty that rumbled in and out of Union Station in the twenties, it may be the beginning of a new era.

Nothing will resemble buying the long green ticket to Paterson for $27.63, boarding the 5:13 P.M. train around Christmas, with snow falling; clattering over Division Avenue into the dark; waiting in the spacious Detroit terminal for the *Michigan Central* to Buffalo, where one arrived in the early dawn; waiting in that snowy city for the *Lackawanna Limited* at 9:30 A.M. This was a crack train, meticulously appointed, on which one often saw boys from Cornell in coonskin coats with flasks in their pockets staggering down the aisle. "Bath, Corning, Elmira, Binghamton, Scranton" still ring through the conductor's voice in my memory. I never tired of the picturesque route Mark Twain often rode when he was doggedly courting a coal baron's daughter. Passengers for Paterson switched to another train at Dover and arrived there at a weathered station on the outskirts of town.

Now the *Lackawanna* is part of Conrail and carries only freight. The parsonage was sold and moved to another street, and the church burned down. I can't go home again. And in Iowa, where no town is farther from a railroad than seven miles, only two passenger trains a day cross the state. Today the great steam engines and the cars they pulled are found in Greenfield Village, originated and initially financed by Henry Ford, the man who probably did more than anyone else to terminate their splendor.

Chapter 11

All in the Family

In August 1933 my father, age 68, had preached his farewell sermon to the congregation of the Fourth Christian Reformed Church in Paterson, a church for which our family had esteem and affection in a city that my parents regretted leaving. He preached on "Jesus Christ, Yesterday and Today, the same, also in Eternity," a translation of the German text, which has been framed in his study and mine for almost a century. It is the essence of the faith that has led us all through joy, tribulation, and death. Paterson Fourth was the church in which I had made confession of faith, the church that held the funeral services for my grandmother, mother, and father. They are buried in the Fairlawn Cemetery, and to my regret I have been able to visit their graves only a few times in all the years since their deaths. Though long gone, they are still part of the family, part of the very texture of my heart and mind.

Immediately after that evening service, I left for Chicago with my friends Andy and Tony Damato, who were going to see the World's Fair at Chicago, while I was going to Grand Rapids to rent a home for my family. My father was to serve as assistant pastor to Dr. William Masselink, who had been his student years before. He was to preach in Dutch for the afternoon service and visit the sick, for which he had an uncommon talent.

For Andy and Tony this was a great adventure. They had never been farther from home than New York City and Newark. On the way we stopped at Niagara Falls and stood under the spray of the thundering waters. When we approached Detroit, Andy asked me, "What is it— Detroit, Michigan or Michigan, Detroit?" We drove nonstop, except for food and gas. They dropped me off in the Loop in Chicago, and I never saw either one again. When I taught at Eastern Academy five years later, they had moved from the area.

Since I had plenty of time, I took a train to Milwaukee to visit my good friend Lewis Grotenhuis in Oostburg, a Wisconsin village. Lewis had been a good friend for many years: when we were in college, he was a model of joviality; in the Orthodox Presbyterian Church he became a model of piety. While I was in Oostburg, Rev. Oscar Holkeboer, also a minister in that denomination, offered me a ride to Grand Rapids, where he was going to be married to Winifred Hager. We arrived at 1348 Alpine Avenue, Winifred's home, late in the afternoon, so I never saw her—and never expected to. I never saw her sister Carolyn either. But when I first saw Carolyn Hager, a year later, I soon realized I would never see enough of her—and never will. Oscar had reached his destination and I walked down the street to Dr. Masselink's impressive manse, where I was treated with uncommon cordiality. During the next week I rented an attractive home for my parents at twenty dollars a month on Tamarack Avenue. But I knew my dad and was not surprised when he bought a house on Myrtle Street, around the corner from 1348 Alpine Avenue—as it turned out, a very convenient location indeed.

The first time I saw my future wife was at a cottage in Grand Haven, where I met not only the vivacious and highly attractive blonde I was to marry but almost the whole tribe: Uncle John, chomping his cigar while illuminating all questions; the three aunts, stately Aunt Cora, Aunt Jeanette, who could sell mud at a profit, and Aunt Nell, who had a gift for tart sayings in spite of a bent back that she endured for her lifetime because a midwife had dropped her as a baby. There was also the mother, Lucy, who hated to part with her daughters; sister Dorothy, dreamy and poetic; her fiancé and my future brother-in-law, Albertus Groendyk, a well of effervescent friendliness. When the time came to leave, the Hagers graciously offered me a couch on the porch. It was a strange experience, with the splashing of the lake in my ears and the friendliness in the rooms. The next morning I returned to Grand Rapids, and I was never at that cottage again. But I determined to be at 1348 Alpine Avenue again, and that resolve flowered into a wonderful wife, two incomparable sisters-in-law, and two brothers-in-law whom I admired. (I have been fortunate in brothers-in-law, because my sister's husband, Rev. John DeBerg, was also a most likable person. It is somewhat ironic that his grandson became a quarterback for the Denver Broncos, which made my father, a profoundly conservative clergyman, the great grandfather of a great grandson who broke the Sabbath every Sunday.) I also admired my future mother-in-law, despite her obvious reluctance to lose her daughters. Her courage, faith, and sense of humor in a life marred by the early death of her husband, relentless poverty, and hard work were remarkable.

My wife's family on her father's side had emigrated from Sneek, Friesland. Her grandfather, Cornelius Hager, a man without formal education, moved from the Paterson silk mills into the ministry of the Netherlands Reformed Church. He had great natural talent: he was a born orator with verve and energy. Years before I met any of the Hagers, he and my father had jointly conducted the funeral service of the janitor in our church, a man with whom I was engaged in an endless feud. I remember my mother's remarking on Rev. Hager's energetic sermon delivery in the living room of the deceased, which almost knocked down the chandelier. He preached a somber religion. In urging his flock to attend church on hot summer afternoons, he told them that they had better come because it was hotter in hell. After I was dating Carolyn, he called me into his study and told me not to worry about being adopted. I told him I never had. When he was in his last illness, he kept his faith and called us to his bedside for a final prayer before he died.

The Hagers had very talented children: Dr. Harry Hager, a prominent clergyman in the Reformed Church; Dr. R. John Hager became a dentist to make a living, though he was by instinct a historian, and he wrote a 900-page history of the Reformed Church, which was never published. Nicholas was a supersalesman of musical instruments who could toot everything, including his own horn. Commenting on his success, he once said to me, "What hath God wrought!" Cornelius, my wife's father, was a banker, a man with a keen mind who for a time took courses at New Brunswick Seminary. His death at thirty-two snuffed out a brilliant career. Titus was a shrewd and brilliant businessman, who not only sold lumber but discovered a new species of tree in Oregon. He had a dynamic personality, impeccable suavity, and great wealth. The one girl in that Hager family, Margaret, was a gentle woman, an aunt my wife loved for her many kindnesses.

My wife's warm-hearted and mystical maternal ancestors, the De Kornes, came from Goes, Zeeland. They departed from Vlissingen, hoping to improve their lot by moving to Grand Rapids, Michigan. In 1895 they moved to farmlands near LeRoy, Michigan, which were more suited to trees than to potatoes, and they had a hard life there for a few years. When Rev. Ekster would come by train once a month, he would hold the services in the home of Grandma and Grandpa De Korne because their house was the only one there with plastered walls. The De Kornes soon returned to Grand Rapids. They were skilled furniture craftsmen by instinct and training, and grandfather began to work in the Gunn Furniture Factory. He worked there until he was seventy-five, and he often said, "Another day, another dollar." They became members of Turner Avenue Netherlands Reformed Church, where Grandpa Hager was the minister. Among their meager possessions was a pet pig who walked with them to church every Sunday and waited outside to return with them. When the father butchered the pig for necessary food, none of the family could eat it.

Uncle Tone was a memorable member of the family, the father of eighteen children, ten of whom survived. His family lived in Jenison, and my wife and Robert Sonneveldt, her cousin, visited them during spring vacation one year. They encountered an uproarious group of boys. The clothesline hung from the house to the outhouse. When Mother De Korne went in there, the boys pulled the rope so hard that the privy rocked back and forth. My wife remembers how she and Bob longed to leave the next day, but the trolley passed them by, and they were in for another night. In the morning they accompanied the cousins to the country school, which housed all eight grades in one room. The teacher asked for a song to begin the day. One of the cousins raised his hand and asked for "K-K-K-Katy." When the song finished, another cousin raised his hand and again asked for "K-K-K-Katy," which was then sung more raucously than the first time. The teacher was beside herself when the students kept singing "K-K-K-Katy" over and over, whacking their desks and whacking each other on the back. She finally got them to come to order.

My wife's great-grandmother, a widow with four sons, sailed out of the mists of Vlissingen and came to Zeeland, Michigan. She married John Den Herder, who later became mayor of Zeeland. She now lies buried in the Zeeland cemetery beside the mayor, with his first wife on the other side of him, each resting in one of his arms, according to the legend on the tombstone.

My wife's father, as I have said, was a banker who seemed destined for prosperity. But he was struck by tuberculosis, and the family was hounded by poverty. Grandfather and Grandmother De Korne converted the upstairs of their small house into living quarters for the family. For a time the father was in a sanitorium in Howell, Michigan, and he seemed to be cured. He came home rejoicing; but the disease was treacherous, and after years of suffering, he died in the windowed annex built for him. He left a widow with three daughters—in a day of no governmental support for the poor—to live lean on gifts from relatives, friends, and the church. It is amazing that none of the children or the mother ever caught the disease. When I first entered the apartment, I was astonished to find gas lights, no bathtub, no central heating—only a coal stove with glowing windows and a limited radius of heat. The girls slept in the unheated annex in the bitter cold of Michigan winters. The one fine possession of the family was a grand piano, which Winifred played with meticulous skill, and Carolyn with self-taught, freewheeling verve.

On Sunday afternoons they amused themselves as children by counting the cars that sputtered down Alpine Avenue, and they devoured the books in the Harrison Park library. They were poor but never knew it, a closely knit group of talented girls who did not need canned amusement. Uncle John Peters and his wife were very good to the children, and the Sonneveldt cousins were the best of friends—and are to this day. On one midwinter day the family was almost out of coal, and they all prayed about it. The next day a ton of coal was delivered from Uncly Ty. Grandfather Hager had paid the two younger girls' tuition at Calvin College, but that did not exempt them from long hours of work to support the family. Poverty, however, did not make these girls envious or greedy; it made them generous all their lives and developed in them a faith like steel.

Some relatives view their poor relations with embarrassment, or, to use Lamb's phrase, "a rebuke to your rising," "a haunting conscience," "the one thing not needful." This was emphatically not the case with Uncle John Peters and his wife, Jeanette, or with Uncle Arnold Sonneveldt and his wife, Cora, or the cousins. Uncle John took them on numerous picnics, brought candy every Saturday, and even attempted—with disastrous results—to cut their hair. Uncle John was an expert furniture craftsman, and that skill spun off a sense of omniscience; his wife was a kind lady with an innate shrewdness that always got the best of a bargain. He was a most generous man, and one of the sad sights in my life was to see him dying thrust into by tubes. Uncle Arnold, who operated Buttercup Bakery, was a splendid baker, an ardent golfer, and hunter of deer, which he pursued in northern Michigan, at times bringing home the results. Bob, his son, was an astute baker who won prizes in his decorating of ornate wedding cakes that had to be transported with consummate care. Josephine and especially Janet were close friends of my wife. Janet was maid of honor at our wedding, and she remained our close friend for fifty years, and neither the sad early loss of her husband nor successive bouts with cancer attenuated her uncommon cheeriness, pluck, devoted friendliness, and faith.

My marriage to Carolyn in 1938 had been eagerly anticipated by my mother, who was already allotting gifts. She died suddenly and unexpectedly a few months before our marriage, while I was still teaching in Paterson. My father married us in a moving ceremony, in which his words to us were a poignant mixture of joy and sadness. We knew Mother had cherished Carolyn. We moved into a six-room apartment that we rented for $20 a month from a Lithuanian woman who had a green thumb with roses but who surreptitiously stole our coal. When our first daughter began to patter over the floor, she would pound on her ceiling with a broomstick; she then told us that we ought to move above a grocery store. Her husband was an inane cripple; her daughter took piano lessons and played the opening strains of *Humoresk* by Dvoràk over and over.

We soon bought a home on Neland Avenue and some years later moved a block down the street. I hired a little fleet of boys with wagons and paid them a quarter a load to help move us. Much of it was transported in my car, through whose floorboard one could see the street moving. Our moving bill was $16.50. We lived on that street for thirty years and saw it change from a middle-class white neighborhood to one half black, from a street where one could leave tricycles on the lawn to one where double locks were a necessity and our big dog Brandy, to whom we owe much, was as valuable as a missile.

It often seems to parents that Francis Bacon was right when he wrote, "He that hath children doth give hostages to fortune"; but in actuality they are gifts from the Lord and hostages to his providence, which often moves in mysterious ways. Children however old, are never far from the thoughts of their parents. I know an elderly lady of over ninety who waits up for her married daughter of sixty to come home. Many parents do not fall asleep until the back door closes for the night. And the worries of parents today include menaces never heard of by my parents. We have had four children to love, pray for, and delight in. When our first daughter, Lucarol, arrived, my wife was a blonde; when I brought them home, her hair was light brown. It cost us $70–$35 to Dr. Ten Have and $35 to Butterworth Hospital for a ten-day stay. No complications, routine bed rest. Our first son, John, arrived with such celerity that I had hardly begun to read a newspaper when the nurse brought him out; such zest for life characterizes him still. They were good babies: they slept in the afternoon *and* at night, and we were placidly unaware of the dynamos that were to come later. Our second daughter, Miriam, eschewed naps and thought 4 A.M. a perfect time to dress her dolls. When our last son, Luverne, arrived and I would take him for a walk, people would say, "What a cute grandson you have." He also thought sleep was for sissies. He unscrewed everything he could at an early age, stuffed the toilet with toilet paper and put a match to it, poured a gallon of paint into his little wheelbarrow and sat in it. When he was three, he poured sand and pebbles into my gas tank; unaware of it, we took a trip. We had to have the stuff blown out of the gas line nine times. He was, as the saying goes, "full of beans."

Our eldest daughter always had a crowded calendar. On one date, her swain kept laughing loudly until midnight; finally, I came downstairs and said, "You get the hahaha out of here." One night we were worried, because she was always home on time, and this time it was very late. Finally, we saw her and her date, Rodney Mulder, pushing an old car down the street to our driveway. He was the last of the suitors and now teaches at Grand Valley College. Our son Tim was mesmerized in high school. He went to Europe with us but returned soon after the New Year. A few years later he married Patricia Knoll, whom he had to leave for a year for service in Vietnam. He is teaching English at Calvin College. Our second daughter, Miriam, met her future husband at the marriage of his best friend to one of her best friends. The next summer she went for a visit to Bob and Mary Meyer in California. We wondered about the long visit until we knew that Steven Lilley was the magnet. He is now working for the National Medical Enterprise. One day after church, a lady was bragging about her son-in-law, "the doctor, you know, in Los Angeles." She kept repeating the reference to "her son-in-law, the doctor, you know, in Los Angeles." Finally, she asked my wife, "What does your son-in-law in Los Angeles do?" My wife smiled sweetly, too sweetly I thought, and replied, "He buys hospitals"—which he actually does as part of a team. Our youngest son, Luverne (Biz) joined the navy at seventeen. After going through the trauma of having our first son drafted and being in Vietnam, we were somewhat dismayed when he entered the armed services. He met his future wife in San Francisco. He operates a huge machine at General Motors; whereas he took everything apart as a child, he puts everything together as a man.

Some time ago I read an obituary which listed among the mourners "some very special grandchildren." There are very many special grandchildren in the country, but whether they are special to other people is another matter. Some of the most tiresome conversationalists exhaust their hearers by detailing the gifts and actions of their grandchildren. However, most people will tolerate a few such stories, and I will tell only a few. One of our grandchildren in the kindergarten was asked on one of these achievements tests, "Where does meat come from?" and she answered "Hondorp's Meat Market." A little three-year-old sat next to me in the driver's seat and asked, "Need any help, Grandpa?" A six-year-old came to me with his usual serious face and said, "Grandpa, I just don't know what I want to be when I'm big. I don't know whether I want to be a paleontologist or a brain surgeon. Now I have been studying the lobes of the brain all by myself."

When one of our adopted grandchildren was very little he was told by his parents that Grandpa had been adopted too. He called up at once and said, "Grandpa, did you know that you were adopted too?" We are all intensely pro-life, and our son Tim has been exceedingly active in supporting that movement by writing, speaking, engaging in fund raising efforts, and offering interim courses on abortion at Calvin. Rodney and Lucarol adopted a homeless eleven-year-old girl who had been abused by a father who extinguished cigarettes on her legs. Luverne has adopted Shane. We all rejoice when the rejected find a good home.

On Christmas day almost two years ago, the four families who live in or near Grand Rapids had dinner at Tim and Patricia's home. We all held Rebecca, the two-month-old daughter of Luverne and Velda. After returning home that evening Vel picked up their baby from its crib to nurse her and found her dead. The next morning was one of the most desolate in our lives. Their home was still glowing with Christmas adornments. We took the three other children home with us. Rachel, five years old, said, "Oh, I'm so mad at myself. If I had been awake I could have run to the window and seen the angel carry Rebecca up to heaven." On the way home she kept singing, "I've got a Home in Glory Land that Outshines the Sun." A little child shall lead them! One of Wordsworth's poems echoes our experience in the first stanza:

> *A slumber did my spirit seal;*
> *I had no human fears*
> *She seemed a thing that could not feel*
> *The touch of earthly years.*

The second stanza echoes the belief of those who lack any Christian hope:

No motion has she now, no force;
She neither hears nor sees
Rolled round in earth's diurnal course,
With rocks, and stones, and trees.

But there was an immortal soul in that little body, and thanks be to the Lord, there is a Savior who can say "Little girl, I say to you, get up."

Chapter 12

Grand Rapids Christian High

In 1938 Grand Rapids Christian High School was located on the corner of Franklin Street and Madison Avenue and consisted of a weathered building, once simultaneously attended by dark-suited seminarians and giggling young girls, and a new addition generally reserved for veteran faculty members. Across the street on one side was an equally antiquated elementary school; next to that school was the residence of Dr. Henry Beets, who would roll in portly fashion to the corner to hitchhike or take a bus for a swim at the Y.M.C.A. Just beyond the corner on Madison was a fire station that disgorged fire engines from time to time with a resonant clatter that so magnetized my class on the corner that I finally had to tell the students, "Get up and look at it." Buses ground to a halt at that corner with irritating regularity and then took off with disturbing gusto. Since the room was on the west and the windows were open on hot days, the ceaseless traffic was irritable competition. In the winter the steam-heated pipes cracked and hissed all day long. It was not the best place to perceive "the light that never was on land or sea," but it was a good setting for Sandburg's *Chicago*. This was Room 7, where I spent seven years—a perfect number of years in an imperfect place with students I remember with affection and regard.

In 1938, Christian High had about four hundred students, a dwarf among the big city schools, whose basketball teams they trimmed for most of the years I taught there. The students came not only from the city but from the suburbs and country towns as well. There was only a tinge of cliquishness in the school: affluent students were few, and most students were sacrificially supported by their parents or by their own hard-earned money. They were young and ebullient and responded to a smile and a sense of humor as effectively as they did to the duress of the stiff-arm approach of a martinet. In the seven years I taught there I do not recall a single angry confrontation. I am not bedazzled by nostalgia: if one remembers anything one remembers insults and rudeness, and I do not. They were not angels, but none had horns.

It would be injudicious and hazardous for me to appraise the faculty, but it, like the student body, was above average in almost every field. In my years there, I witnessed but one disaster. One teacher was a soft-hearted young man who knew his material but could not keep the lid on. His class could be heard in the hall like the sound of many waters. Once Mr. Post, the principal, and I were standing in the hall, and he asked me, "What's he teaching in there?" I said, "Shakespeare's *The Tempest*," and he replied, "It sounds like it." That teacher could not control the imp in the best of us. One time I heard two seniors talking about an older member of the faculty. One said, "He's getting senile," and the other said, "What do you mean, *getting* senile? He's always been senile." Apart from these comments, I heard little severe criticism of any teacher and very high praise for some of them.

We did have one "character" on the faculty, one Frank Vanden Berg, teacher of bookkeeping. He was a stocky, shortish man with a square face, determined jaw, and a shimmer of reddish hair. He had a distinctive, rolling walk, and he was smoking a cigar whenever possible. When I referred to the cost of cigars, he said, "I forget about it." He had a gruff voice and rather stern expression, but I enjoyed his salty independence. He had very strong opinions about the administration and carried on a running opposition to it, always referring to it as "the office." He taught bookkeeping for a living but wrote novels for recreation. *Rusty* and *Westhaven* are not American classics, but they do indicate imagination and a good sense of characterization and dialogue. One would not expect them to emerge from a bookkeeper's desk any more than one would expect Wallace Stevens' great poems to emerge from an indemnity insurance office. His remarks may have been inept at times, and his voice and manner intimidating, but he added spice to faculty meetings. I enjoyed his bold individuality and memorable person.

The principal, Mr. E. R. Post, was a unique blend of humor, firmness, and pedagogical insight. I had quite a few "practice teachers," and the final evaluation of their performance was made by a Calvin professor, Mr. Post, and me. Mr. Post's comments on the teaching were incisive and perceptive; he knew the techniques that work. He never interfered with a teacher if the latter did his work well; he stressed high standards and Christian commitment. On the occasions when I was ill or injured, he was a sympathetic friend. He handed me my contract for the first year as I was boarding a Michigan Central train for New Jersey. It was the first step toward seven years of rewarding teaching under a distinguished administrator.

During these seven years I taught English III, an introductory course in grammar and composition, English IV, American Literature, English V, Advanced Composition, English Literature, and a course called "Commercial English," which I escaped as soon as possible—and that was very soon. I was also drafted to teach courses in Latin and church history. Few students relish grammar, and it is difficult to dramatize the

semicolon. In the literature courses I tried to relate biography and literature, a process that illuminates both and often gives authenticity to a
poem or story. After all, Mark Twain himself was a complex synthesis of
Tom Sawyer and Huckleberry Finn, a realist and a romanticist, though
the realism became pitch dark in the end, and the fantasy turned into a
nightmare in *The Mysterious Stranger*. I assigned books for outside
reading that I believed they would enjoy, never a showy reading list to
prove that we were intellectuals. I would rather have them enjoy *The Red
Pony* than be puzzled and proud at having read *The Brothers Karamazov*.
Of course, if some brilliant student wanted to test his or her mettle by
reading *Moby Dick,* I gladly acquiesced.

Room 7 was separated from a large session room by sliding doors,
under which there was room to slip notes during session periods. I soon
noticed some sly slipping of notes under the door. After I intercepted a
few of them and answered them myself, the mail stopped. My good
neighbor in Room 6 across the hall was Sidney Stuk, a popular teacher
and a delightful person. One semester I had to take charge of his study
session while he was engaged in other duties. During the period, a boy
fell sound asleep. I told the class to leave most silently at the end of the
hour, and I informed Sid's class in the hall that they should enter most
quietly. In the middle of the next period, the lad awoke with embarrassment.

A portion of English III was devoted to oral composition; I never
knew why. It was often uncomfortable for the students, and this was not a
speech class; but some rejoiced in doing it. One session remains clear in
my mind. A young girl, athletic and strong, gave a talk on the process of
resuscitation. Her partner in the demonstration, a little guy, had presumably drowned and was lying on the floor, and the girl gave him the works.
She pummeled and bounced him while she explained the process. During
the exercise the class was convulsed with laughter, and the tears ran down
my face. She got the A she deserved.

Although real discipline problems were rare, there was whispering
sometimes, especially during study periods. As punishment—deliberately somewhat silly but acceptable at the time—I made the students
write lines. Joe Stevens, a brilliant boy who later taught at Harvard, told
me years later with a grin what I had made him write: "The Franklin bus
is big and brave." I told a surly girl to write, "I want to be a sunbeam."
There was also a boy named Bishop, who had to write the biblical text
describing the duties of a bishop. Nobody would or could do that today,
but forty years ago it worked.

I did not especially welcome the introduction of "practice teaching," but I learned as much as I taught from the experience. Success in
teaching can be helped by creative imitation; one has to integrate what
one learns with one's own gifts. To try to imitate what is contrary to one's
nature is perilous: one should learn from others but be oneself. I gave the

practice teachers as much freedom as possible to do that. Lesson plans are important, but one has to sense when to deviate from rigid patterns to make a point unmentioned in the pattern. I had some excellent apprentices: Bert Bratt, who taught for many years at Oakdale Christian; Tony Brouwer, a pugilist and later a teacher at Calvin; Miriam Stevens; and Julianne F. Steensma. The last was a vivacious and imaginative teacher who dressed sharply and wore bobby socks—at that time a daring innovation. She also sat on the desk while teaching. There was also a young lady with a marked poetic gift but little skill in teaching; she tried so hard but lacked the talent to communicate her enthusiasms. Today, of course, this training is far more lengthy and doubtless more helpful.

Miss Helen Zandstra was the head of our department. She was a notable Christian lady whose works live after her. She was helpful without being officious, sensitive to beauty in art and life, and she was never scanty in encouragement. She made a career of welldoing in and out of the classroom, and she modified many lives through her sympathy, knowledge, and Christian witness. When she retired, I was happy to be able to arrange her appointment as an assistant in English at Calvin College for several years.

Christian High had three excellent Bible teachers while I was there. Dr. John Bratt was there for only a few years, but his strong commitment to the Reformed faith, his keen and balanced perception of biblical truths, and his interesting chapel talks were greatly appreciated. Rev. William Stuart was white-haired but young in spirit. He had a razor-sharp mind, abominated pretense and stuffiness, and gave terse, illuminating chapel talks. He was a provocative teacher, a sharp conversationalist, and a good friend to colleagues and students. He died suddenly on his way to preach a "nice Christmas sermon." His sudden death shocked our community, and I remember the packed auditorium at LaGrave Christian Reformed Church for the funeral, to which I took my father, who had long admired him. He was a man of memorable talents.

Dr. Leonard Greenway was the teacher of Bible during my last years at Christian High. He was a musician, orator, and pastor. His Wednesday chapel talks were fresh, interesting, and stirring: the announced titles caught the eye and the mind, and the messages went to the heart of the matter and into the hearts of the students. He, like the other Bible teachers, was devoid of ministerial pomp and without a trace of self-importance. He could give compliments as well as receive them. Dr. Greenway was a kindly, dynamic man who served his church nobly and untiringly until his late seventies, and his death was a personal as well as ecclesiastical loss. He was a bright and shining light, and all who knew him benefited from him. He lived to serve, not to be served.

All of the teachers were competent, but three had unusual gifts as well. Earl Strikwerda had a Ph.D., rare among high school teachers—as he himself was a rare person and teacher: an unremitting inquirer of truth, a ripe scholar, a master of the telling phrase, and a connoisseur of railroads. Bernard Fridsma, teacher of Latin and German, was an acknowledged authority on Frisian language and letters. Mrs. Trena Haan was an accomplished singer and choir director; many of her choirs received statewide recognition and often deepened chapel experience for us.

Sometimes chapel was varied by outside speakers and educational films. Two of these modifications glow in my memory still. On one of those oppressively hot September days in Michigan, a psychologist from a university spoke to the packed auditorium, where the heat was intensified by the presence of many bodies. Technically he was a psychologist; but as a speaker he was a prime example of elongated dullness, and he spoke for a full hour. There was no air conditioning, only increasingly hot air. On another occasion we were treated to the showing of an educational film. These were chosen by a very conservative man who usually previewed the films, but this time he had evidently neglected to preview it. The film was about the planting, cultivating, and marketing of tomatoes (whatever that had to do with chapel, I do not know); but that film was a mini-blockbuster. Scantily clad girls were picking tomatoes; beautiful, curvaceous babes in tight clothing displayed them; there was a sort of tomato dance. Before long, the catcalls and sharp whistles echoed throughout the auditorium, and the applause came. For some reason I still don't understand, the teacher allowed the film to run its full course, a world of luscious tomatoes and incendiary lassies.

In the spring of 1938, the school, for some years a formidable power in basketball under the coaching of Claus Beukema, decided to field a baseball team. Since I had played a great deal of baseball, I was appointed coach. The first year was almost an experiment in misery. We had to play large schools with a long tradition in baseball; most of our boys had little experience in baseball. Some of the boys were ludicrously inept: they would rush in for fly balls that sailed fifty feet over their heads. One player, a good fielder, did not get a single hit all season. Another, an all-state basketball player, wanted to re-enter the game after he had been removed from the lineup; when he found out that this was impossible, he quit. Fortunately, we had a good pitcher and won three games. Gradually the team improved, and one year we finished a game behind the leader. If I could have had all the good players in one season, we would have been unbeatable: players like Maurice DeJong, Jimmy Swart, George and Joel Worst, and Leonard VanderLugt were as good as high school players get. Over the years we won more games than we lost, largely because we beat Holland Christian twice a year.

Memories of these seasons are still vivid: playing at Creston's field in early spring in falling snowflakes; the time I had so many boys in the car that the axle broke and I had to pay the repairs out of the small honorarium I received; the deft fielding of Jimmy Swart; the profane coach of Catholic Central; upset victories over Ottawa Hills and Central. The most irritating memory is of a game we played at Valley Field against Union. We were leading by one run in the bottom of the seventh, the last inning of the game. There were two out and two strikes on the batter, a weak hitter. The game seemed to be in the bag, when our catcher tried to pick off the runner on first base. He threw the ball into right field. It was *the* bonehead play in my experience in baseball. But I said nothing to the catcher—out of discretion.

Coaching baseball with these boys was a pleasure. In many cases, being on the team made them work harder in their classes than they otherwise would have. Sports, if kept in proper perspective, are a valuable feature of school life. Baseball at Christian High School also caused me physical pain. One day after a game at Garfield Park, where I drank water from a fountain, I came home with a high fever. There were no antibiotics in those days, and my recovery was tediously slow. When I returned to school and led chapel, I told the students—who had been markedly sympathetic—that I had been so ill that the hearse had waited at the door for three days. But the worst was yet to come. While I was watching a baseball game on a school picnic in late spring, a batter lost his grip on the bat and it slammed into the left side of my face. I woke up in the hospital with a surgeon stitching the abrasions on my face. Dr. Laird said I had a classic black eye, and I still have the scars. When I reflect on what could have happened, I am grateful that I had only scars and pain. Add to these events the broken fingers I received in playing baseball, and one can see that it has expenses as well as pleasures.

The Board of Grand Rapids Christian was a largely invisible power. No board member ever visited my class, and reappointment was routine if services were satisfactory. Usually I met them only on a spring picnic. They were highly visible only once—during the years when movie attendance was strictly forbidden. The matter of amusements greatly concerned the president of the board, Henry Hekman, whom I remembered because he once visited my parents in Paterson and kept the taxi waiting for him for over an hour (such affluence amazed me then). He called a special meeting of the faculty to interrogate us on our attitude toward movie attendance. There we sat as if before a judgment seat, and each one was asked to profess his steadfast allegiance to the rule. When my turn came, I got away with saying, "I have better things to do." There was something eerie about that meeting and, in the light of later synodical decisions, something bizarre. I have never been a movie fan: I doubt whether I have seen a dozen movies in the last forty years; but I do remember that the movies we were denied were infinitely better than many of the films one may now freely attend. It was also an exercise in hypocrisy because every teacher knew that some films were wholly above reproach and even inspiring. A sort of tyranny prevailed then, because to have defended movie attendance at that time would have made one suspect. It wasn't worth the battle.

Some board members also had some extremely right-wing attitudes toward politics. One member of the faculty was in jeopardy because of his outspoken sympathy for labor, and it took the mettle of Drs. Ryskamp and Jellema at Calvin to preserve his status. I don't think Democrats are in peril at Christian High today, but in the forties, though they may not have been in peril, their political convictions were not welcome in class or out of it to most supporters of the school.

During part of the time when I taught at Grand Rapids Christian High, the janitor was Henry De Good. We both came from the western fringe of the American heartland, and we enjoyed telling stories and smoking pipes. He was Mr. Fixit. I doubt whether Christian High ever had to replace anything during his tenure. One cold day in early November my furnace at home ran into trouble. I called Holland Furnace Company for aid, but the man who came dismantled my furnace and left it that way. They insisted that I needed a brand new Holland furnace at a time when such a purchase meant real hardship. Henry came over and put in a new grate for $16. (Incidentally, Holland Furnace went out of business some years later because of numerous such ripoffs.) Henry De Good has been repairing troubled machines, inept fixtures and lamps, broken furniture and other things for us for over forty years, always asking far less than union labor and receiving more than he asked for. Henry, however, is more than a handyman; he always has a new story. He and Richard Tiemersma know more stories than I can possibly remember. Henry was also, before his stroke, an accomplished accordionist. He has given free concerts and spiritual encouragement to numerous audiences in jails, old people's homes, churches, nursing homes—all places where people need cheer without charge. After his stroke he had to turn from the accordion to a musical saw, on which he can play an extensive repertoire to similar audiences. His devotion to spiritual and human need and his willingness to help at inconvenient times have endeared him and his wife, who is similarly endowed, to our family.

Curious little incidents linger in my mind and I will pack them into a paragraph. One day in chapel, as we were singing "God of Our Fathers," a faculty member not noted for vocal supremacy began loudly by singing a solo, the word "Trumpets." When our first daughter was born, students brought various gifts to class, among them a dozen diapers and safety pins. I had a box of little cigars, which I offered to those who wanted them—to the displeasure of some parents and colleagues. Over a Memorial Day weekend, my wife and I chaperoned a group of girls at a cottage on Spring Lake. When some boys came flocking to the honey hive, my wife said to the girls, "If they waited until now to try to get a date, tell them to go blow," which they did. It was a cool evening and we were sitting on the floor in the living room telling ghost stories, when we heard a sharp knock on the door. It was Dr. and Mrs. Clarence Bouma, asking, "Where's Thea?" They had searched all over the park and the pier for the girls, only to find them safe in the cottage inventing ghost stories. We also had faculty parties. At one of them a young lady was giving a piano solo while the faculty and their wives kept talking. My wife, who was the chairman of the party, asked the pianist to stop and said, "As soon as Mr. Post and all of you faculty keep still, we will continue with the program."

* * *

The years at Christian High were not without sadness. I attended untimely funerals of two sixteen-year-old students, and the war ended the lives of some of our most promising students. Rev. Stuart, a landmark in the church and school, died suddenly. The saddest experience, however, was watching the physical deterioration of Frank Driesens from an incurable disease that caused painful eruptions on his body. During the last days of his service, he came to class with heavily bandaged hands. Finally, he literally died of starvation when the disease ravaged his throat. I will never forget the funeral at Twelfth Street Christian Reformed Church, with his wife and six fatherless children sitting in the front. I doubt whether there was a dry eye in the church.

I left Christian High for Calvin College in 1945. It was an excellent school then, and it is an excellent school now, with an enviable reputation and far superior facilities. The old building I taught in has been reduced to discarded rubble, and the voices of many of that faculty are only memories, but the memories of both and that of the extraordinarily likable student body are unforgettable. History is the fever that destroys the champions of vision and tradition, but my hope is that the tradition will never fade.

Chapter 13

Brave New World with a Bramble Bush

In the summer of 1946, Calvin College was on the edge of a dramatic expansion for which it was impossible to be adequately prepared. None could have predicted how or when World War II would end, nor expected the tremendous influx of students that followed. In the fall of 1946, Calvin was overwhelmed when its student body doubled: 1400 students crowded into facilities that had been inadequate for the 700 of the year before. Classrooms bulged; dormitories were wholly inadequate; there were no empty seats in the library; and classes ran from dawn to dusk and through Saturday morning. Every light was green and the traffic tremendous. Enthusiasm, industry, and almost extemporaneous provision and vision were the marks of the time.

In the spring of 1945, I had been interviewed briefly and cordially by President Schultze and two members of the executive committee in an enlarged cubicle called the president's office. I was never interviewed by the full board because I was lying on a davenport recovering from the effects of the baseball bat accident. This, the board felt, was hardly a condition under which one should be interviewed concerning his stand on amusements. At the end of the board's sessions I received a letter that began "Beer Brother." I remember my pain in laughing about it. I was appointed for two years; but in those days of hectic expansion and appointments, the board forgot to reappoint me, so I served for some years without a contract.

President Schultze was a highly gifted man, but the administration was actually a sort of troika that consisted of Prof. Ryskamp, Prof. Dekker, and the president. Prof. Dekker, however, was a very efficient registrar and was often wroth with the faculty for not following his instructions about registration. Once he said something like this: "You expect your students to follow directions, but you don't follow mine. You mess things up." Excellent administration did not come in until the arrival of William Spoelhof, Henry De Witt, John Vanden Berg, and Lester Ippel.

I had taught at Calvin's summer school for five sessions preceding my appointment. In the spring of 1940 the Grand Rapids Board of Education began requiring public school teachers to attend further schooling, and it asked Calvin to offer summer courses. That summer I started teaching on the sixth floor of Davis Technical High School, now occupied by Grand Rapids Junior College. There was no air conditioning, and some days were so hot that the tar on the roof that projected over another part of the building beside our windows buckled in the heat. The class contained a striking and histrionic redhead from Union High who knew Amy Lowell and other contemporary writers. She had a gift for reading poetry and provided a delightful asset to the class. Some years later I taught a class containing a Miss Dilley, the daughter of a Grand Rapids attorney who opposed aid to private schools as vigorously as his son does now, and Lewis B. Smedes, a brilliant student who later wrote superb books. Since they held to radically different perspectives and were both highly articulate and keen in argument, their differences of opinion provided both amusement and illumination. Only once in later years did I experience such charged debate. That was in a class containing Robert Staal, the *Chimes* editor at the time and a very bright young man, and Henry Pietersma, who was classically trained in the Netherlands and possessed a philosophical talent. One day, in disagreeing about the value of Whitman's poetry, they argued so vehemently that they rose in their seats and almost came to blows. Since most Americans hardly know that poets exist, I have never forgotten the incident.

During my first semester at Calvin, I taught three sections of Freshman English, whose size ranged from thirty-five to forty students. Freshman English is difficult to teach, not only because of the inexhaustible need for red ink but also because of its manifold objectives and the startling range of student aptitudes. One meets students to whom grammar is an already mastered bore, writing well is easy, and term papers are a challenge. There are also those for whom instilling grammar is almost like pounding a nail into stone. I have received brilliant papers from students like Martin Wyngaarden, Mary Holtrop, and Peter Kreeft—and eighth-grade performances from some who should never have been admitted to college. The course was enjoyable when the second semester was largely devoted to literature; but the 4-1-4 curriculum, by concentrating mechanics, the term paper, and *The Edge of Experience* into a little more than three months, became a shining example of "in-depth" education.

American Literature is a delightful course to teach, with its sweep of thought from the fierce faith of the Puritans to its even fiercer rejection by the naturalists. When I first taught the course, our text was an 800-page volume; when I retired, our two textbooks numbered 3,600 pages. Small fry from earlier periods had been eliminated to make room for a host of small fry from later periods, many of them included for nonliterary reasons. I always preferred a text called *Major American Writers*. I could get along without D. H. Gass and Allen Ginsberg, but modern editors prefer a smorgasbord.

Over the years I have taught fourteen different courses in the English Department. In addition to American Literature, my favorite courses were Chaucer, the History of the English Novel, and Victorian Poetry. Anyone who does not enjoy teaching and taking Chaucer is allergic to literature. The English novel was not only inherently fascinating but always enriched by students from other disciplines. I always assigned twelve novels to read, and I do not remember any complaints. Victorian Poetry was exciting to me because it was a highly literary reflection of my own struggles with the dilemmas of faith and reason. Though not the greatest of the Victorian poets, Matthew Arnold spoke most poignantly to me in the indigo moods of the poems that reflect on lost loyalties, ebbing ideals, and the search for certainty.

Teaching in a college like Calvin is done in a distinct cultural and religious ambience. One is not a philosophically neutral member of a pluralistic community; in fact, one is employed to be the opposite. This ambience was marked by clearly identifiable characteristics during the 1940s, 1950s, and early 1960s. In the thirties and forties the intellectual life of Calvin focused on the word *integration*. That there was an "antithesis" everyone affirmed, but the question was: How shall faith and learning be related or integrated? How shall a fundamental unity of faith and scholarship be achieved? It cannot be achieved by either closing the books or blandly accepting them. No scholar can be at once a behaviorist in psychology or a mechanist in physics and at the same time a Christian in faith. How does the religious professional view all learning, and how does the Calvinist "make the principles of the Reformed faith fundamental in all his teaching," as Professor Berkhof put it in "Our School's Reason for Existence"? The "Committee of Ten," appointed by the Christian Reformed Synod, requested and received statements from all faculty members on this question in 1940. The effort to find and apply answers to the question of integration was intense during these years, and the quest involved amusements as well as philosophy.

During the fifties, the so-called silent generation had a great deal to say about *commitment*. In the "Foreword" to the *Calvin College Prism* of 1950, we find these words:

> We feel that Calvinism, far from being dead or dying, represents a segment of that orthodox Christianity which holds the hope of a world that needs salvation in blind alleys where no salvation is to be found.

Commitment to God's Word and the Calvinistic heritage, commitment to making that Word critically relevant in thought and life, commitment to Jesus Christ as its energizing source—this was the spirit of Calvin during the fifties. It manifested itself not only in teaching but in student publications, not only in officially pure statements but in journals and public lectures. Successful integration, Calvin professors and students believed, presupposes intelligent commitment.

Until the college moved to Knollcrest Farm, faculty offices and departmental secretaries were nonexistent. Professors had studies instead of offices. One is a creature of habit, and when I was assigned my first office I could not stand to sit in it; I used it for interviewing students. The absence of secretaries, incidentally, put an additional burden on my wife, who cheerfully and meticulously typed many letters of recommendation; one year, when I was chairman of the department, she typed more than fifty. In many cases the adequate differentiation of qualities in students becomes a problem in writing recommendations: imagination, scholarship, mental acuity, and even winning personality are common to bright students. Recommendations to the seminary were a different problem: obviously, criteria other than those used for admission to a graduate school, such as piety and personal conviction, were in order. At one point I became impatient with the fact that intellectual mediocrities were being admitted to the seminary. Finally, I sent a letter that said: "This man, though obviously a saint, can neither think, write, or speak. Since you will admit him, make sure he lands in an obscure charge where he can do little damage." Needless to say, I also had the pleasure of recommending outstanding preseminary students, who later proved their promise.

Alexander Lodge, a kind of dump with an aristocratic name, was a decaying elementary school that the college renovated to house students. Conditions there were spartan: bare rooms with double-decker beds, no closets, two tiny lockers for each student, no showers or bathtubs. The lodge happened to be across the street from our home, and we frequently invited the young men to our home, many of them veterans who had gone from army barracks to college barracks. Some of them were almost speechless, with handshakes like the touch of a fish; others were great company. Here we struck up a permanent friendship with Richard Tiemersma, a suave, eloquent young man who was loaded with spicy stories, solid convictions, and keen insights. He became a colleague at Calvin and enriched our living room as well as his classroom for many years.

Every faculty worth its salt is full of salt: it tries to follow the light but uses dietary precautions against sweetness. Every faculty also has a considerable number of highly intelligent, articulate, and strong-willed characters; and when the righteous are right, they are very right. Consequently—in the days before most matters were shifted to committees and passed without much murmur—our faculty meetings were often colorful affairs. As an example: formerly, each preseminary student, as well as every student recommended for a certain scholarship, had to be recommended separately and approved by the faculty. Partisan eulogies sizzled with praise, and the ensuing debates on the merits of these candidates were often sharply candid. (Today a committee settles the matter.) The appointment of new faculty members also had to be approved after open, frank, and sometimes stormy discussion. And new courses were sometimes acrimoniously debated before approval. In some cases there was a distinct afterglow of chagrin and even hostility.

From the time I entered the faculty, pieces in *The Literary Review, Chimes,* and its satirical spinoffs, *Spoofs* and *Bong,* involved hours of discussion. I remember a faculty meeting at which one professor was violently upset because the word "whore" appeared in a story. How far away that seems now! During some of those sessions, our former colleague Bernie Van't Hul would draw snide cartoons for his own amusement and our edification. Some faculty members were frank to the point of presumption; at times speakers had to be curtailed. During his many years as president, William Spoelhof exhibited a great deal of forbearance, tact, and wisdom chairing faculty meetings. When done well, it is an art.

In the 1950s, President Spoelhof introduced faculty retreats in the early fall, which have continued to the present day—except that the faculty now retreats to the campus instead of outlying sites. For some years these retreats spanned two days and a night, and the discussions sometimes continued into early morning. On our first retreat at Camp Geneva on Lake Michigan, I saw Professor Wyngaarden promenading through the woods in the hot night at 3 A.M. in full dress: hat, vest, and watch chain dangling across his chest. Later, the retreats continued at Castle Park, a luxurious resort where we sat beneath a tin roof under a boiling sun or in a cool, informal semibasement. Here I heard Cecil De Boer, who feared no man, reduce an argument to shambles, and I heard the touted Dr. Dooyeweerd of the Free University deliver a learned lecture, which Harry Jellema, who was reading a novel in our room, did not attend. I always liked Cecil De Boer's abrupt honesty. If you asked him who was at a meeting where you should have been, he would say, "Everybody that counted." As the faculty grew in size, the expense involved limited the retreat to one day, and the sheer number in attendance restricted intensive discussions to small groups.

Churches and colleges take great pride in growth, but it always proves to be a bittersweet benefit. I recognize that growth is essential to the acquisition of facilities, equipment, and books; but it is not without a cost in intimacy and even in learning. On the one hand, a large faculty offers opportunities for greater selection of teachers; but it also limits one's exposure to the best. The faculty tends to split into departmental enclaves. In my early days at Calvin one could have coffee with members from ten departments; now certain departments have coffee in their own parishes. The large college runs the risk of impersonality.

On the subject of growth, I was an ardent and futile nonsupporter of the 4-1-4 curriculum, which, in brief, means that a student may take only four courses a semester, plus an interim course in seventeen days on an astonishing variety of subjects. Taking thirty-two courses in college simply does not seem equal educationally to forty-plus courses. What it gains in depth it loses in exposure. When we considered the proposal, I remembered all the courses I would have missed had it been in effect in the twenties. The interim offers many courses, but the students who really push themselves in these courses are not abundant.

* * *

During the summer of 1946, I was granted $100 from the college for a summer session at Northwestern. The keeper of the books was a prim, bossy, mincing little man: if he could deter a buck's departure, his day was glorious. When one professor complained mildly to him about his high water bills, the bookkeeper replied, "Take a bath like I do—with an inch of water." I went to him in June to get my check, but he said, "I'm too busy with Synod." During the summer I asked him again, but he was too busy with other matters. When the fall semester began, he said, "I'm too busy with registration." By this time incensed, I went to President Schultze, who said, "Come with me." He went to the bookkeeper's office and said, "Write this man a check—now!" Little boys have big ears, and one day when our three-year-old son saw the bookkeeper prancing by our house—as he did twice a day—he said, "Hi, Poopy" (he was yanked into the house fast). A meticulous financial martinet, the man would not pay for the removal of a tree unless the executive board ordered it (in those days the executive board discussed the removal of trees). Yet, despite his minute observance of order, he forgot to pay me my last check in the spring of 1935. Calvin still owes me $22. I remember that little man well.

Ultimately, all faculty members are under the Calvin Board of Trustees, which was called the Curatorium when preseminary students still learned Latin. The board has been and is an excellent body of dedicated, competent, and generous men and women. However, as a pious elder in an appropriately quavering voice said to a professor's son during house visitation, "Well son, we all sin, your father and mother sin, elders sin—even ministers sin . . . " (to which the boy replied, "No shit!"). Some curators have had minor faults as well. One board member known for brains and brass visited us in our apartment, and as he left he asked, "Is this all you've got?" I replied, "I ain't got it yet."

During my thirty years of teaching at Calvin, I had four unannounced classroom visits from board members. The first visitors were the president of the board and another clergyman—both first-rate theologians. I was discussing Jonathan Edwards' *The Freedom of the Will,* a knotty, slippery book, and I offered them an opportunity to participate.

But they slipped out of it. The second visit came when my freshman class was studying Ring Lardner's classic baseball story "Alibi Ike." No room for interpretation there. The third visitor was a staid gentleman from the plains who suffered through Emily Dickinson's "Some Keep the Sabbath Going to Church" and "I Taste a Liquor Never Brewed"—plenty of room for "integration" there.

The fourth visit riles me still. I had an exceptionally able class, and as we were studying Thoreau's art, an exciting discussion with both drive and direction ensued. I am not known for boasting, but this was an excellent period. Afterwards, the board member, whom I knew from the days we both attended Calvin, said nothing at all about the class. I was sure that he had stood many times at the back of his sanctuary awaiting praise for a wonderful sermon. Forgiveness is a splendid virtue, but one that I can't live up to in this instance. I still remember this clerical clod with resentment.

I have one final example of doltish behavior on the part of board members. On the twenty-fifth anniversary of my teaching at Calvin, the board sponsored a dinner at which several of us were honored. The speaker, supposedly selected to congratulate me, was a fellow alumnus of Eastern Academy, and he spent all of his time describing pranks I had initiated or participated in during my high school days (fortunately, he was only partially informed). I thought he would at least have congratulated me on longevity. All of the foregoing pales, however, compared to what happened to a fellow retiree at a similar banquet. After he had put in many years of hard work at the college, a board member presented him with an enlarged plastic golf ball and a large plastic club and said, "Now you can play golf," a statement imbedded in a tinhorn introduction and an irrelevant conclusion.

Every teacher has unpleasant experiences with students. Mine came in waves. The first was an attack by seven students on six professors, which they made without prior complaint. The subjects of the complaints ranged from merely silly minutiae to serious and fundamental issues. The students often ripped the teachers' positions out of context and clouded them by misapprehension. Doubtless, the professors could have been clearer, and the students certainly could have been more charitable. When the seven students and the six professors met with members of the board, however, Prof. Harry Jellema confuted them with superb effectiveness. The second wave consisted of a militant nucleus of the disciples of Cornelius Van Til of Westminster Seminary. They were constantly in battle gear in my classroom, until I said to them, "Let me write on the board the essence of your critique." After writing it out, I said, "Am I representing you fairly?" When they agreed, I said, "I will take this statement to President R. B. Kuiper of the seminary and ask him whether you are right or wrong." I went to Prof. Kuiper, who had taught for many years at Westminster Seminary, and I was happy to return to the class with his statement: "You students are wrong." This was a kind of unpleasant experience that does not occur in elementary German. The third wave involved disciples of Dooyeweerd, about whom I knew very little (one can't read everybody). They had a code of words that nobody at a normal college could have followed. I told them, "Write in English or explain your terms." Later, one of them became a good friend and even gave me a box of cigars.

The fourth wave requires a new paragraph. Since I taught mainly courses not directly involved in this surging wave, I was not as thoroughly inundated by it as was the college as a whole. The late sixties, with its storms and stresses, severely tested the commitments of Calvin College. American society was in turmoil: protests, marches, confrontations, and riots boiled over the land; the Vietnam War, pollution, crime, and drugs worried us all. The youth movement, beginning in 1960, shouted answers followed by action. Calvin became involved, as *involvement* became the slogan of the era: the faith of the ages had to meet the needs of today. Many students demanded involvement all the way from the classroom to administrative affairs. But the mood of the suggested solutions was often far from the moorings of the college; involvement sometimes led to identification with the wrong kingdom, and the sense of *antithesis* was often lost. The steady, wise leadership of President Spoelhof, supported by an able administrative staff and faculty, preserved the integrity of the college up to a more peaceful era.

The students of the late 1960s were a very diverse lot, in which the intelligent, vocal minority in control of college media received most of the attention. That era is familiar enough; I wish only to comment on my relations with these students. Whereas President Schultze, in an earlier time, had told a student to go home and put on a tie and coat, some of my students came in bare feet, jeans, and an avalanche of hair, in addition to a sprawling beard. But there were always conventionally dressed students in the class as well. The leading rebels were exceedingly well read, unusually literate, and, as far as my experience was concerned, polite and even affable. They did their work, and in some cases it was brilliant work. They supported causes, some of which I also did.

These were not the people I disliked. I met the latter in the Fine Arts Auditorium, where I participated in a panel on the subject of chapel attendance. It didn't feel like I was at Calvin College. The speakers and the audience were drowning in self-pity: they were utterly humorless and fanatical. My predecessor at the podium greatly overexpended his time; yet when I came up and remarked, "His speech could have been cut in half if he had left out the 'you knows,'" the audience groaned. Speaking to that audience was like trying to reduce granite with soft soap. I had had but one of those characters in class, a boorish boy who did failing work in Chaucer and wrote a note on his bluebook complaining that I did not use a translation—and that he would be happy to talk to me about it. Later on, my wife and I attended a poetry reading in which he participated. With his fly open, he read a bawdy poem about love in the back seat of a car. The girl sitting behind us had her bare feet on the top of the seat next to me. This was not the style of the gifted rebels who were marked by civility in class.

What I resented in many of the rebels was a sort of highbrow philistinism. Some think that the essence of philistinism lies in an immunity and hostility to ideas. Its exemplars are the "standpatters"—in Arnold's phrase, so "resolute and unintelligent." However, the battle cry of the sixties, "Trust no one over thirty," the superficial hostility to tradition, the immersion in the present—these struck me as equally authentic symptoms of philistinism. To deride the past at twenty is merely showing off.

Teaching at Calvin involved benefits beyond the classroom. So many became available that there wasn't time to enjoy them all: the tensely exciting basketball games, interesting and often excellent stage plays, the noon-hour lectures during interim, the beauty of musical performances. The campus in spring was an ever-recurring delight. There was always construction booming along: even if there had been no available and supportable project, the college, in its compelling zeal, would have replaced sidewalks.

Then there were the inestimably transforming powers of evaluation sheets. Words fail me to record what they taught me! One year, many professors consented to have written student evaluations printed in a booklet. Each course was evaluated by a student with impressive scholarly and pedagogical attainments, and some of them were so devastatingly penetrating that the professors who consented to them may have regretted submitting to this surgery without obtaining a second opinion.

The college introduced square dancing, which only squares avoided; and aesthetic dancing illuminated scriptural truths with moving effect. In the meantime, chapel was reduced to twice a week—without a surge in attendance. And the library continued to expand its excellent services, a real tribute to the staff and the administration, which provided generous support.

The 1970s, as I experienced them, were largely a return to normalcy. The recession sobered freedom of expression; the blaze of publicity and the blare of assertion diminished. The Johnsonian era of almost unlimited largesse to colleges was over. Civility and conventional dress reappeared, student attitudes were less critical, and people over thirty were trusted again. Religious life quickened; lively, independent chapel services reappeared. The college I retired from in 1976 was markedly different from the one of 1966.

During the recession of 1972, retirement policies at Calvin were altered. Early in the history of the college, professors had been appointed *ad vitam*, a perilous policy that was later changed to mandatory retirement at seventy. The financial stringency of the early 1970s made the college change mandatory retirement to sixty-five, with limited additional employment for those who had long served, financial benefits to those so affected, and the opportunity to teach one course each semester for two years. Some people welcome retirement; some have it thrust upon them. I found that what I was competent doing was replaced by innumerable requests to do what I didn't care to do. Of course, one has to face the end of "westering." The physical strength that once enabled me to work from 6 A.M. to 6 P.M. in a silk mill and then run home for a bite to eat before pitching seven innings of baseball is long gone, as this poem by my son John indicates:

Ascension

Father, climbing ladders
at 63 to paint the house,
towers above me.

I probe the groundwork looking
for stairways to meet him.

That summer day
father on the wooden ladder
ran his hands over blisters
in the skin of the house
that knows him so well,
knows his morning laugh ringing
through paneled corridors,
his songs filtered to wake us
through knots in the wood.
Father touched the cords with his voice
and set them daily singing.

That summer day
the old thirty foot ladder gave way
as father turned to wave at me
coming home from a six month's absence;
turned tumbling through the split rails,
lying with cracked ribs
among his roses.

That summer day
I picked up his worn tools,
searched the blistered house
for father's touch and found
his hands grasping mine in the wood.

No one can have taught at Calvin as long as I have without gratitude to God. I also owe a large debt to an overwhelmingly pleasant student body: most of my students were good, and quite a few were brilliant. In the course of the years, I have taught not only Christian Reformed students, but Netherlands Reformed, Protestant Reformed, and Orthodox Reformed; Presbyterians and Orthodox Presbyterians; various branches of Baptists, a few Quakers and Methodists; Jews and Catholics. They have all added both spice and zeal. I have taught the literally blind, halt, and the lame—and was impressed by their astonishing courage. I remember them with affection and regard. I owe a debt to the administration and to my colleagues, especially those in the English department.

I am proud to have been associated with Calvin College. Born of a noble vision, it was brought to a distinguished maturity through sacrifice (often anonymous), idealism, intelligence, and faith. My prayer is that it will remain an outpost of faith in a deteriorating world, a city set on a hill, where its founders, could they return, would still feel at home in the essentials.

Chapter 14

Land of Conquered Waters

As the stately ship *The Rotterdam* glided into the Dutch harbor of Rotterdam, the first large advertisement we saw was for "Lucky Strikes," a good omen for our ten-month residence there. The first large truck we saw had "Bulgaria" printed across the side, a sign of an old continent. Our first stop in the Netherlands was a luxurious inn, where we were surrounded with legendary elegance, were served a splendid meal, and received 2,100 guilders in cash. We were on our way to Amstelveen to live while I was teaching in the Vrije Universiteit, which was founded by Abraham Kuyper with the magnificent support of the "little people." Now the university is 95 percent supported by the Dutch government, with the resultant loosening of its ties with the Gereformeerde Kerk. When I was there, it really had no campus: its buildings were widely scattered all over Amsterdam, and I lectured in a former castle.

In 1963, the Netherlands was a human beehive, with over twelve million people crowded into an area one-fourth the size of Michigan, much of it consisting of canals and other water. State planning and government control were central to survival. Some of the green land had to be preserved at all cost. And the government controlled inflation by decree: one could not buy or sell a house without state approval, which determined not only the price but the number of occupants. Two people were not allowed to rattle around in a huge house. Such regimentation would seem to ensure a sheeplike population; yet one must never underestimate the fiery independence of the Dutch. The beehive had many nonconformists, even in the royal family.

Dutch life offers many paradoxes: among them, a democracy that supports a costly royalty and class distinctions that are palpable. In the university, janitors and secretaries did not drink coffee with the professors, and professors did not associate with instructors. The Dutch seem to love liberty, but they practice little fraternity and do not positively affirm equality. This would seem to deaden variety, but the Dutch are colorfully varied. Half the people in Amsterdam were unchurched, and many of the second half rarely attended church. But in Staphorst, fifty miles away, austerity prevailed: the men wore black, the women wore black that covered everything but the face, and newborn babies were fined for indecent exposure. In Catholic Nijmegen life had a bright and sunny aspect, and in Zeeland one felt a mystical warmth and the influence of mist and water. In Friesland one saw many large farms (for the Netherlands), eighty acres and more, and thousands of cows grazing on dark green grass under a spectacularly clouded sky. On the island of Marken there were ugly people practicing a harsh Protestantism; however, in Volendam, a stone's throw away, there was relaxed Catholicism. Although the country was largely flat, there was a large forest in Gelderland and hills in the south. The Dutch practice variety in unity; they specialize in splinter groups, but they number all the splinters.

Our townhouse, similar to an American condominium cluster, was on Urkerstraat, which had once been water. It was fronted by a patch of grass, and in the back was a small barn for storing bicycles. Everything in the house was small: the refrigerator; the washing machine, which held one sheet at a time; the kitchen, in which three were a crowd. But it was completely and neatly furnished. There was a winding stairway, which our little boy used as a slide. A few rods to the west was a canal of dirty water from which the ducks would come regularly to our house for bread crumbs. To the east was the home of our sunny Catholic neighbors, the Postmas; across from us, in a small house, lived the Bloemesteins, a large, boisterous, and hospitable family. They were gems in a block where the Gereformeerde people greeted us with a cold nod. When we were saddened by the death of President Kennedy, all of our neighbors hung their flags at half staff and visited us with their condolences. The Bloemesteins invited us to witness the funeral on their television, and they served us Genever (Dutch gin) to soothe our sorrow.

Amstelveen was a prosperous suburb seven kilometers outside Amsterdam, to which it was united by a superbly efficient bus service. But one could easily walk to Amsterdam, and the picturesque architecture on the way was entrancing. The streets in Amstelveen were often bordered by multitudes of gorgeous roses, and almost every home had a bed of variegated tulips. Near our home the canal moved slowly through a vista of homes almost buried in flowers. In the center of the city was a modern shopping center and supermarket that was cramped by American standards.

What struck us most forcefully was the specialization of the shops. In Amstelveen a pharmacy was a pharmacy, not a smorgasbord of liquor, tobacco, cards, paperbacks, and toiletries. Vegetables were sold in a shop that sold nothing else: it was the *groentemarkt*. We went shopping with the whole family so that each one could stuff his pockets with potatoes. We soon learned that we had to shop with a basket, because nothing was wrapped. We saw a woman buy half an onion in one of these stores. A tobacco shop was drenched in the aroma of nothing but tobacco;

there one could buy the best Dutch tobacco for a great deal less than the cheapest American tobacco. Little kiosks sold fat-drenched *potata frites* ("french fries"); another sold fish; and another sold *ijs-koud-ijs* ("ice cream"). Even the bakeries were distinct: one sold breads only, another sold *gebakjes,* elegantly sweet pastries. Dutch bread and raisin buns were delicious. A baker came to our door every noon, and we bought a half loaf of *wit* and a half loaf of *bruin;* in between each, he would wipe his nose with his hand and then wipe his hand along his heavy pants. One day my wife asked him if he ever sold graham crackers. He puzzled over that one and said, "Graham, net zo als Billy?" The encounters between two languages made for some interesting linguistic creations. At the beginning of our story, my wife, who knew no Dutch but had made up her mind to learn it, came up with a few notable constructions. One time, as we were about to board the train to Nijmegen, she said, "That's not our train. It's going to Niet Roken" (No Smoking).

We had to make adjustments in our diets. The Dutch water was plagued with little worms and was well nigh undrinkable. The newspaper had headlines that the water was "echt vies maar niet gevaarlijk" ("real dirty but not dangerous"). So we ground more coffee and supplemented it with milk, Coca-Cola, and beer, which we bought from the milkman who came to our door every day. The Dutch had excellent pork, but the beef was tougher. It may have come from cattle that had been around the canals too long. It was interesting to us how habit changes taste. We had taken a tin of Hills Brothers coffee along for Christmas week, but when we used it, it seemed lifeless compared to the strong Dutch coffee we had become used to.

One day an internal revenue agent in uniform (every official in the Netherlands wore a uniform, including the official rat poisoner) came to our door looking like an officer from the Gestapo. He had come to levy a tax on all our furniture; but after quite an argument, he accepted the fact that we were American renters and did not owe him a thing. The postman came to our house twice a day, and every once in a while a gaudy barrel organ came down the street grinding out melodies; the grinder always got the tip he expected. Young boys who could not make it in school past the sixth grade regularly pounded the bricks of the pavement into place.

When we went to the Paulus Kerk the first time, we were ousted from our seats because they were reserved. After the service, the flock butted its way out like rams, and never did anyone in that church say a friendly word to us. If members of the Christian Reformed churches are cold to strangers, these parishioners have been in a deep freeze for years. So we went to the Scotch Presbyterian church, where the preaching was mediocre but the people friendly.

During a two-week orientation period for Fulbright teachers and students, I had the privilege of a free room at the Nijmegen home of Baron van Wijnbergen, who practiced law, taught political science at the

university, and was also a member of the Dutch parliament. He was a
brilliant and cordial man whose external polish reflected an inner graciousness. His wife was a garrulous and friendly lady who was neu-
rotically concerned about her two beautiful children, a picture-book boy
and girl exquisitely dressed and mannered. They were far removed from
the rough-and-tumble life of most American boys and girls their age; they
did not know how to play, how to relax. My wife and our three children
were invited to their home the day before we returned to Amstelveen. Our
boisterous little boy of seven tried to play ball with the Dutch boy, who
couldn't catch a thing, while his mother hovered at the window anxiously. He was a gracious, polite boy, but rigid discipline and his mother's wing had kept him from being a boy. On the other hand, the two girls
had little difficulty in enjoying each other's company.

The orientation period was held at the Catholic university in Nijmegen. The lectures were on Dutch art, politics, and hydrology, a science
concerned with the function of water in Dutch culture. Nijmegen was a
picturesque city where the people were friendlier than in Amstelveen. I
noticed many German hitchhikers passing through the town and remembered that twenty years earlier such boys had tramped down the streets
with irresistible force.

The final party in Nijmegen was typically luxurious. The next
morning the baron drove us to the station and waited to wave good-bye
until the train moved away. We were sorry he was later unable to accept
an invitation to our home. He was an impressive man with a profound
insight into Dutch life.

It is often said that whereas God created the world, the Dutch
created the Netherlands. If they did not create it, they certainly made a
great deal of it. One of the most astonishing scenes in the Netherlands is
the sight of the stormy North Sea on one side of a highway and the quiet
Zuider Zee on the other. This brilliant feat of engineering thrust a twenty-
mile dam through rough waters and built a splendid highway on it. If one
stands on the windswept highway with the gulls sweeping about and
crying overhead, one is amazed that they ever did it. It is thrilling to see
how the Dutch reclaim the floor of what was sea by building a dike around
a portion of water, draining a section by pumping water into the ditches,
planting desalinating grasses on the sea floor, and finally erecting a city
where fish had swum and gulls shrieked over them. For an American, it is
an eerie feeling to walk on a road many feet below towering water.

Canals, large and small, flow through the Netherlands, serving
almost as fences; in the cities large canals serve as waterways on which
some people live the year round. In the spring the canals are opened to
change the dirty water. The canal near our home was almost drained, and
we could see discarded tires, broken chairs, old mattresses, worn-out
corsets, newspapers, and other junk moving slowly through the low
water as it drifted toward the sea.

Amsterdam, whose main railroad station is built on large poles driven deep through the underlying water, is a magical city, a blend of brilliance and decadence. Kalverstraat, the Fifth Avenue of Amsterdam, is a narrow street lined with elegant little shops selling exquisite jewelry, vases, dishes, and other quality goods. There was no rip-off on that street, no fake elegance. Yet near the railroad, not many blocks away, painted prostitutes advertised their profession openly.

One day I was browsing through a bookstore without noticing that I was standing next to an electric brazier. Pretty soon I heard a woman say, "Wat een ontzettend gestink!" ("What an awful stink!"), and then I realized that my overcoat was burning. My wife rubbed the fabric with her gloved hands and got the flames out. (Later, my friends at the university told me that I should seek insurance compensation because I was unaware of Dutch interior heating. However, knowing Dutch rigamarole, I figured it wouldn't be worth the trouble.) How we laughed getting on the bus for home with my coat in shreds! Prof. Geschiere of the French department graciously loaned me a coat until the weather warmed. In another store my wife told our daughter to talk to the clerk; since she had to speak it in school, her Dutch was so much better. But the clerk approached them and said, "May I help you?" My wife asked her, "How did you know we are Americans?" The clerk said in Dutch, "You don't have such big derrierres."

We first learned of President Kennedy's death in November 1963, when a newscaster on a German radio program said, "President Kennedy ist todt." The memory of German terror and American generosity was still vivid in the minds and hearts of the Dutch, and there was genuine national grief. All Dutch flags were at half mast. In the afternoon, on a prominent street in Amsterdam, we saw a very large portrait of Kennedy buried in flowers. The line in front of the portrait was long. People who could afford it brought armfuls of flowers, and those of little means stood with a single blossom in their hands to lay at the foot of the portrait. Immediately, the Dutch named a prominent street Kennedylaan. Just the Sunday before, a clergyman from Scotland had prayed for Julianna of the Netherlands, Elizabeth of England, and John of the United States; my wife had written the president a note to tell him of the prayers being offered for him in the Netherlands. We received a note from Evelyn Lincoln, Kennedy's secretary, thanking us but saying that he had never seen the note because he had already left for Dallas.

In the Netherlands I often heard about the furious recklessness of Parisian drivers; but there is nothing conservative about Dutch drivers. More than once we saw a cyclist lying in the road, and one was badly smashed. Prof. Aalders and his wife drove us to the Kröller-Müller Museum in the Veluwe, a wooded section of the Netherlands where the trees wear a grey-greenish bark intermingled with streaks of yellow. The museum houses many priceless paintings by Van Gogh, exotic and memorable; but so was the ride itself. I sat in the front seat of Aalders's small car anxiously watching the speedometer. That little car was going 130 kilometers an hour and vibrating dangerously. He never slowed down, and he drove as if he were calmly delivering a lecture on Greek history.

During the trip Aalders said that someday he would like to see the "grote land of America"; but like most Hollanders, he did not have any real sense of American space. For example, I heard one professor excuse another for not coming to a meeting because he would have had to come "all the way from Ede"—fifteen miles distant. Some years later, the affable gentleman who had taught Dutch at our orientation in Nijmegen called me at home in Grand Rapids from Chicago and invited me to drive over there to have lunch with him. He had no sense of the distance the trip involved. American spaciousness is an overwhelming experience for a person who can cover the longest distance in his country in five hours.

Dutchmen have little houses and big dogs. Whether one walks down Rembrandtplein or Vaart Straat, strolls through a supermarket or a large department store, rides on a bus or a train, one sees or encounters dogs. Dogs ride the bus and pay fare if they are over a certain size; if they can be contained in a basket, they ride free. They use the streets as commodes, and to walk on the street in the dark without gaining odoriferous adhesions on one's shoes is almost impossible. There's an imperious stance in some of these dogs. I have seen Great Danes almost filling a large window, gazing on passersby with inordinate disdain. My wife and I saw a woman clean a dog's rear end with tissue paper that she carried in her purse for that purpose. When my wife took a picture of it, the husband said, "Kiek nu, zij maakt een foto daarvan." When dogs fall ill, they run up big bills at the veterinarian. If they are prized dogs with wealthy owners, they are buried in a nifty little cemetery in Amsterdam. When one uses the expression "a dog's life" in its usual sense, one does not refer to the dogs in Delft.

We had two unusual experiences with dogs. The first occurred on a Dutch bus. After some argument with the driver, a woman was allowed to board carrying a sizable dog in a basket. She sat right in back of us, with the dog literally squeezed into the basket. Pretty soon the dog began to squirm and fret under a natural pressure. The basket was much too small, but the woman did her best to confine the results to the basket. By this time our family was roaring with laughter, and soon the Dutch riders joined in. The woman finally triumphed over disaster, and the dog settled down in his achievements. Only in Amsterdam.

The other occasion was frightening. Our younger son, seven years old, and I were out walking. Nearby a man was walking a Great Dane, a beast of formidable ferocity. Suddenly the dog broke loose, jumped on our little boy, and began biting him. I kicked the dog as hard as I could, and finally the man dragged him away. The boy had scratches on his neck and back, and we hurried him to the Free University hospital. The doctor, a stolid, man, cleansed the wounds, administered medicine, and calmly told us, "If this doesn't work, he'll be dead in twenty-four hours." It worked. The next day the owner came to bring our son a candy bar. I can't repeat what my wife said to him at the door (she could speak Dutch by this time).

We left the Netherlands with bittersweet emotions. We had made friends we would never see again. We had seen much: a moldering thousand-year-old church in Friesland; the idyllic beauty of Delft; the spectacular cloud formations that drifted over us; the open sea in a drizzle at Vlissingen; the Pieterskerk in Leiden, where the Pilgrims worshipped; the Rotterdam harbor dense with great ships bound for the ends of the earth; the many marvelous museums in Amsterdam, The Hague, Veluwe—one after another. We enjoyed the radio broadcasts from Germany, Spain, and France, and we laughed when one German announcer, after playing "I Got a Hammer," said, "Beethoven schrikt."

We had experienced much kindness, not only from our precious neighbor Mrs. Postma, but from fellow Americans like Dr. and Mrs. Dennis Hoekstra, Dr. and Mrs. Carl Kromminga, Dr. and Mrs. Clarence Vos, and Dr. and Mrs. Sidney Rooy. Mrs. Postma was the hardest to leave. She and my wife were in tears when they waved their final good-byes. Originally from Maastricht, she was a light-hearted little lady, the soul of helpfulness and hospitality. It was in her home that we received the telephone call from Dr. William Vander Ploeg in Grand Rapids telling us the operation on our older daughter, Lucarol, had been successful. Mrs. Postma was a symbol of the way we had been treated by our hosts, the Vrije Universiteit, and the United States Educational Foundation.

Part II

No One Knows When Teaching Stops

Chapter 15

░W░hat Teaching Taught Me

I drifted into the waters of teaching and discovered that I could swim. In my junior year at Calvin College, I was offered an appointment to teach Freshman German. When I said to Prof. A. E. Broene, "I think that this will be a good experience for me," he said, "We are not interested in giving you experience; we are interested in the good teaching of German." With that exuberant encouragement in mind, I faced my first class of students in the fall: classmates, campus celebrities, and some who thought friendship would ensure a good grade. The only course in education I had taken was the superb History of Education, an admirable fusion of biography, educational principles, and cultural history. My philosophy of education was simple: "Here's the text [Vos's *Essentials of German*]; learn it." It was a good class, and they did. My agonizing perplexities about what to major in and what to do about it afterwards were solved by my experience in that class. Most of what I learned about teaching was through teaching.

Later on, the Depression forced me to return to Calvin to earn a Michigan Teacher's Certificate. I learned a great deal of physiology in Educational Psychology, a few things about the principles of education that I had not learned in Prof. Broene's class, and how to make lesson plans after having done so for three years. I also "observed" a number of high school and junior college teachers. The one bright spot in my program was "practice teaching" at Oakdale Christian school. These ninth graders were intelligent and lovable youngsters, and after six weeks they presented me with a booklet I still cherish. I taught them *As You Like It*, and I liked it.

Almost all teachers try to be good teachers. There are drones and moonlighters, but they are few. I can only portray the kind of teacher I should like to have been. The first thing I would say is that good teachers follow their own rhythm. Good teachers must mediate imitation with their own gifts. Good teachers are all different, and evaluation sheets rarely do justice to the fact that a few outstanding strengths may overwhelmingly outweigh a few weaknesses. Good teachers should be interested in their students; yet I know effective teachers who seemed to care little about their students. Impressive knowledge, clarity of presentation, and rigid standards achieve valuable fruits.

Good teachers transcend the text on whatever level they teach. This is not an irrelevant platitude. I have known teachers who did not. In elementary and high schools they tend to be unmitigated bores; in college they are disasters; and they rarely occupy a chair in a university. Enrichment, stimulus, and memory originate in wide reading and study that complements the text. An empty pitcher pours no water. It was with real regret that I saw teachers forced to supplement their income with manual work all summer long. It may have enhanced their wealth, but it rendered their teaching hackneyed. Unless a person has an extraordinary imagination and winning personality, he will fail as a textbook teacher; but persons with imagination and personality are generally not textbook teachers.

Good teachers are critical without being abusive. A friend of mine took a course with the famous psychologist McDougal. While a student was reading a mediocre paper in a seminar, McDougal said to the student, "Do you intend to insult me with such work?" Why not quietly let the student seal his own doom and rebuke him afterwards? In a philosophy seminar at the University of Southern California, a professor went up to a student reading a paper and said to her, "My dear girl, this is no place for you." Some teachers use their sharp minds to embarrass rather than aid students. But criticism should be moderated by praise, if at all possible. One can make a point without striking it into someone's hide.

Teachers should conscientiously comment on papers they assign. I have seen both a stack of bluebooks and a stack of term papers on which there was nothing but a grade. That is professorial indolence at its worst. Sometimes, of course, papers are so outstanding that there is room for nothing but compliments. They should be given—and given specifically. I have read many student papers I could not have written. Why not say so? Other papers need extensive red-penciling, the bane and bore of teaching, especially English teaching; but omitting it is a dereliction of duty.

Some teachers openly show favoritism. Although the teacher may like or admire some students more than others, that should not become apparent. Some time ago, an alumnus of a school I taught in said to me, "Did you know that Mr. X seated all the girls with attractive appendages in the front seat?" He may have been favoring them, but he was gratifying the old Adam. Favoritism poisons the atmosphere. Avoid the hand of the student who always wants the floor. I had such a handwaver in class once, and I finally said to him, "You will be allowed only one question a period. Make it a good one."

Favoritism and justice are closely allied, and assignments and examinations should always be just. Any pedant in college teaching can compose a test that no one can pass. This is not teaching; it is showing off.

A University of Michigan professor who taught a graduate course in logic gave a final examination that consisted of one question only, written on a slip of paper and handed to each student. On the slip was the number of a chapter: the student's grade depended on his knowing that chapter and that chapter only. That is not even pedantry; it is cruelty. A good examination involves the knowledge of important elements discussed in class and the ability to generalize fruitfully on the impact of the entire course in good written English.

A good teacher is a showman without showing off. Every good teacher I had possessed some qualities of theater. Prof. Broene would walk back and forth as he discussed the Socratic method; Ralph Stob would adjust his nasal whine to situations with skill; Harry Jellema could play the part of an inquisitor with amazing skill; Roozeboom used voice and manner to dramatize history. I have known a Sunday School teacher who could dramatize Bible stories unforgettably.

There are two valuable qualities I have never seen mentioned on evaluation sheets. One is voice quality, and one of the deadly sins I have committed is envying teachers who have clear, resonant voices. I frequently had students in class who could read poetry better than I could—whose readings, in fact, vivified dramatic poems like Frost's "Home Burial"—and I would ask them to read passages for the next class. Strange and interesting things can be done with the voice. Some years ago, in a large shopping center, I heard my name clearly called. I was alone in the aisle, no one was looking at me, and I was bewildered. This happened several times. Later, in a much smaller store, I heard the same insistent calling of my name—with nobody in sight. Finally, a Mr. Groot came up to me and said, "I'm sorry I've been bugging you." I asked, "How did you do it?" It turned out that he was a ventriloquist. Now that man I envied. Imagine directing a tough question to a poor and hesitant student and having a perfect answer emerge from his lips. I can't even think about it.

The other quality never mentioned in teacher evaluations is a sense of humor. It is the pause that refreshes, the change of moods that makes for good feeling, illuminates foibles painlessly, and gives us the power to see ourselves as others see us. It should avoid personal abuse, but almost anything else is fair game. It also should come out in an effervescent burst; plotting it destroys the effect. Sometimes I felt that the chaps who made up the evaluation sheets had a somber outlook on life.

Although I said above that some teachers are effective without having much sympathy for or interest in their students, they are few indeed. When one asks the question "And what do you think, Miss Cheney?" one must be prepared for anything. A colleague once told me that he had a student who would begin his answer to the professor's question by saying, "This is a very good question; you do well to ask it." Poems often offer more than one interpretation: they are deliberately ambiguous in a good sense, because they have layers of meaning, especially if they use myth and are freighted with symbols. Some student reactions to them are ludicrous. But the teacher should try to make something out of nothing, unless the answer is so inept that the entire class laughs. The same is true of student writings, which they sometimes shyly hand in for private appraisal. What would one say to the lad who handed this in?

> *My muscles acke*
> *My mind flots*
> *My lungs whezz for air*
> *Clean air*
> *There was none.*
> *My lungs had none*
> *My mind had none*
> *The city had none*
> *I had none . . . no air.*
>
> *My muscles were tight*
> *My mind was tight*
> *My lungs were stretched for air*
> *Clean air*
> *There was none.*
> *My lungs couldn't agree*
> *My mind couldn't agree*
> *My muscles couldn't agree*
> *The city couldn't agree*
> *I couldn't agree . . . couldn't move.*
>
> *My muscles had to move*
> *My mind had to think*
> *My lungs had to breath clean air*
> *Clean air*
> *There was none.*
> *My lungs whezzed for air*
> *My mind couldn't agree*
> *My muscles acked*
> *The city had none . . . no air*
>
> *The country had air*
>
> *I moved*
> *I had some*
> *I agreed*
>
> *It was Spring-air.*

All I could say was, "Brother, what you need is artificial respiration."
  The students who are hardest to deal with are not the sharp scholars

but the self-appointed literary geniuses and those dull to poetry and literary excellence. It is the ultimate in frustration to read Dickinson's great poem "I heard a fly buzz when I died" while some dullard watches one buzzing on the window pane. The self-appointed literati are energized by the artistic temperament, and that temperament is seldom placid or receptive; it is generally high-strung, often arrogant and iconoclastic, prone to art for art's sake, a sophomore's dream of the relationship between art and life. There he sits—

> *A most intense young man*
> *a soulful-eyed young man*
> *An ultra-poetical, super esthetical*
> *Out of the way young man.*

He is weary of received traditions, eager to beat his music out in his own way. He is inclined to follow subjective rather than objective patterns and resents institutional control. He is a product of critical and artistic chaos, the whirl of experimentation with a cynical bent. He likes Ginsberg's "Howl."

One of them, with a glow of genius on his face, once handed me a four-page poem composed entirely of adverbs. It reminded me of the horse who managed to stand on a relatively small block of wood at the World's Fair in Chicago. So what? Such a poet thinks he is touched but wants to be untouched. However, I have also had in my classes gifted poets who were eager to learn and later produced excellent poems.

I have always taught in Christian schools, and that adds a difficult dimension to the teaching of literature: a serious application of Christian principles in the evaluation, a conflict of basic perspectives. The antithesis runs deep and is often tricky. In class, but especially in papers, I have had to confront agnostics, atheists, persons who believed in human engineering, rejectors of the Bible as determinative, adherents to the poem for the poem's sake—whatever its moral content. The problem ranges from profanity and obscenity in masterpieces to bitterly hostile world-and-life views. I know that some students have considered me chicken for not reading these profane passages in class. Sometimes they are, indeed, an integral portion of the poem and support the entire impact of the piece, which is often ennobling; but I could never bring myself to read them. I agreed and taught that the passage should be evaluated in the light of the entire book; but I preferred the silent reading of profane passages. I always held to the principles stated or implied later in the chapter.

I believed in a student's right to express a wrong opinion, and I treated it with courtesy. Yet, as a Christian, I held to a higher loyalty than broadmindedness. If, however, I was proved wrong, I didn't try to weasel out of it. We are all wrong at times. All, that is, except theologians: they disagree but seldom admit error; they simply start another denomination. I have been reading our church papers for many years, and I do not remember a theologian ever saying, "I goofed. I was dead wrong."

*   *   *

What was I trying to accomplish in the literature classes I taught for so many years? My immediate objective was to arouse students' pleasure in the poem, novel, play, or essay under discussion. Poems that students take no pleasure in are never lodged in their memories or modify their natures. They may grasp the poems intellectually and answer questions on them accurately, but they will remain an inert addition to knowledge. This meant, of course, that I taught effectively only the pieces I took pleasure in myself. No pleasure in the teacher, little pleasure in the class. Enthusiasm is contagious. I have had to teach pieces that bored me, and when I taught them I did not fake delight in them. I simply told the class that for historical reasons, critical acclaim, or the editor's personal judgment, the poem had to be mastered. If a student took pleasure in a poem that bored me, I was pleased rather than affronted.

To achieve that pleasure, I often found it important to elucidate the poem by explaining the author's meaning on his own terms, in his own time. This attempt at illumination often changed a student's opinion. Everybody likes *Huckleberry Finn*—except some contemporary racists in reverse who refuse to read the book in the light of Twain's age. On the other hand, the satirical masterpieces of Alexander Pope, in their measured eloquence, need to be clarified, often in detail, before they are understood and enjoyed.

That is why I believe that biographical data are relevant—not necessarily to evaluate the poem but to understand it. Frost's magnificent poem "Home Burial" takes on a new dimension when one knows the poet's experience that engendered it. And who can understand Coleridge's "Dejection: an Ode" without a knowledge of the circumstances propelling its composition?

The evaluation of a literary masterpiece ranges from taking simple pleasure in it to applying profound psychological and philosophical principles. There is little consensus among critics, and their internecine warfare becomes apparent when one scrutinizes critical dicta. Starting from different premises, they often tend to negate each other. Henry James, for example, has said that "an enthusiasm for Poe is the mark of a decidedly primitive stage of reflection"; on the other hand, Edmund Wilson ranks Poe with the "great inquiring minds like Goethe." Stanley Hyman estimates Veblen as "one of the two or three creative thinkers of undoubted genius in America"; Mencken dismisses him as a "geyser of pishposh." Most of us have been taught to admire Milton and to idolize Shakespeare. It comes as something of a shock, then, to see Ezra Pound describe *Paradise Lost* as a "conventional melodrama" written by a "coarse-minded, asinine, disgusting, and beastly man." Rymer, a prominent eighteenth-century critic, declares that Shakespearean tragedy "raves and rambles without any coherence, and spark of reason, or any rule." As for Shakespeare's poetry outside drama, Rymer dismisses that with the statement that "the neighing of a horse or the howling of a mastiff possesses more meaning." Yvor Winters describes Henry Adams as "the radical disintegration of a mind," and Van Wyck Brooks calls Joyce "a sick Irish Jesuit" and his work "trivial, salacious, bad-smelling." It is no wonder that William Faulkner never read criticism and that Swift describes the critic as a "discoverer and collector of a writer's faults."

After acknowledging that there are few universally held criteria in the evaluation of literature, a good student and a good teacher will strive to arrive at a set of principles that are valid for them. It strikes me as inept and unfair of teachers, after allowing and encouraging students to express their convictions, to conceal their own. Teaching taught me that I ought to reveal mine, and I now do so—at my own peril.

Literature is significant verbal *form*—form in the sense of technique. The terse couplet and the sweeping epic must exhibit pattern. Chaos is not art. Furthermore, structure must have meaning on some level of experience—sensuous, moral, intellectual, spiritual, or all four. Pound's imagistic poem "In a Station of the Metro" is a miniature, but it is art:

> *The apparition of these faces in the crowd;*
> *Petals on a wet, black bough.*

It is a minimal example of significant form; it gives immediate pleasure. Furthermore, the creative writer is, as Allen Tate has said, intent on communion rather than communication: the shared experience, the transfusion of emotion. A work of literary art always tells more than it says. Communication is getting the meaning across in its essentials; communion moves on a deeper level of emotional experience and spiritual sympathy. The poet wishes to give the reader the feel and tone of experience rather than a shorthand transcript. We say in our prosaic way, "All must die." The poet says:

> *Beauty is but a flower*
> *Which wrinkles will devour,*
> *Brightness falls from the air,*
> *Queens have died young and fair.*
> *Dust has closed Helen's eye,*
> *I am sick I must die.*
> *Lord have mercy upon us.*

We say in our commonplace way, "I long for the past." Housman put it thus:

Into my heart an air that kills
From yon far country blows:
What are those blue remembered hills,
What spires, what farms are those?

That is the land of lost content,
I see it shining plain,
The happy highways where I went
And cannot come again.

In each case the thought is interfused with emotion that is tellingly transmitted through simple but brilliant diction and metrical pattern.

Such significant form, transmitting experience as intensely and fully as possible, whether in works of great scope or of miniature range, must exhibit certain universal principles. The work must be unified: it must add up to one total experience, and the delight from the whole must be accompanied by pleasure in the parts. There must be variety in unity and unity in variety. Form and content must be mutually adapted and fused. And if the work is to attain wide influence, it should concern itself with the primary emotions exhibited in revealing actions.

Now works of art become increasingly valuable as their range of significance and excellence of pattern widen and deepen. Pattern is a formal matter that involves sound effect, versification, emotive diction, structure, architectonics, and the like. Formal merit lies in an organic fusion of medium and experience so tight as to make paraphrase impossible. Upon formal values as such, theology and philosophy can have little to say. But a work of literary art is always written by the whole human being—mind and heart, for the whole human being—mind and heart; therefore, it inevitably involves moral and philosophical values. Thus upon the contained experience, that is, the total impact of a piece of writing, theology has the final word. In support of this opinion, I offer four authorities:

> The "greatness" of literature cannot be determined solely by its literary standards; though we must remember that whether it is literature or not can be determined only by literary standards.
>
> —*T. S. Eliot*

> But as long as poets speak, and use words that have a meaning, I think we may ask what they mean and where their meaning stands in our scale of values.
>
> —*D. Bush*

I think it can be said that we regard a work of art as good or bad because of the way its formal qualities are combined with what we roughly call its vision, or its value, or its range of consciousness.

—W. PHILLIPS, PARTISAN REVIEW

It made me impatient with anything, including art, which pretends that it can exist for its own sake, and still be of prophetic importance. A great drama is a great jurisprudence.

—A. MILLER

Consequently, the final value of a literary experience is determined by one's values, philosophical outlook, or theology. For us a literary masterpiece increases in value as it moves in the direction of a fuller containment of truth, assuming always that the pattern is commensurate with the experience.

In great literature, meaning and form tend to be commensurate: the best form best expresses the content; and the greatest literature expresses the truest vision of life in a correspondingly effective form. To illustrate: Dreiser's *American Tragedy* is a great novel because it is a richly detailed illustration of American experience in an effective form. Hardy's *Tess of the D'Urbervilles* is a greater novel because it presents a more compelling picture of life in a superior pattern. Melville's *Moby Dick* is greater still because it presents the agony of the agnostic, the very truth of the universe seen without God, in a form of surpassing brilliance. *The Divine Comedy* reaches the heights of secular literature because it presents in supreme verse the truth of the universe as seen with God. In each case the contained experience is presented in an organically related medium.

What is literature for? Obviously not merely for entertainment, or sheer technique, or self-expression, or adjustment to society, or pure play—although it may accomplish all these objects. The ultimate object of literature is to glorify God, and that it does in various ways. It may do so through explicitly religious verse, as in Francis Thompson or Christina Rossetti; but it may also do so implicitly through the work of unbelievers because it reveals, in however shattered a fashion, the imperial glory of the image of God. Great writers illuminate life, restore our wholeness. Literature changes the tone of fact and transfigures the commonplace. It may even, as in the case of *The Sound and the Fury*, arouse our sympathies for an idiot. The greatest literature heightens the quality of experience and involves the total personality with reality. It deepens our awareness of God and the world. It can do all this without being Christian if it is read by a Christian.

If one sums up what one thinks a good teacher should ideally be, one sees how far one falls short. How does the ideal teacher shape up?

The good teacher is intelligently sympathetic, always cheerful, broadly human and understanding. He is neat in appearance and exact in language without being fastidious in either. He is orderly without slipping into the ways of a martinet. He should be, not only competently, but rather profoundly acquainted with his subject matter. He should impart meaning and attitude as well as fact. He should be a gracious listener to the question. His assignments should be perfectly clear, definite, and moderate. He should be able to distinguish betwixt south and southwest side of a hair when it comes to marking. He should be as impartial as sunshine. He should be eager to aid in distress. In fact, this ideal teacher is part of the staff of the schools of the New Atlantis, is as rare as the phoenix, and if found will be as hard to domesticate on humble mother earth as Coleridge's "footless birds of Paradise."

Yet one "chooses something like a star," and if there are disappointment and frustrations, one echoes Browning's "I was ever a fighter, so one fight more"; and if the going is really tough, one thinks on an old Anglo-Saxon line: "Fight the hardest, when your strength is least." It is the height of naiveté to think that teachers are always full of ginger and as effervescent as uncorked champagne. However, I found the teaching of literature a delight that transcended the ache of blue books, term papers, uninterested students, and the 4-1-4 curriculum which cut my Chaucer course in half. William Somerset Maugham said in his *Summing Up*, "Philosophy never lets you down." It let Maugham down; in old age he regarded his life as pointless. Literature at its best never let me down. I thank the Lord for allowing me to teach "the best that has been known and taught" to students whom I liked—and many of whom I admired.

Chapter 16

The Very Free
Vrije Universiteit

To Americans of Dutch descent who belong to the Christian Reformed Church, the Vrije Universiteit means—if it means anything—the genius of its founder Abraham Kuyper, the monumental works of Herman Bavinck, the views of biologist Lever, the philosophy of Dooyeweerd and Vollenhoven disseminated by American disciples, and the doctorates earned there by a considerable number of Christian Reformed scholars. It also bespeaks the myth of ecclesiastical support: 95 percent of its income derives from the Dutch government. The nature of its income determines its admission standards: any qualified Dutch student has to be admitted upon application.

What were the students like? How had they been trained? My answers are twenty years old, and much may have changed, but I should like to say something about the Dutch educational system as I knew it. The Dutch educational system is a remarkable consensus, an ingenious blend of meticulous control and striking individualization. There is a diploma for every occupation—from selling books to cutting meat—and almost everyone can get a different diploma. Dutch education regulates schools very closely, but in such a way that each individual has the opportunity to develop his unique talent, or what at an early age appears to be his unique talent. Dutch education specializes early in life; therefore, many Dutchmen are denied what I would call a liberal education. Growing tulips does not nurture the mind like reading Shakespeare does; but if a youngster has no academic gifts, he is channeled into manual labor at an early age. The Dutch seem agreed on this system, although I noticed worried faces.

The primary schools correspond to our grades one through six; but at the end of grade six the massacre of the mediocre begins. The academically average are then channeled into advanced primary schools and domestic science schools; the corridors to academic education are closed to them. The survivors, about 50 percent of the students, go to the Gymnasium, the elite schools; the *hooger-burgerlijke* schools, which are more concerned with modern languages than is the Gymnasium; or the

Lyceum, a working combination of both. All these schools are arduous indeed: only 50 percent of the freshmen survive the course, which lasts from grades seven through twelve. Upon passing stiff entrance examinations, students are admitted to the universities. Here they remain for varying lengths of time, until they receive either the *doctorandus* degree, roughly equivalent to our master's degree, or the doctor's degree. If they study medicine or engineering, the degrees are, of course, different.

The school our children attended, like the Catholic and public schools, was financed by the state but was allowed to pursue its own religious emphasis. The children were taught languages in rote fashion. I have heard the murmur of voices reciting declensions and sentences in unison. Our children had to memorize many Dutch sentences. However, as old-fashioned as the teaching of languages was, it was highly effective. The high school girl across the street read novels in French, German, and English. The teacher had great authority. When the Dutch version of P.T.A. met, the teacher told the parents what the score was. He or she uttered, and the pupils regurgitated. The Dutch teacher's American counterpart probably knows less, especially in secondary schools, but he or she is likely to be more imaginative. In the Netherlands the burden falls on the pupils; in the United States it falls on the teacher. If a Dutch Johnny does not like Poe's *Bug* or *Raven,* it's his fault. In America the teacher is expected to do the impossible—interest everybody. In the Netherlands, then at least, the pupil was expected to be interested.

The Dutch university student has an unusual command of languages, because the mastery of various languages is considered essential for the college-bound. The average freshman at the Free University has had years of Latin, Greek, German, and French or English. And the interest in languages is not limited to these students. A great number of Dutch youngsters learn German, French, and English; many of them can not only read these languages but speak them.

When the Dutch student enters the university, he has notable qualifications and notable deficiencies. He has a superb mastery of the tools of learning: languages, mathematics, and natural sciences. His memory has been superbly strengthened: he can memorize rapidly and accurately. He knows how to study; to give Dutch university students lectures on how to study would be beyond contempt. And he has become involved in the past, in the mainstream of Western culture. But that student also has deficiencies. The constant emphasis on fact and rote mastery has not stimulated his critical faculties. He has translated ad infinitum, but a sound training in critical analysis has been denied him. I was strongly impressed by this fact. Formal literary criticism was foreign to my students. A question such as "What makes this a good poem or a good novel?" was new to them; they had no standards of evaluation. Finally, their imaginations had not been sufficiently stimulated. In America we may rate self-expression and creativity too high, but the Dutch educational system underrates it.

I also found in my classes that the students who were studying English had done very little writing in English. They spoke it accurately in the British manner, but they chose to escape writing it. I offered to read any themes, essays, or stories they might submit, but in a class that averaged between fifty and sixty students I received one paper, and only sixteen students chose to take the final written examination to obtain credit for the course. I was amazed when the English section, as they called the department, passed a resolution to limit student papers to eighteen pages and to require no more than two papers from a student before admitting him or her to candidacy for the doctorate. While the American professor groans under paperwork, his Dutch counterpart outlaws it.

What immediately strikes a visiting teacher at a Dutch university is the idyllic student-teacher ratio. The English department at the Free University had 80 students, with eight professors to teach them. That makes a ratio of ten to one. At Calvin I was accustomed to a ratio of thirty-seven to one. Translate that into student papers. Add to it the fact that the Dutch professor teaches eight class hours a week, and you can see why it is a university—a place where one can find time for sustained and rewarding research.

Another notable difference is the extraordinary student freedom. There are no deans upon deans. There is no rigorously inspected student housing, and there is no organized student counseling. There is simply nothing paternalistic about the system at all. The student, presumably mature, stands on his own feet, basically sets his own pace, attends classes as he sees fit, takes examinations when he wishes, stays almost as long as he likes, and, when he lacks fortitude to persist, vanishes without a ripple.

There was no Bible department in the Free University. There was a famous theological school, but no student had to take courses in it. Chapel services were unknown.

The professorial staff was rigidly structured in a steel hierarchy. The chairman of the department—and usually its only professor—did not associate with an instructor, who in his turn was frozen in his echelon until enrollments increased or a person with higher status retired or died. And enrollments increased very slowly.

The head of the English section when I taught at the Free University was De Hooggeleerde Professor Dr. Klaas Fokkema, a fine scholar in Frisian literature but poorly acquainted with English literature and almost ignorant of American literature. Fokkema had wangled his way into the chairmanship, but that never bothered him; he always forged ahead. He was a gruff, outspoken man, a gifted storyteller, and an amazingly generous host. At the first party of the English section, we were astonished at the variety of drinks on the table. My wife and I each took a glass of sherry. Dr. Fokkema came to my wife and said, "Sherry? What for a drink is that? You have to have some Genever." We each took a swallow and felt as if we had imbibed liquid fire; a full glass would have eviscerated a mustang. When Fokkema went to visit, he always carried a pack of Willem II cigars in one pocket and a bottle of Genever in the other, from which he would sip occasionally, no matter what was served. He was never drunk. In fact, I never saw a Dutchman drunk. Dutchmen drink a lot, eat a lot, smoke a lot, and die at eighty-five and beyond.

Fokkema was a good scholar but was indifferent to theology, philosophy, and the *Wetsidee*. Kuyper and Bavinck never entered his conversation. And though he was a member of the Paulus Gereformeerde Kerk, he was not even interested in ecclesiastical gossip. He was a smart and delightful man, completely free of the waspish remarks with which professors sometimes impale each other.

Dutch professors are an exalted species. The first letter addressed to me from the Rector Magnificus was addressed to De Hooggeleerde Heer, Professor Doctor _____. At Calvin I received mail that omitted the "Mr."; and to some secretaries we are all buddies, as if we were in high school. The one system illustrates ridiculous pomp, the other lack of elementary courtesy. Professors in the Netherlands also receive free treatment at the university medical school. They move and act like royalty and have autocratic power. The students, docile in class, assert their independence by skipping it. In one class, a professor lectured to one student, who sold his notes to the others. The professor, however, had the last word in the oral examinations.

Calvin College has faculty parties and banquets, but these constitute only a first course compared to the luxurious feast the Free University served on *dies natalis*. The university celebrated its founding with a cornucopia of wine, mixed drinks, that bottled lightning called Genever, and a first course of succulent fish. I thought that that was the menu, but it was only the beginning. Then came large servings of excellent pork and something they call beef in the Netherlands, vegetables of many kinds, and a never-ending refilling of wine glasses. Finally came dessert, a mountainous dish of ice cream with fresh strawberries. Some of the professors ate the whole of it. Afterward, the acrid smoke of Dutch cigars billowed through the spacious hall. It was a high and formal affair for which one had to rent a tuxedo. Before the meal, one professor had some wine spilled on the coat of his tuxedo. My wife, typically American, said to him, "Geef mij uw zakdoek, and I'll wipe it off." Flustered by her half Dutch and half English, and looking down to see that his button fly was undone, he said "Pardon, Pardon," and rushed off to rectify it in the *heren kamer*. I had never been to such a stupendous feast. These Dutchmen lived it up. Dutch professors—at least then—ate more, drank more, smoked more, and lived longer than I could believe.

In the Humanities department I never heard talk of the integration of faith and learning; they were either past it or not up to it. My colleagues were good scholars, interested in their subjects, but I never heard the endless conversations about learning and piety that I did at Calvin. They were, doubtless, all "Pro Rege," but they seldom talked about his kingdom. I enjoyed their company and profited from their scholarship, but in practice I might as well have been teaching at Michigan State. Once, when we were invited to a dinner at the home of one of the professors, he asked his son to get the Bible, and the young man said, "Hoeft dat?" ("Is that necessary?") Our regular church attendance was a quaint anachronism to some of my colleagues. I am not saying that these faculty members were not Christians; I am saying that the kind of Christian education we strive to achieve in our institutions was not a matter of concern with them.

I taught three classes during the year: American Literature in two successive periods, Victorian Poetry, and a seminar in Literary Criticism for six weeks. The sixty students, who attended with amazing faithfulness, rose from their seats when I entered and rose again when I left; I asked them to cut the calisthenics. There were no textbooks, so I had to rely on lectures and mimeographed copies of poems, which the genial secretary of the section prepared for me. The students were bright but shy, and they brought forth next to no discussion. They liked American literature but had few American classics. The American chief of cultural affairs, with whom we had become very friendly, came to my rescue with a splendid donation of over fifty American classics to the library of the Vrije Universiteit in my name. We invited all of my students to our home in groups for dinner. On one occasion, a diminutive Nigerian took about half the meat at his turn, so that by the time the platter came around to my wife and daughter there was only a very small piece left. Whatever was passed, he selected a major portion. When it came time for dessert, he suddenly shouted, "Mijn buik, mijn buik!" ("My belly, my belly"), and ran out of the house. His hoggishness prompted my wife to call out, "Good, I hope he dies!"

The seminar in Literary Criticism was composed of bright students whose training in formal criticism consisted of what they had read on their own. They had written few papers, so the class was largely a matter of discussing Cleanth Brooks's *The Well-Wrought Urn*. Only one lad attempted to give a paper orally, and he did a poor job. The class stomped its disapproval. I rose, put my arm around his shoulder, and told the class what he had intended to say.

The school year, whose pace had been leisurely throughout, subsided into a crawl in April and ceased in May. Our friendships in the university were almost wholly confined to the Department of Letters, and they hosted us most kindly. I must mention the unusual cordiality of the Rector Magnificus, Dr. De Roos. He lived on Amsterdamseweg, a street gay with flowers most of the year, and he diffused some of the same gaiety himself. New Years' Day in a foreign land can be a long, cold day—and would have been but for his hospitality. It was a day of freezing sleet, and one walked at one's own peril. He walked six blocks to our home and invited us to his home for the whole day. He waited for us to get ready, and then we slid half the way there and had a joyful time. He was a man of great talent and influence, but he never lost the human touch.

My year in the English department concluded with a farewell in a historic inn. I liked and respected these Dutch colleagues; they had color and learning. Dr. Meier, imported from Switzerland, had the south German temperament (he translated *Paradise Lost* into German blank verse—no minor achievement). We were drawn together also because our families were strangers in Amsterdam. Our closest Dutch friends were Dr. and Mrs. VanBeek. He had taught for a year in Dallas, and he proved an enlightening and welcome friend. We had planned a tour of the Netherlands in their van, but he was stricken by a heart attack, and we said good-bye to him at his home bedside. It was a pleasure to compare notes on the relative merits of our educational systems: he ardently wished for Holland a less rigid structure that would allow the "late bloomer" to bloom. He also wished to see a shift in the department from a heavily linguistic program to a more balanced course in which literature would be more closely examined.

Chapter 17

An Excellent Speech, Would It Were Done

Traveling speakers and lecturers enjoy a long tradition in our country. Ralph Waldo Emerson initially received only five dollars a lecture from his New England sponsors; but as the years passed he expanded his fee and his circuit—as far west as Minnesota. At one time he traveled by railroad to Kalamazoo and from there to Grand Rapids by horse and buggy to deliver a lecture on "Manners," which aroused no enthusiasm. Today poets, celebrities, and clergymen crisscross the continent and often receive enormous fees. Among the highest paid are James Kilpatrick, a renegade Democrat, and Bob Hope, a comedian. The latter receives $40,000 a talk.

There was, however, a vast difference in the expenditure of vocal effort between lectures before and after the microphone. It is now hard to believe that Abraham Lincoln, with his high, thin voice, could be heard by 15,000 people in an open field, or that Whitefield could address audiences of 20,000 and be heard at their fringes. In my youth, speakers had to have clear, resonant voices whether they spoke in a grove or a large church; today electronic devices, if they work, carry squeaky voices to the last row in the balcony. I marvel at the stamina of the speakers of years ago, preaching to a thousand people in the heat of August, wearing a Prince Albert and a stiff celluloid collar, and facing waving fans and noisy babies. Furthermore, such speakers had to have both substance and length. A puritan preacher who could not outlast the hour glass was obviously a lemon. Some outlasted two.

I have heard many speakers of varying competence. I heard Richard Nixon speak on the steps of the Calvin Library on Franklin Street. Despite his friendly smile, there was a glint of glower in his eyes. I heard Senator Fulbright give a clear, well-reasoned speech on foreign policy in The Hague. When Roosevelt spoke in Soldier Field in Chicago in 1935, I did my best to get in; but the press of people and traffic made that impossible. Wendel Wilkie, a forceful and appealing speaker, stood a few yards from me as he spoke eloquently—with a voice almost ruined by hoarseness—on the necessity of a new order in one world. Queen

Juliana spoke in the Calvin auditorium, and Prince Bernhard, obviously amused by the deferential pomp, winked at me as he passed by. I expected a little speech when John Kennedy stood on the end of an observation car at Kalamazoo Avenue in Grand Rapids, but he only handed out a few dollar bills to the youngsters.

Robert Frost came to Grand Rapids to read some of his poems in the Fountain Street Church. I had been invited to a luncheon in his honor, but it was canceled. The auditorium was packed a half hour before Frost's appearance, but we were all evacuated because of a bomb threat. No bomb was found, and I never understood why anyone would want to bomb Robert Frost. If it had been Allen Ginsberg, it would have made some sense. After we reassembled, Frost walked briskly down the center aisle, jaunty with his white hair bouncing. For over an hour he delivered, solely from memory, a selection of poems. It was a superb demonstration of memory. He interspersed wit, insight, and innuendo amongst the poems. His voice was not magnificent like Dylan Thomas's, but its Yankee articulation fit the poems. And he generously responded to deafening applause with encores. He included not only the well-known poems but also some of the darker poems, such as "Design," "Acquainted with the Night," and that masterpiece of domestic tension, "Home Burial." Afterwards we shook hands with him.

Frost at his best was a great poet, one of the last masters of narrative verse in rhyme. Behind the mask there was a man who had grievously hurt others and who had been poignantly hurt. He was indeed acquainted with the night, but he always chose "something like a star" to follow. I am glad to have a signed edition of his collected poems, which was given to me by Betty Duimstra, who attended the Bread Loaf School of Poetry in Vermont.

I have heard some fascinating speakers over the years. When I was a little boy, my father and mother and I went to hear Billy Sunday in Chicago. What I remember was the physical antics: he soon peeled off his coat, pulled off his tie, rolled up his sleeves, and assailed the evil one. In the course of his gyrations he slammed a chair on the platform and broke the legs. In Paterson, mother and I went to hear Harry Lauder, a famous Scotch lecturer and singer. At the end we all had to sing "Auld Lang Syne." Many years later, Uncle John Peters asked my wife and me—and also persuaded my mother-in-law and her three sisters, all conservative and three of them Netherlands Reformed—to attend a service led by Campbell Morgan, a literate and perceptive spellbinder. The evangelical fervor put grim looks on the sisters' faces. When the pianist pulled out the throttle and the audience began tapping to the jazzy tempo of "Grumble on Monday, Grumble on Tuesday . . . Grumble the whole week through," they were grumbling, while Uncle John was bobbing up and down and my wife was belting it out. The four sisters sat in gloomy and disapproving silence.

At Northwestern University I heard two of the most prominent university professors in the country. One was George Lyman Kittredge, the Chaucer and Shakespeare scholar who never earned a Ph.D., for, as he said, "Who would have examined me?" His face, bearing, and stature reminded me of a Viking warrior as he spoke on Macbeth and in that fascinating address defined evil as "the wrong use of energy." It was a strange definition, but there is truth in it. The other speaker was William Lyon Phelps, who could popularize Browning so that the course was always packed, including a regular contingent of football players. He also organized a *Faerie Queen Club,* which a person could join after declaring that he or she had read all the cantos of Spenser's epic poem instead of merely the first two that were usually assigned. His books were delightful reading but markedly different from those of the "New Critics": he did not squeeze the lemon but tried to make readers like literature. Popular, somewhat superficial, but fascinating—as was his speech, of which I remember nothing but his outstanding exuberance.

Since I regard a sermon, whatever else it may be, as a speech, I have heard thousands of speeches. Brevity may well be the soul of wit, but well into the 1940s at least, and in some churches longer than that, a sermon worth attending to had to be at least fifty minutes long. Brevity was regarded as shallowness or lack of preparation. The Dutch Reformed farmer didn't drive ten miles to hear a twenty-minute sermon. All this has changed today: sermons and speeches seldom exceed thirty minutes. When one is asked to speak, he often hears hints about the excellence of brevity. "If you can't say it in twenty minutes, you can't say it." Well, it all depends on what you are saying. When Lincoln was once asked how long a man's legs should be, he replied, "Long enough to reach the ground." Flexibility is a key element in a speech; it should not have to be squeezed into a scheduling framework, and often it cannot be.

The sermon was formerly the centerpiece of worship; now additions and adornments, creative participation and additions, sometimes reduce it to a sermonette. There must be the murmur of many voices in responsive reading: and children now enjoy a sermon, often a good one. Fixed, synodically approved forms have become a spur to originality. The long prayer is now written down and read to God. The sermon is in danger of becoming a diminishing dot in a flurry of addenda. Recently I heard a minister in a church, not my own, say, "I see a member sleeping. Praise the Lord!" I suppose the sermon was too long. I sometimes think the sermon is in many churches a diminishing island in a surging sea of activities.

The Christian Reformed Church has produced eminent preachers from the beginning of the century to the present. What sticks in my memory is the variety of their styles of preaching, even when, as for many years, they used the formula of three points. The sermons varied from densely packed theological exposition to freewheeling dramatic presentation. The microphone has great value, but it inhibits gestures and movements—the histrionic panache. One can still wipe tears from the eyes, but not in affecting gestures. The three-point system, despite its often boring rigidity, did prove mnemonically effective, because the audience had landmarks to remember. But I make no case for its supremacy. I have heard topflight exegetical sermons founded on a story in the life of Jesus, or on an entire parable, without such divisions. The important point is that the preacher gives his audience, through vivid presentation and illumination, something to remember during the week.

I have seen some strange things during sermons. Twice I have seen the minister bowl over the glass of water. I heard one minister who momentarily forgot a portion of the Lord's Prayer. On one occasion, when a minister paused in the long prayer to offer the opportunity for parishioners to pray silently, my little niece, unaware of the nature of the pause, said in a loud voice, "Is he stuck, Mama?" One preacher paused dramatically and lengthily after asking the rhetorical question, "What time is it?" Finally, a member of the congregation called out, "It's 2:45, Dominie." One dramatic preacher said, "Where are Job's friends?" and then turned around to see if they were behind the pulpit chair, in the organ loft, or elsewhere. I attended a German church in which the consistory members were fast asleep, and the minister thundered, "Aufmerksamkeit, bitte!" ("Attention, please!") One of my preachers delivered an entire sermon walking up and down the aisles dragging a long coil behind him. He went up to the alcove, where he preached with his back to most of the congregation, as the Lutheran preachers in Evanston had, they who sang and prayed with their backs to the audience. This man also encouraged comments from the congregation by asking questions. One day he got a ridiculous answer and stopped the practice. My most memorable experience in church was watching President Schultze suddenly suffer a stroke while reading a Bible passage before he was to preach that morning; after he was helped from the platform, Rev. John Weidenaar delivered an excellent and moving extemporaneous sermon.

I have given many speeches over the years—after breakfast, after lunch, and after dinner, to crowds ranging from a small group in a Sunday school room to several thousand in a large auditorium. The easiest speeches to prepare and deliver were those with a specific topic for a specific audience; the most difficult were those given in response to "speak on whatever you wish." In the latter case, one knows he will face a heterogeneous audience to whom the talk may be inappropriate. But I enjoyed all of these talks. There is always the curiosity about the audience and the exhilaration of a responsive one, the unpredictability of the introduction, and the ruthless inappropriateness of some questions, (some of which are little speeches of dissent), if questions are part of the program.

Mark Twain once said—quite untruthfully—that the only reason he wrote was to make money. He made a lot of it. I, on the other hand, have never had to worry about making such a claim. In terms of preparation, travel, and giving the speech, I never made much. In fact, on some occasions I have just dismissed it as charity. One of the embarrassing questions one is sometimes asked is "How much do we owe you?" It is embarrassing to see a person fumbling for a bill in his billfold. At times one gets nothing. I have found that colleges and other educational and ministerial associations are always fair and often generous. They know what goes into a speech. The real tightwads are the church members who ask a speaker to while away the time they have to wait for their children to erupt from Sunday school.

Introductions have varied from the simple mention of my name to embarrassing flights of eloquence. At a Calvin junior-senior banquet the toastmaster spent a good deal of time involving me in stories about cows, and there was nothing I could do but thank him for revealing the fact that "all that I am and ever hope to be I owe to udders." At a talk in the Grand Rapids Public Library, I was introduced as "having no special interests." There have been times when the chairman said that they really wanted to have Mr. X speak; and sometimes, when my talk was part of a series of talks, the chairman has spent most of my introduction praising my illustrious successors. If the crowd is small, the chairman states that the quality of the audience compensates for its poverty. The best introduction I ever received was given by Rev. Esler Shuart; he should have framed and sent it to me for therapy at blue moments.

It is interesting to watch a face growing grim as one is speaking: it is the intimation of verbal lightning to come. I was once savagely attacked for praising the liberal arts program at Calvin instead of pleading for courses in furniture design, crafts, horticulture, and the practical arts. An interdenominational ministerial group in Iowa asked me to recommend a book that they would study and I would speak on a few weeks later. I made the huge mistake of assuming that *Pragmatism* by William James would be a good introduction to understanding American culture. They did not want to understand American culture; they wanted to refute it. The toughest time I ever had, though, was at a Teachers' Convention in Chicago. I was asked to choose twelve novels all high school students should have read before graduation and to support my choices. I expected some disagreement, but I did not anticipate Armageddon. The list, as a whole, was liked by nobody, and the speech was an exercise in futility.

Twice I was really rooked. The first time involved a trip of 1,600 miles and two speeches before a crowded auditorium. I received a check for $35. Since the trip was in the interest of Calvin College, the college administration generously covered the rest of my expenses. The second time, the trip was about 1,200 miles, and I spoke to the alumni and later to a large, crowded auditorium. It involved two nights at a motel. Much later, when my check came, accompanied by a letter scratched on a scratch pad, my net profit was $7. The time I was given two dollars reminded me of the times my father married young couples in our living room: the groom would give my father two dollars, which he would return with a year's subscription to *The Banner*. I do not specify the times I received nothing.

The speaking engagements did not lack minor adventures. After one heavy downpour, during which I had to work fast to prevent a flooding of our basement, we set out for Fremont. On the way the slippery, sometimes icy, roads were hazardous, and we finally slid into a ditch. Fortunately, there was a garage nearby, and the operator hauled us out. When we arrived at the church, the Calvin alumni were loyally waiting for us—an hour late. I still remember the fine spirit there. I have been thoroughly drenched and received scarcely enough with which to have my suit dry-cleaned. In addition to giving agreed upon speeches, I have been asked to speak extemporaneously, as if I had a little button to press that caused a speech to emerge. I have been lost in Chicago, and once I gave two speeches putting all my weight on one foot because the other was so swollen by infection that I could hardly wear a shoe on it. But my most embarrassing moments came after a talk on good writers, when I was asked for my evaluation of a number of religious potboilers by an audience that evidently thought they were classics. That was an ordeal demanding tact and courage.

Chapter 18

Our Little Magazines, and *The Reformed Journal*

Little magazines have for over a century played an important, and sometimes even a crucial, role in the life of our church. Running from fifteen to thirty-five pages each, written in three languages, read by between 2,500 and 50,000 subscribers, dedicated to molding the hearts and minds of our constituency, and almost always subsidized by a kindly angel or the denomination, these little magazines, together with the pulpit and our educational institutions, have to a marked extent formed our faith and practice. It would take a page to list them all; many of them are unknown today, and some are in a foreign language unintelligible to most readers today. *De Wachter,* after serving our church well for almost a century, has ceased to be published. *The Calvin Forum,* after twenty years of bright achievement and promise, had so few subscribers that the Calvin Board of Trustees extinguished it. *The Banner* is over a century old and still perennially young and flourishing. *The Reformed Journal* and *The Outlook* retain a loyal readership, and *Christian Renewal* is trying to get one. As James Bratt has demonstrated in his impressive book *Dutch Calvinisn in Modern America,* no historian of our cultural and religious development can afford to neglect them. In a sense, they have helped form the minds that we think with. And at their best they have gone beyond being parochial magazines in which we simmer in our own ethnic juices to become vigorous engagements with contemporary culture.

From the beginning, we have been a verbalizing religious/ethnic group, a predictable result of a distinctly articulate and often irascible American subculture that was marked by a penchant for solid thought, verbal skill, theological concern, and unremitting argument. We regularly launch, as Auden put it,

> *Our intellectual mariners*
> *Landing in little magazines*
> *Capturing a trend . . .*

or initiating one. We have taken our faith seriously, as the titles suggest. There was a *Wachter* on the walls of Zion, a *Banner* floating over it, a *Torch and Trumpet* to enlighten and alert us, a *Forum* to challenge us, a *Christian Renewal* to reawaken us to our duties to *Religion and Culture*. We love writing about each other, for each other, and against each other. One rarely picks up one of our periodicals in which someone is not pommeling somebody else.

This literary tradition of small magazine writing reveals only a part of our verbal output. An astonishing number of able book writers have emerged from our small group as well: our novelists have produced over a hundred novels, from pulp to classics, many books of scholarly merit, and admirable poetry. When I attended Calvin, only Professors J. Broene and R. B. Kuiper had written books. Today Calvin professors produce a book almost every other month, from scholarly study to fiction.

Mr. Peter DeKlerk's impressive bibliography of the writings of Calvin Seminary professors runs to over nine hundred pages. Yet I have heard complaints that these professors have not spoken out. A bibliography of the writings of members or former members of the Christian Reformed Church would produce three such volumes. All this from a denomination that after 130 years numbers only about 300,000 persons, many of whom as yet can only color. Whatever the worth of these publications—and some of them are masterpieces—the rank luxuriance of such a verbal flowering is startling. I don't know who reads all these pieces, for I know many people who don't read any. But the authors pop up from every hamlet—

> *Pen in each hand, fire in each eye*
> *They rave, recite, and madden through the land.*

The best known of our magazines is *The Banner*, now 121 years old but alive as never before. Its original name was somewhat presumptuous, *The Banner of Truth*. In 1906, *The Banner* and *De Wachter* became official publications of the Christian Reformed Church. *The Banner* has survived high blood pressure, occasional anemia, savage indignation, almost uninterrupted dispute, and 5,247 "Voices." During all these years it has reflected and reflected upon the life of the church, often with insight, imagination, and significant influence. Under the editorship of Henry Beets, it developed an ecumenical interest, which at later times was restricted, but under the editorship of Andrew Kuyvenhoven has been substantially renewed. Over the years the editorials have ranged from competent to excellent. It has been and is an outstandingly good church paper.

I have known all the editors of *The Banner,* one of whom, Dr. Beets, I have written about in this book (pp. 156-58). When I was a freshman at Calvin, Hero Bratt and I boarded at the home of the mother of Rev. H. J. Kuiper. He would visit her regularly, and we were once invited to the parsonage of the Broadway Christian Reformed Church, which he served at the time. He was in several ways a remarkable man, the pastor of a large city church while simultaneously editing *The Banner* for many years. Personally he was a genial, approachable man, a poised and gracious gentleman. When he spoke editorially, however, he was magisterial and dogmatic, a militant defender of the faith who used his considerable rhetorical talent to deflate all dissidents. If he made an error, and he made some, I never observed that he admitted it. And he could be a little pompous in the use of the editorial "we." At one time he reported on the suffering of his toe, saying, "We are glad to report that our toe is improving." He was continually concerned with Calvin College, which he often upbraided "out of love." He was also at considerable odds with Lester De Koster, whose political views at that time he tried to shoot down with the sizable arsenal at his disposal. I still largely hold to the views that De Koster then championed.

Rev. John Vander Ploeg was the first *Banner* editor to ask me for contributions. He was an honest, courageous, and cordial man who knew how to write for the audience he addressed. His conservatism was always clearly and forcefully expressed. When he retired from *The Banner,* I was a guest at the synodical dinner in his honor, since I had completed twenty-five years of teaching at Calvin. I was seated next to him, and he was very nervous. The satirical *Bananer,* produced in sport by a group of Calvin students, hurt him deeply. He would not deliver a satirical riposte but resorted instead to bitter indignation. His retirement speech was both moving and depressing; it was not pleasant to hear anger and sorrow in a retirement speech from a man who had served the church laudably for many years.

During the five years of Lester De Koster's editorship, I, as a member of the Christian Reformed Periodicals Committee, saw at first hand the prickly, tough job the editor of *The Banner* endures. Gertrude Haan, the amiable and gifted associate editor during these years, once said to me concerning *The Banner*'s reception among the constituents: "We are glad when we hear nothing." This was a reference to the abrasive letters it received for the "Voices" column, many of which were unpublishable either because they were irate blobs of nonsense or excessively mean. De Koster, like his successor, was honest enough to publish the ones that were harsh and even unfair attacks; but both had to draw the line at the silly and the vicious. An editor of our little magazines has the dour task of rejecting articles of which the authors are proud as well as the delight of printing pieces of which the editors are proud. I was on the committee for six years, and it was an education in the art of public relations as well as an opportunity to profit from the diverse company of men and women from various walks of life.

Dr. De Koster was a creative editor and enriched *The Banner* in many ways. Some of his innovations, such as periodic movie reviews by good writers who were not meticulous about limiting their reviews to bland and inoffensive films, sparked a good deal of criticism. Anyone who solicits reviews on films or books for *The Banner* has a problem. One does not wish to publish reviews of sentimental religious slush on the one hand; neither, at least in my case, do I wish to review highly heralded books that portray evil for evil's sake, or portray an abominable lifestyle with literary skill without portraying it as an abomination. I wish to review books that are artistically excellent and contribute to the spiritual life of the readers. Sometimes that may involve reviewing a controversial book in a spiritually helpful way.

Some of De Koster's strongly held convictions, expressed with verbal skill and a keen debater's verve, also created tension. This was especially the case on the matter of women in church office. The Periodicals Committee spent hours once debating whether or not to print a certain article. However, De Koster was in these matters, as in all others, a poised and courteous gentleman and an exceptionally encouraging friend. Whether one agreed with him or not, whether one applauded his wide shifts of opinion or not, one would admire him for his array of talents as debater, writer, collector, and reader of many books and as a distinguished library director at Calvin College for many years.

Rev. Andrew Kuyvenhoven, the present editor, speaks his mind eloquently, has greatly diversified the content of *The Banner*, has spent much time and skill in assembling issues that focus on a single topic, and has thereby guided the magazine to a new peak in circulation.

* * *

Although the Christian Reformed Church had for many years enjoyed a remarkable consensus among its membership, with some dramatic exceptions, this consensus began to unravel in the early 1950s. The Synod of 1951 faced difficult options, and the Synod of 1952 even thornier problems. *De Wachter*, under the editorship of Rev. H. Keegstra, was a moderating influence, but its circulation was relatively small. *The Banner*, under the editorship of H. J. Kuiper, was strongly conservative and highly influential. Since the demise of *The Calvin Forum*, responsible alternatives seemed a dire necessity to the founders of *The Reformed Journal* and its sponsors.

The five founders of *The Reformed Journal* in 1951, now enshrined on its masthead, were Harry Boer, James Daane, George Stob, Henry Stob, and Henry Zylstra, four of whom were theologians. The Dutch have always been noted for theology and mercantilism, and the birth of the *Journal* resulted from the union of theological heavyweights and an unusually gifted and theologically minded businessman, whose profound convictions and largesse made the maturation of the *Journal* possible. Over the years writers for the *Journal* have been numerous and from many places; but what they have written—brilliantly, engagingly, mod-

erately, or dully—was made possible by the spiritual and financial support of William B. Eerdmans and his son. It has also been greatly aided
by the unheralded and time-consuming work of the editor, first the late
Calvin Bulthuis, then Marlin VanElderen, and now Jon Pott, whose
literary abilities and editorial acumen have enriched not only the readers
but the writers. All three helped to prevent the magazine from being
inundated by a wave of theological and philosophical élan.

The first issue of the *Journal* clearly stated its objective: to address
the problems and interests of the Christian Reformed Church particularly
and other believers generally. This emphasis has undergone considerable
modification and broadening. The founding editors wished especially to
appeal to the "more thoughtful and responsible members of the church
assembly and to write plainly and understandably." They obviously did
the former. They dedicated themselves to the illumination and perpetua-
tion of the Reformed faith, and they promised forthrightness in expression and opportunity for responsible dissent. As the years have passed,
they have applied their understanding of the Reformed faith to the examination of labor unions, separate political organizations, worldliness, the
nature of the love of God, the character of Scripture, divorce, abortion,
the role of women in the church, reprobation, and many, many other
issues that confront Reformed believers in a complex world. The *Journal*
has also published a sizable number of poems, stories, informal essays,
and book reviews. This list of items merely suggests the contents of the
over 300 issues published since its founding.

I am a long way from being a founder, still further from being a
theologian or philosopher, but I have written for the *Journal* during its
entire existence. It is a good magazine to write for: editorial changes
suggested by the editors have always, in my experience, been an improvement; the writer has a good idea of the audience he writes for; there
may be hostile readers, but they are neither oafs nor philistines. The
readers subscribe because they enjoy the magazine rather than to have a
symbol of piety on a coffee table when church visitors come. The magazine has a fine reputation, and having one's work printed in it is a source
of pride. There have been pieces in the *Journal* that transcended my
understanding, but none without literary competence. May I add that
under the rubric "Review," the *Journal* has for many years reviewed
films and books with artistry and insight. Though few people seem to
think so, writing a review that stimulates interest in a film or book without
leaving the reader with the impression that he has seen the film or read the
book is in many ways as demanding as writing a good article. This is no
apologia pro vita sua; it is a fact.

Fourteen years ago I was invited to serve on the editorial board,
whose meetings were then held at the homes of the members, where the
hospitality was cordial and abundant, the discussions ardent, and the
swirl of tobacco smoke like a growing blue mist. The chairman tried to

adhere to an agenda of articles to be approved, rejected, or sought; an issue or issues devoted to a single topic; and the never-ending discussion of the nature and future of the *Journal*. However, sustained attention to these matters was constantly interrupted by circumlocutory comments, numerous extraneous asides, initiations into the deviousness of church politics, heated homilies, autobiographical addenda, anecdotes, and stories, one of which concerned Mr. Rabbít and his friends. We had heard it before, but were always glad to hear it again. Convictions were strongly held, challenged, and usually unchanged. Some articles augured a storm; but if the rain was worth the lightning, they were courageously accepted. Somehow the business, except for the ever-recurring discussion of the goals of the *Journal,* got finished. Then for a period we met in a seminar room of the philosophy department at Calvin with bag lunches and something called coffee. Since the efficient editorship of Van Elderen and Pott, we have met less frequently and in more elegant surroundings. These editorial meetings have resembled elite bull sessions, and, except for occasional reiterations of well-known convictions, have proved to be both a delight and stimulus to me. I have not often dwelt nostalgically on faculty meetings; but these *Journal* meetings are a precious part of my personal experience.

　　Some "thoughtful and responsible members of the church" did not and do not always appreciate the *Reformed Journal;* they identify "progressive" with "liberal." That has been true since *The Torch and Trumpet* appeared a week after the *Journal* was founded. Whatever the reason for its appearance, this magazine (now named *The Outlook*) had a different outlook. It was and is an honest, forthright magazine, perspicacious in style and intent. Sometimes it reads as if it should be called "lookout," but it has over the years published many worthwhile articles, including some of mine. *The Outlook,* whether one agrees with its thrust or not, serves a useful purpose. We need open discussion magnanimously conducted.

　　Magnanimity is hard to practice; slugging is easier. At times we all react a bit as Matthew Arnold did when he was reproved by a niece for being too dogmatic: "I'm not dogmatic, I'm right." The issues are often discouragingly complex, at least to me, and we would be more magnanimous if we more frequently treated controversial matters with phrases like "it seems to me" or "an alternative conclusion could be. . . ." Paul said, "We see through a glass darkly," and it is just possible that some of us do too.

　　I regard the *Journal* as an admirably written and edited magazine on whose pages a great deal of outstanding talent has been verbalized, at times with moving skill. However, some pieces are not at all "plain and understandable." Plato said, "Mere technical display is a beastly bore," and I have been bored. Ideally, we should write so that "the more responsible and thoughtful members of the church" can understand us. We do not always do so. Perhaps inherently technical subject matter cannot attain such an aim.

Since March 1951, the *Journal* has been altered significantly in visual appearance, the number of issues per year, the number of pages devoted to an issue, the origin of the authors, and the range of readership. In a *Journal* of twenty years ago, all the authors were of Dutch descent, and all had attended or graduated from Calvin College. In the last issue I read, half the authors were not of Dutch descent and had not attended Calvin. In 1951 the vast majority of subscribers belonged to the Christian Reformed Church; now only about half of them do. Twenty years ago we had no rubric called "As We See It." Twenty years ago we published two advertisements; in the last issue there were four (if our readership had increased so dramatically, we would have rejoiced). The notable increase in writers of differing ethnic and religious orientation has enlarged, enlivened, and deepened the quality and vision of the *Journal,* and the increase of non-Christian Reformed readers has broadened its goals and scope.

I look at magazine racks in stores with nostalgia. Some of the best magazines, such as *The Atlantic* and *Harper's,* have greatly changed. *Scribners, The American Mercury, Colliers, The North American Review,* and *The Saturday Evening Post,* which published almost as many classics as commercials, are gone. What now calls itself *The Saturday Evening Post* is a poor postscript. Disraeli once said to a friend who had given him a novel to read, "I will lose no time in reading it." This double-entendre applies especially to "opinion" magazines today. We send more and more young people to college, and they seem to read less and less. Recently I went to the magazine rack in a fine grocery store and found it loaded with booze.

An anonymous writer in *Newsweek* recently wrote: "Little magazines, as Lionel Trilling once said, are invaluable cultural gadflies." The *Reformed Journal* is, in my opinion, a valuable cultural and religious gadfly. It has a distinguished readership, which I only wish were larger. The *Journal* editors and contributors endeavor to emulate William Morris in his wish "to see the vision and not deny it, to care and to admit we care."

Chapter 19

o Exit?

As I reflect on my years at Calvin I appreciate the fact that teachers of literature there have certain advantages not common in many colleges. A teacher generally knows how much the student knows: most of the students are familiar with Reformed doctrine and the Bible. I doubt whether I ever had a student who did not know who Bathsheba was; at Northwestern the professor received no answer to the question of her identity from a large class. Anyone teaching English and American literature knows how much familiarity with the Bible means in understanding writers from Chaucer to O'Connor. The Bible is woven through many writings through reference, allusion, theme, symbol, and myth. And this is true even of non-Christian writers like Hemingway and Steinbeck. Many footnotes are superfluous for Calvin students. Furthermore, the awareness of and belief in Reformed doctrines renders the choice between options much clearer. In my last year at Calvin, I noticed a diminution of such knowledge, largely, I suppose, because of the way it is being taught. Formerly, the Bible courses in the grade schools and high schools were taught historically, book by book; now they are often taught thematically, and the results are obvious.

The classics of English and American literature are not only inherently excellent but often astonishingly contemporary. Chaucer's characters are not extinct: the zeal of the studious clerk, the good shepherd, the parson of a town, the hypocritical and mercenary pardoner, the pious plowman, the shrewd merchant, the acquisitive physician, and even the Wyf of Bathe, who said, "Alas! alas! that evere love was synne!" So one could continue from Hamlet to Flem Snopes. Fate struggles with providence in *Beowulf,* and Hardy's dismal vision of man's destiny is still shared by many. It was an unending pleasure to illuminate memorable thought in undying words, poems in which no word could be bettered. But best of all was the opportunity to observe the mental and spiritual growth of students. Furthermore, one discusses not only great literature but magnetic people. What was life really like in the Brontë parsonage, where genius rampaged in three women, a dour pastor, and an alcoholic son? What a contrast between the immured genius of Emily Dickinson and the worldwide showmanship of Mark Twain! What a contrast between the disciplined genius of Eliot and the verbal heroics of Dos Passos! If one can make a dull affair of all this, one deserves to be in Pope's *Dunciad.*

Two of my favorite poems are Matthew Arnold's "The Scholar Gypsy" and "Thyrsis," with their poignant blend of aspiration and nostalgia. The scholar gypsy had "one aim, one business, one desire": he waited for "the spark from heaven to fall"; he was more than a "half-believer of our casual creeds"; he strove against "the divided aims" of modern life. Calvin and its staff, in its own way, sought "to see life steadily and to see it whole" from a biblical perspective. I am glad to have had a part in that effort.

In a recent conversation, a young man asked me, "What are your plans for the future?" It was a natural question for a young man whose life is in the green leaf to ask; when one's leaf has changed color, one has to learn how to make the most of a "diminished thing."

Although few leaves cling to the trees and only the sturdiest flowers survive, the grass is still dark green. Soon everything will be covered by the beauty and discomfort of snow. The circle of life has been rounded again. Many old, familiar faces have vanished in the storms of life, and the dead lie under the heavy earth. Are they permanently snowbound, imprisoned in the earth? Are we earthborn and earthbound? Is there only silence after we pass through the western gate?

Atheistic naturalism asserts that we live in such a world, as E. A. Robinson said:

> It's nature and it's nothing. It's all nothing.
> It's all a world where bugs and emperors
> Go singularly back to the same dust
> Each in his time.

There is no tomorrow for the dead. Men try to record their existence by cutting into stone, but the cuttings "wear in the rain" and are no more. In the words of Robinson Jeffers:

> Man will be blotted out, the blithe earth die,
> the brave sun die blind, his heart blackening.
> The earth with everything in it will disappear.

Stephen Crane's short story "The Blue Hotel" gives us a spectacular picture of a naturalistic world of existence, death, and oblivion. Three men are struggling through blinding snow to the Blue Hotel, an eerie inn whose shrieking, garish blue is a symbol of the pitiless world. The main character is a paranoid Swede. After some drinking, cheating at cards, and a challenge to fight, the men flounder through the huge drifts to settle the quarrel. The big Swede wins and, half-crazed with victory, returns to the saloon, where he is soon engaged in another fight. His opponent stabs him, and he dies on the floor with his sightless eyes glued to the cash register, which bears the legend "This is the amount of your purchase." Men are equated with lice, "which cling to a whirling, fire-stricken, ice-locked, disease-stricken, lost bulb." Whatever happiness a person may have is transitory and doomed. In such a world one may well applaud Swinburne's words:

> *I thank whatever Gods there be*
> *That no life lives forever,*
> *That dead men rise up never,*
> *That even the weariest river*
> *Winds somewhere safe to sea.*

Some are so bewildered by the mystery of human life that they cease to seek an answer: whatever ultimate principle rules the world, if there be one, is unknowable. Multitudes, however, believe in God. But what God? The god of deism, who made the world but does not tell us what to do in it? The god of pantheism, of whom we are a part? Man makes a god that satisfies the reason, imagination, fears, or hopes. E. A. Robinson said, "We are children in a spiritual kindergarten trying to spell God with the wrong blocks." Through faith I believe that only God himself can spell out his being, and that he does so in the Bible. His beautiful world surrounds us, and his grace sustains us. We can through faith in Jesus look forward to the true country, where no thing is diminished. Though many believe they are on a road that leads to a dismal exit, there is a right road through a narrow gate to that true country.

The giant Despair in Bunyan's *Pilgrim's Progress* had put his prisoners, Christian and Hopeful, into a "dark Dungeon, nasty and stinking to the spirit of these two men." There he beat them fearfully "in such sort that they were not able to help themselves, or to turn them upon the floor." There seemed to be no exit, but Christian remembered the "Key in my bosom called Promise," a key that would free them from Doubting Castle. Because of their faith in the promises of God, the bolts of the castle gave, and they found escape.

This famous episode shows the only exit from modern despair: faith in Christ and his saving sacrifice. We remember with great sorrow and great joy what our Lord did for us. Our Lord was a "man of sorrows," and as the road began to end, the sorrows thickened. The vision of what lay ahead drew sweat like great drops of blood in Gethsemane. In that lonely garden agony thickened; there was no exit for him then. He was derided and reviled at Gabbatha—the innocent one bearing our guilt. The way led to Golgotha and the heart of darkness, where God forsook him. Forsaken, he endured the pangs of hell to provide an exit for us: Gethsemane, Gabbatha, and Golgotha, the unforgettable way stations for our redemption.

Jesus did this for us, the despairing and the lost, the no-good and the naturally God-abandoned. He led us from the bleak desolation of *The Blue Hotel*'s world to the inn of tranquillity. He transferred the grim despair of "no-exit" into "enter ye," lane's end into a never-ending highway. This is the victory of grace abounding, upholding to the uttermost even the broken reed.

Part III

Miniature Biographies

Chapter 20

The Sage of Siouxland

"Pa, what shall I have done and did Before the sexton rings my final bell."

—F. M.

In 1979, Fred Manfred wrote a wonderful piece entitled "Ninety Is Enough: A Portrait of My Father." In *Green Earth* (1979) he gave us a touchingly tender portrait of his remarkable and saintly mother, who in her younger years helped preserve my precarious life. She was always a nourisher and preserver, a memorable Christian lady. They both saw much of what Fred had done, and it was impressive.

I first met "Feik," as we then called him, in the northwest corner room of the old Calvin dormitory, hardly a poet's corner, adjoined as it was by a bathroom, where one constantly heard toilets flushing, and the north entrance, whose stairs resounded with voices and trampling feet from dawn till late at night. He was a long way from the quiet of the prairie; but his room faced west, and his western voice was heard in the college publications *Chimes* and *Prism* for four years in twenty-five contributions. As an associate editor of *Chimes,* I was there to hear and talk about his poems. Impressed as everyone was by his commanding presence, I was intrigued and stirred by his devotion to words, his compelling urge to write well, and his unusual devotion to great literature— extraordinary in a freshman. His captivating personal charm enhanced our discussion.

I shall never forget that tall young man standing up to read his poems and swaying in consonance with the roll and rhythm of his verses. I do not remember the poems he read, but I was impressed by his acute observation of details and the thoughts they engendered. He already saw

The eye of a robin at dawn
Waiting for a worm in the garden.

He was a see-er who became a seer. In *The Primitive,* that curious conflation of realism, fantasy, and myth, there is a sour note of disenchantment with the lack of student and faculty recognition of Thurs's (Feik's?) abilities, something I never really detected and certainly never shared. I thought he was a celebrity, not a nonentity.

All fiction is to some extent autobiographical. Manfred's *The Wind Blows Free* is almost wholly autobiography. And though *The Buckskin Series* is the most objective of his works, one finds Manfred in them too. The careful reader must avoid the pitfall of identifying Manfred with the words and actions of his characters. Some of the novels are raw, violent, and spotted with profanity; but these elements are not consonant with or reflective of Manfred's character. He explicitly says that he is "a very fine recorder of what people say and do." That is true, and in his recording he has sometimes offended Christian readers; but their identification of such materials with Manfred as a person is unfair. I have spent many hours in his company: he has visited with us and dined with us, and he has attended church with us. He is a most courteous gentleman whose company has enriched us and has never offended the Christian sanctions of our home.

Except for the trip to Iowa with Henry Zylstra and him in 1933, which I have described above (chapter 7), I did not see Manfred again for many years after college. For him these were years of wandering and working various jobs, and ending up in a sanatorium with tuberculosis. He then made the courageous decision to become a writer. After a number of successful books, he paid a return visit to Calvin College. Because of various hostile reactions to *The Primitive,* some of us were nervous about his reception. But it turned out to be triumphal: he spoke to a densely crowded audience in the chapel, and he was superbly "lionized," with students following him around as if he were the Pied Piper. He fraternized freely with groups of students, suffering or enjoying repeated interviews. During that visit and subsequent visits he always graciously talked to one of my classes. He would come partly to answer questions, but a question would prompt an answer that would trigger an anecdote that would produce a theory that would turn into an exhortation. What we got was Manfred talking, and that was something special—a mélange of story, advice, reminiscence, and humor. He gave much time to students, autographed books as if he were on salary, and presented formal lectures. The campus seemed a little empty after each leaving, as though an authentic mountain man had left us.

My wife and I visited him several times at Blue Mound, his home on the prairie near Luverne, Minnesota. On the first visit, as we entered a gate surrounded by signs saying "Private" and "Keep Out," a huge dog came to greet us, barking ferociously. My wife hollered, "Feik, get that big dog out of here." Fred emerged from the garage and called his protector in. We sat in a large room facing a huge window, and Fred said, "I still see the buffalo there." That is one of his great gifts: seeing the past through a creative imagination that has authentically re-created the world of the Sioux when white men were only a rumor.

My wife had brought cookies, and Fred furnished the coffee. We spent an unforgettable afternoon reminiscing and discussing works in progress and artistic ideals. As we left the house to see his workshop and sanctuary, he gave us some sage, which *he* said made wonderful tea. The cabin where dreams were turned into fiction was tightly constructed to weather the intense cold, icy winds, and snow of Minnesota, and it was surrounded by the vast vistas of Siouxland. There was always something about Manfred's eyes that suggested exposure to distance, and his western novels move in great spaces.

At home Fred was encased in books—old favorites like Chaucer, Shakespeare, the Bible, Plato, Whitman, Faulkner, and others. There were the books of friends, some famous; and the Frisians were there too. There were many word books, reflecting Fred's interest in words that has a philologist's zeal. He sought the exact word, and when—especially for onomatopoetic effects—he could not find one, he invented it. There were the first editions of his own books, now quadrupled or more in value; a first edition of *The Arrow of Love* may fetch $200. Here for at least four hours every day he has written and rewritten his books; he wrote *The Golden Bowl* seven times.

This place was, for an urban resident, unusually quiet, disturbed only by the never-ending Iowa winds, the moo of a cow, and the small sounds of the creatures of earth and air. On leaving, I asked him, "Do you have these books insured?" When he said no, I replied, "You must feel a lot safer here than I do on Neland Avenue in Grand Rapids."

The last time I saw Manfred was at his interesting lecture, sponsored by Calvin's English department, "The Mind of the Artist," which turned out to be about Fred's mind. The subject is always fascinating: where do stories come from? where do ideas originate? Some rise from experience, others appear unannounced out of the blue. Stephen Spender says some of his poems originated in a sudden striking phrase that rose in his mind. Historical novels have a substratum of fact, but it is enriched and vitalized by the imagination. Fred has always talked about the "Old Lizard" spilling ideas into the unconscious, which then rose mysteriously to consciousness. He also says, "I've dreamed all the characters in every one of my books." I dream stories too, but in the morning they are sheer mist. The raw materials have to be given form, and Fred has plotted his stories to the last detail. Structure and style are conscious procedures.

Age has treated Fred gently: his verve and vitality seemed undiminished. The day after the lecture, he had a bad fall in the snow, but he emerged unscathed. What is most memorable about Manfred is his literary corpus of twenty-four books, some very long. In that body of work are what I, not as a friend but as an honest critic, would regard as genuine additions to American literature—books that face the future with serenity. They will not perish soon. Among the best are, in my judgment, *Conquering Horse, Lord Grizzly, This is the Year,* and *Green Earth;* they excel in story, style, structure, theme, and vision. His books are now no longer waifs that are viewed as the products of a minor writer by the eastern critical elite. His name is now regularly coupled with those of Walter Van Tilburg Clark, Vardis Fisher, A. B. Guthrie, Jr., and Wallace Stegner as major writers of western fiction. The definitive bibliography of Manfred's works up to 1981, compiled by Rodney J. Mulder and John H. Timmerman, lists 600 entries, including reviews, critical essays, theses, books, and fascinating interviews. If "Pa" were still living, he would know that Fred has done very much very well "before the sexton rings the final bell."

Chapter 21

Remembering Peter De Vries

In May 1931, Peter De Vries, editor of the Calvin College *Chimes* and extraordinary orator, debater, and journalist, closed his academic career at Calvin College, which, whatever its vagaries in academic achievement, indicated an uncommon future. That future was realized in an outpouring of creative fiction unlike anything else in American fiction. It was rewarded in May 1983 by De Vries's election to membership in the American Academy of Arts and Letters in the footsteps of Mark Twain and E. B. White.

Peter De Vries is not forgettable. I met him as a fellow freshman on a bus trip to the beach at Grand Haven, which was sponsored by the college to divert homesickness. His already scintillating wisecracks sparked the bus and the party at the beach. He was entirely worthy of Chicago. I admired him at once and throughout college for his exuberant presence, chic clothes, rare brilliance, verbal daring, and winning personality. I sat in various English classes with him, worked with him on *Chimes,* rooted for him at debates and oratorical contests, and participated with him in various bull sessions. Calvin was then a very small college, and one had to be half-conscious not to know him. He was exceedingly bright, but he chose to reveal it only in carefully selected courses. He was popular but distant; very few knew him well because he had a shell of reserve around his deeper convictions. I never knew him well, although we were friends. I saw him three times after graduation, each an occasion I savored and still do. Although our perspectives on life differ sharply, I have been enriched by some of his books and the memory of his extraordinary presence. One does not often associate with a genius.

This is not the place and I am not the person to count the ways in which De Vries has enriched American literature. The sophisticated intellectual set on the East Coast do that well and frequently. *Time* magazine loves him, and *The New York Times Book Review* celebrates even his failures. Writing in the latter publication, Ben Yagoda claims that De Vries has an unwavering core of 25,000 devotees, including a considerable British audience. I am not a wholehearted devotee. But I would

serenely predict that five of his novels and his volume of short stories will
have a permanent place in American literature. Sometimes I find his
subject matter unsavory and his style overbearing, but at his best
De Vries is a great comic writer who knows that comedy is often the other
side of tragedy and seldom confuses the two.

De Vries's literary gifts are well known: the verbal dazzle, the
memorable characterization, the satirical thrust, the good story, and the
underlying serious criticism of life. I have always relished the unexpectedness, the twist with or without the barb. Nowhere, in my judgment,
has De Vries exhibited the unexpected better than in the beginning of *The
Vale of Laughter,* with its ironic title. The book begins thus:

> Call me, Ishmael, feel absolutely free to call me any hour of
> the day or night at the office or at home.

When one thinks of Ishmael in *Moby Dick* hunting a whale in the trackless
seas, this beginning is hard to beat. The unexpected erupts everywhere, a
constant source of surprise, shock, and pleasure.

It is always encouraging to see a long-held personal conviction
corroborated by a writer of distinction. In his *NYTBR* article, Yagoda
quotes De Vries as saying, "Humor deals with that part of our suffering
which is exempt from tragedy." I have long believed that. Tragedy stifles
humor, and that is why "black humor" (which has nothing to do with
race) has seldom amused me. That is also why a statement by Flannery
O'Connor, a comic writer I admire, has puzzled me. O'Connor says in a
letter to "A":

> In my experience, everything funny I have written is more
> terrible than it is funny, or only funny because it is terrible, or
> only terrible because it is funny.

Flannery O'Connor's grotesques can be very funny; they can also be
terrible, and then I don't find them funny at all. The misfit in *A Good Man
Is Hard to Find* is a terrible man; what he does is bloodcurdling. Certainly, he is not terrible because he is funny. Humor ceases when the
terrible strikes. I think De Vries is entirely right about this, although we
all know that sometimes tragedy and comedy are grotesquely related.

Peter De Vries grew up in a parochial society made for a satirist's
delight—a bustling, paradoxical community crammed with contrast and
opposition. He radiantly exercised the satirist's franchise of exaggeration
and dared to risk the alienation that came with the appreciation. I have
lived in his early world and remained in it for most of my life, and I have
enjoyed the spectacle. It is a fairly tight world with many dimensions,
some of which deserve great praise rather than censure. On the one hand,
I know many stories of outlandish behavior on all its levels: I know and
have known paradoxical people who were memorably gifted and pitiably
vain; savage in-fighting by saints who celebrate agape; overblown and

overpaid pomposities fattening themselves on the idealism of others without practicing it; moneyed men who didn't want their left hand to know what their right hand was doing because it wasn't doing anything; and I have known screwballs and cheats in sacred places.

But that is far less than half of the story. I would need many pages to describe the goodness, unwavering integrity, and unstinted sacrifices I have so often observed. The immigrant community in which I grew up has become, through uncommon persistence, native ability, and God's grace, a community that serves many noble causes in many places and provides leaders in almost every walk of life. What a gift it would be to achieve comic distance with intense appreciation, to re-create the complex texture of this society in the light of the convictions it much more frequently honored than betrayed. Peter De Vries could have done it, if one considers only his great gifts. Stanley Wiersma did it well in a restricted locale. But I envy the talent that could have done it, even when it didn't.

Chapter 22

Dutchman from Dachau

When we lived in the Netherlands for ten months in 1963-1964, the physical devastation the Nazis had wrought was largely gone. In Rotterdam, for example, gleaming new buildings replaced the ruins. However, the psychological scars were strikingly apparent. Memories were still hideously vivid, and we hardly had an acquaintance without a searing story of oppression, robbery, and stark brutality. What amazed us at times was the fact that some of the tourist shops sold objects obviously once found in Jewish homes. Germans were tolerated for mercantile reasons; but they were generally disliked, and often hatred seethed beneath the mask of the tradesmen. The Germans were prosperous and flooded the Dutch beaches, often preempting the resorts and crowding the sands. For some reason we were at times mistaken for Germans, and it was amazing to watch the facial expressions change when they heard us speaking English. The Dutch had existed on the edge of famine, precariously surviving in the cold damp of winter at the end of the war, and not a few commented tearfully on their overwhelming joy when the packages of American food dropped from the skies. Their love of Americans, however, was sometimes tempered by the brash ways some rich Americans drove their big cars through narrow streets designed for and crowded with bicycles. But in 1964, the Germans still seemed like invaders rather than tourists.

We observed a vivid instance of hoarded hatred in Waterloo Plein in the heart of the famous Jewish quarter of Amsterdam. During World War II the Germans had ransacked and then demolished the picturesque Joodenmarkt, the unique Jewish flea market. It had now been rebuilt and restocked. In its dense order or confusion—or something of both—it was a bizarre accumulation of an immense variety of objects: books, magazines, kitchen utensils, obsolete models, stepladders, watches, furniture, and a potpourri of other stuff. We saw a balding Jewish salesman sitting on an elegant chair beside a curtained fourposter bed; an enormous woman pounding out jazz on a piano; a man playing an organ, another a violin. We bought a superb manger scene, which the

seller packed in boxes almost too heavy to carry to the bus (when we were
half a block off, he came running and called, "Hier is ook nog een
schaapje!").

Among the objects for sale was a large bust of Hitler, which sat
there glaring at his escaped victims. Before the bust stood an elderly
Hollander chewing a wad of tobacco. When he had accumulated sufficient ammunition, he spat the whole of it on Hitler's face, whence it
trickled down the bust. Neither the seller nor the spectators said a word in
the heavy silence; then the Dutchman adjusted his cap and walked slowly
away. It was not the monument erected in "The City of Widows," where
the Germans had machine-gunned all males over twelve because a Nazi
had been drowned in the canal. But it was memorable, and, as Bacon has
said, "Revenge is a wild justice."

In the Netherlands, birthdays are celebrated with unusual zest. One con-
gratulates not only the honored guest but his relatives. People of moderate means in America have a special meal, gifts, candles, and cake; the
Dutch roll out a cornucopia of delicacies. Our neighbor, a butcher, celebrated his birthday with an overwhelming abundance of food, pastries,
drinks, flowers, and interminable singing of "Lang Zal Hij Leven"
whenever another bottle of Heineken was opened.

A Dutch townhouse living room is small; two large windows en-
closing about thirty square feet of space flanked by a wall and a tiny
kitchen and hall. This living room was crowded and swirling with the
smoke of Dutch cigars. The center of attention was a "huge hill of a
man," sixty-five and jovial, even raucous, whose belt hung low to ac-
commodate his prodigious belly, which in turn had accommodated many
bottles of the Heineken beer he sold. During the evening, according to
our tally, he drank seven bottles of beer, each preceded by an entire circle
of liverwurst sausage; at intervals he would pop in a stinging Genever and
tidbits. He was flushed with gusto and happiness. He led every chant of
"Lang Zal Hij Leven." When the party ended, his daughter was at the
door to drive him home.

The next day my wife said to Mrs. Postma, our neighbor, "That
man must have had a happy life." "No, no," she said, "he had a miser-
able life." She told us that when the Germans came, he refused to
knuckle under. First they put his home under surveillance, and as he
continued to resist, they tore his little baby girl form his arms and threw
her in front of an oncoming tram to be crushed before his eyes. They
slashed another daughter's leg so severely that it left a long, gaping sword
wound that never healed. Finally, in the dead of a winter night they
hauled him out of his home wearing only a suit jacket, and they marched
him all the way to Dachau. He subsisted on scant rations and occasional
snacks sneaked to him by sympathizers. In Dachau he was put in a quarter
that housed dissident Netherlanders; they were utterly downcast and

mistreated, and were fed so little that they often ate grass. But he roused them from their inertia, got them to exercise, made them sing songs and psalms—and live on hope. His ineradicable buoyancy strengthened them until the Americans came. His was the quintessence of the Dutch spirit that has walled in the wild sea and built fields and cities on its once salty floor.

Chapter 23

![A] Humble Saint

Jenny was born in the little village of Yrseke, Zeeland, one of six sisters in a poor family that was barely subsisting on the produce of their tiny field. The future was grim. Marriage in Yrseke usually meant moving to an even poorer home. Thus a door of escape seemed to open when a letter arrived from Kees Van Norden in the United States. Van Norden had been a village nuisance whose departure no one in the village regretted; but maybe he had changed. The letter was alluring: he promised to obtain a position for one of the girls in a New York mansion, where life would be luxurious and the pay sufficient to not only cover the cost of her passage but enable her to procure fare for the other sisters as well. Van Norden's shady reputation dissolved in the sunshine of this opportunity.

The father promised to read the letter after the Sunday morning service, which the daughters attended wearing stiff white caps, immaculately cleaned and stiffened with heavy starch. Lost in speculation, the girls heard nothing of the sermon. After the scanty Sunday dinner, the father read the letter; after some thought, he said that he had determined to select the invited daughter by lot. Not one of the girls really wished to go, and they drew their straws with fear. The lot fell to Jenny, twenty years old, who had hardly seen another town. Tears came to her eyes as she thought of immigrating to a strange land four thousand miles away. The father tried to encourage her with a lavish description of her new life and its opportunities. There was no way out; she had to go, lonely and afraid.

Some weeks later, in early darkness, the family set out for the port of Vlissingen, twenty miles away. They walked every inch of the way. The mother had provided her daughter with twelve hard-boiled eggs to add nourishment to the expected meager fare on an immigrant boat at the lowest prices. As they walked down Pardonstraat to the wharf, they shivered in the icy blasts of sea winds. Grey mist, heavy and sullen, wrapped the harbor in mystery. They could hardly discern the merchant ship Jenny was to board. Their farewells were brief, and Jenny embarked, a badly frightened girl without a friend on board, into an unknown future with only faith and the dubious integrity of Van Norden to sustain her for weeks of travel on a slow and pitching boat.

Finally, the ship moved into the calmer waters near the coast of America, and she saw the wharves of New York. Her wonder at the bustle around her changed to fright when the immigration officer told her that she would not be permitted to disembark without a sponsor, for she had no money. How could she embarrass her family by being shipped back at a dreadful cost? They and their friends had raised every guilder they could to pay her fare. Apprehension turned into terror.

But the immigration officer approached her again and said, "There is a man standing on the dock who claims you are to be his wife." That was a lie, and Kees Van Norden had grossly tricked her and her family. She hardly remembered what Kees looked like. But there he stood on the dock, a slightly bent man, seedily and loosely dressed, a silly grin revealing his buck teeth, smirking at his successful trick. She was married to him on the deck of the ship, a pious Christian girl forced to marry a man who had the reputation of a scoundrel, a ghoulish, repulsive figure. What else could she have done so many years ago in such a web of inescapable intrigue?

Instead of serving at damask-covered tables, Jenny had to board the train with Kees for Grand Rapids, where she lived all her life in a tiny house in northwest Grand Rapids. Her husband, a cruel oaf, fathered three children in four years. After the third child, she suffered from severe depression and spent weeks in a mental hospital. She could hardly stand this man who slouched along with his silly grimace, his crude behavior, and his total lack of affection. But she remained a faithful wife and became well known as an astounding Christian lady. Out of her poverty she squeezed pennies to give to those even poorer than she—a meal, a blanket, friendship. Though her husband disdained the church and never attended a service in his married life, she took her children to church until they too rebelled. "The Lord loveth those whom he chasteneth" could well have been her epitaph.

Her three children were a shattering disappointment. When one of her sons was sent to the Michigan penitentiary at Jackson for a second armed robbery, her minister persuaded her to accompany him to the judge to plead for leniency. But she said to the judge: "He has had several chances already; if this is necessary to make him realize the error of his ways, let him stay in jail." One time she was giving a party to support a missionary. The refreshments were humble enough—coffee and cookies. The other son came in and shouted, "Huh, ya give all the good grub to everybody else; ya don't give us nothin' to eat." It was an odious untruth. This son also ended up in jail. The daughter, though better than the sons, was a hypercritical snob who ridiculed her mother for taking in washing after Kees died and she never helped her. She turned out to be a nonentity who drifted into obscurity.

My wife and I knew Jenny Van Norden for years. She was one of God's jewels polished by affliction into a rare, self-sacrificing sweetness. She would spend what little she had to help the afflicted, and I never saw her without a smile. When God gathers his jewels, she will be there.

Chapter 24

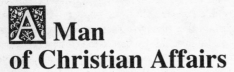Man of Christian Affairs

Dr. Henry Beets deserves a full-fledged biography. Fascinating in manner and personality, he was an eminent churchman; eloquent preacher; editor of *The Banner* from 1904 to 1929 (while serving large city churches); author of forty books and pamphlets, including the still readable and valuable *The Christian Reformed Church in North America* and the perspicacious *Compendium Explained;* a primary energizer of the missionary spirit in the Christian Reformed Church; a suave and canny mixer—in short, a man of many talents that he employed with extraordinary success and vigor. He was, in addition, as Herbert J. Brinks has effectively pointed out in *The Banner* (July 7, 1978), an admirable conciliator of the two dominant theological strains in his church. In his day he was the most widely known member of our church.

Short in stature, round-faced with a wisp of a mustache and a gravelly voice that always struggled with the pronunciation of the English *th,* he had a memorable presence. He was my father's best man and best friend, and he frequently honored our home with his presence, where he treated a little boy as if he were somebody. He could converse with a tramp, fellow passengers on a bus or train, a governor or a senator with ease and poise. He glided into the company of the great with finesse and talked effortlessly to the humble and obscure. He was a social infiltrator par excellence: when Charles Lindbergh came to Grand Rapids after his solo flight across the Atlantic, Beets was in the Cadillac with him. And wherever he went he carried the name of Jesus with him; he was always a missionary.

He applied his unique fusion of gifts in the church at home and in the organizing of mission churches abroad. He served Calvin College and Seminary so well that they gave his name to a building; but he also sympathized with and defended the aspirations of the German element in our church against bitter opposition. During World War I he vigorously defended certain Calvin professors when the local press accused them of pro-German sympathies. I can still see him in the blazing Iowa sunlight addressing a large crowd at the laying of the cornerstone of the new dormitory in Grundy Center. On the seventy-fifth anniversary of our church he gave a memorable speech to the "sons and daughters of Luther and Calvin." He was a nonmilitant editor of *The Banner* who sought to unify the church. While seeking other quarry in old *Banners*, I came upon a perceptive article he wrote on Benjamin Franklin's influence on American culture. He was an able preacher, a three-point man; and his own dramatic conversion sparked an emphasis in his preaching as to conversion's meaning—not once for all but from day to day. Though awareness of his contributions has greatly diminished in the church today, Beets left a permanent stamp on the Christian Reformed Church.

Neither Henry Beets nor my father had their roots in the Christian Reformed Church. My father was for the first twenty-two years of his life a member of the German Reformed Church. Beets grew up to about the same age as a lukewarm member of the Dutch Reformed Church; he became acquainted with the Christian Reformed Church in Luctor, Kansas. They were classmates for six years in the Theological School of the Christian Reformed Church, where both were profoundly influenced by the teaching of Dr. Geerhardus Vos. They came into our church out of strong conviction. They were both staunch supporters of Christian education as a hedge against worldliness and an instrument of a Calvinistic appraisal of learning.

Dr. Beets's physical appearance, his memorable voice, his efforts to conquer the English sounds, his buoyancy, his unflappable poise, and his interest in people and love of the limelight were of great interest to me. On one occasion he was hardly in our house in Paterson before he was calling Senator Arthur Vanden Berg to ask that he open Congress with prayer. And he did. On another visit he took me on the bus to the main library in Paterson to acquire a library card. He then selected three volumes of Scott's novels for me. Now Scott is very good when he gets his story cranked up; but it takes a long time, and at eleven I was not ready for *Ivanhoe*. He gave his nephew, Dr. William Vander Ploeg, a book with some raw passages in it. But he said to him, "Eat it like you would a fish; eat the meat and leave the bones." He lived for years directly across from Grand Rapids Christian High, and I often saw him thumb a ride downtown to the Y.M.C.A. to swim. As an example of his flexibility and poise, he once stumbled onto a bus and landed in a sitting position on the floor; looking up at the bus driver's name, he asked, "Are you a Westside boy too?"

Dr. Beets was a family friend before I knew him. It was to him that my father turned for advice about Grundy Seminary. And he was also shrewd about money. He told my father once: "I don't invest in Christian institutions; I invest in General Motors and give to Christian institutions." He attended our wedding and spoke at the reception. After the wedding, he and his wife came to our apartment to decide upon an appropriate gift; and later they gave us one.

Dr. Beets was a great solace to our family in times of trouble. When my mother died, he spoke at the funeral—as he did some years later, when father died. Beets was a Hollander, but he understood Ostfrisians; he understood a disciplined mind that was softened and illuminated by a mystical strain. His remarks revealed a sensitive perception of his friend, who gloried in the cross yet worried about his sins. He was in tune with a man who relished dogma and doctrine but was also inspired by the words of the hymn: "He lifted me, from the depths of sin and shame, He lifted me." Beets spoke freely to friends and strangers about the only One who can do so. He was a bright and shining light, and we were privileged to rejoice in him.

Chapter 25

Diamond in the Rough

Dr. Peter Hoekstra, chairman of the discipline committee when I began teaching at Calvin, used to say that dormitories were a necessary evil. He also thought that a wayward student was an unnecessary evil. One morning I came to class to find the doorknobs removed from all the classroom doors. One had to open and shut the door by maneuvering one's finger into the lonely empty space. When the class met again, the perpetrators had been discovered, and one of them was in my class. We were studying a poem by Whitman, and I asked this young man to read a passage that contained the appropriate line "Unhinge the hinges, unlock the doors." Such a halfhearted reproof did not satisfy Dr. Hoekstra, who wanted him suspended. The boy was very bright, and though he seemed to think that knowledge came by osmosis, he had unusual potential. I asked Dr. Hoekstra to allow him to room with us and to remove the suspension if he did; he agreed provided the student were under strict discipline.

He arrived early on New Year's morning, and the "stag had drunk his fill." For some time we heard the results in the bathroom. Later that morning, he came downstairs and said to my wife, "I guess you'll want me to move now." My wife said, "No, I will make you breakfast, and in the future you will never do that again." He didn't. When he was leaving for the church service, he had only a suit on in the bitter chill of January. Fortunately, I had an extra overcoat, which he wore for the rest of the winter. His entire wardrobe could have been squeezed into a briefcase. But somehow he managed to pay for his room at our home and board at the dormitory. Although it was 1948, the effects of the Depression were still with us.

His mother had died some years before and had been replaced by a stepmother he found unsatisfactory. At fifteen he enlisted in the marines, and was promptly ejected when they discovered his age. He was a young man in need of sympathy and attention; and he was not eager to hide his candle under a bushel. At Calvin he suddenly developed an illusory brain tumor and visited several of his professors for advice. The sympathetic attention he received dissolved the psychosomatic tumor. When he roomed with us, he expressed profound admiration for Prof. Jellema and his teaching, and he decided to be a philosopher. He had imagination and creativity, but I saw in him no pronounced gift for abstract thought. There was a grandeur for him in being a philosopher king, in being one of the arbiters of human thought. His gifts, however, were clearly in concrete, imaginative thinking and language. So I said to him: "Do this before you make up your mind. Read the first fifty pages of Kant's *Critique of Pure Reason;* if you read it with unappeasable delight, you are a philosopher." I never heard the results of the experiment or if he made it, but he did not major in philosophy.

After graduation he enlisted in the navy as a cadet. One warm summer day some years later, he flew to Grand Rapids in a small navy plane and offered our two small children a ride over the city. Lucarol and Tim were dancing with anticipation, and we reluctantly consented to the ride and watched the little plane become a dot in the air and fade out of sight. We were unabashedly thrilled to see the dot reappear and the plane bob upon the runway. Some time later, he had to fly an admiral from Florida to Las Vegas, at government expense, for a weekend of nonmilitary maneuvers. During one of these trips, he flew into Grand Rapids in his huge jaunty plane, a superb machine whose wings lowered when at rest and rose into place when the plane took off—almost straight into the air like a rocket. He received permission to "buzz" the airport, and he took a taxi to our home to collect as many little spectators as he could. We jammed our car with children to watch the flight. It was a solo flight. The plane was out of sight in a few minutes, and a little later it roared low over the airfield at 800 miles an hour and vanished on the way to Las Vegas and the relaxing admiral, whose every flight cost the government 1,600 gallons of gasoline.

Robert Van Kluyve, about to be commissioned lieutenant commander in the U.S. Navy, was engaged to a pretty, petite, and brilliant girl, whose slight size was dwarfed by her swashbuckling swain, but not her intelligence. We were happy to be invited to their wedding on June 6, 1952, which the navy postdated to June 25, since he was not supposed to be married before being commissioned. As the hour of the wedding approached, and the wedding guests were mostly seated, Libby was waiting in her bridal array, but there was no Bob. My wife said to her, "Don't worry, Bob will be on time." He was. He had driven all night from Florida, the gas pedal to the floorboard, had bathed in a gravel pit in Grandville, and he came in glittering regalia.

When released from the navy, Bob enrolled in Johns Hopkins University and became a medievalist. He wrote his thesis on *The Archana Deorum* of Thomas Walsingham (a far cry from Kant's *Critique*), and it was later published by Duke University, where he had joined the English faculty and become associate professor and chairman of the honors program. In 1969 he joined the faculty of the University of the District of Columbia, the first land grant college in the country.

Although he has continued to teach, Bob diversified his career by expanding a hobby into a triumph: the fashioning of exquisite pottery. He began this work in 1967 in North Carolina and finally set up a working studio in 1969. In 1975 he set up a studio "The Swinging Bridge," in Criglersville, Virginia. His pottery, of which we are the proud owners of five plates featuring Chaucerian characters, have been on exhibition in Baltimore and Washington, D.C.

While deciphering abbreviated Latin manuscripts as a graduate student, he became interested in the art of calligraphy. Evidences of his growing mastery of this art were put on exhibit at Duke University and in a one-man exhibition at the Anne Hathaway Gallery in the Folger Shakespeare Library in Washington. Expanding his interests in 1983, he worked for Amtrak in its restoration of the Baltimore railway station and developed a glaze to match the original Rookword tiles, many of which needed replacement. He is constantly experimenting in pottery, and he is now engaged in sculpting original pot handles; at present most are lizards, but he projects grander beasts to come.

When Bob and Libby visited us a few years ago, she had become so severely crippled by arthritis that he had to carry her into our home and had to cut her steak for her. However, despite her bent fingers, she has created delicate and intricate stoneware sculpture, which has also been on exhibition at the Folger's Anne Hathaway Gallery. To make such figures with strong hands is admirable; to make them with crippled hands is a remarkable example of endurance and skill.

Libby and Bob Van Kluyve have unlocked many doors since we first knew them. One day, after Bob had left and my wife was engaged in a bit of housecleaning, she noticed the following words on a slat of the bed he had slept in in college: "150 wonderful days." We are grateful for that tribute and the opportunity to have known and loved such extraordinary students.

Chapter 26

Four Majors

Robert Walter had lived only a few blocks from us for years before I met him. He went to Central High School in Paterson, while I went to Eastern Academy; he belonged to the Madison Avenue Christian Reformed Church, with which our church had strained relations for a time because its pastor was stealing our sheep. Between Fifth and Sixth Avenues there were large lots on which boys played baseball. It is hard to believe today how many such empty lots there were in Paterson at that time, where taped baseballs were being hit by taped bats. Walter was a catcher and a good one; in fact, he prided himself on his catching. One of the boys said to him, "Have you ever caught for that kid from Fourth Avenue?" They arranged that he did, and that was how we met sixty years ago. I can't throw much of anything with that arm now, and I doubt whether he can catch much of anything either.

Baseball brought us together often in the twenties. Bob was manager of some of the teams I played on. The Parkways, composed of fifteen- to eighteen-year-old boys, was a crack junior team that included the amazing Tony Presto, who caught fastballs, drops, and curves without a mask, was a good batter and a gutsy, unforgettable guy.

I had already known Bob's future wife, Ada Kuiken, for some years; the classroom had brought us together. There were so many Kuikens in our church that when one of them died, the Riverside Christian School was closed on the afternoon of the funeral. She excelled in mathematics, and I was pretty good in Latin, as Mr. Kooistra, our Latin teacher, once said between tapping his teeth with his finger. We often supported each other. Bob and Ada were married in 1930 by my father. (They have one son, Robert, who is now the pastor of the Milwood Christian Reformed Church in Kalamazoo.)

Robert Walter began his first career as a construction engineer on the Delaware, Lackawanna and Western Railroad, a first-rate line that operated the fabled "Phoebe Snow" from Hoboken to Buffalo on a meticulously maintained roadbed through scenic landscapes. After that, he worked on constructing a new line for the Erie Railroad—which doubtless needed additional repair, since it was never in a class with the D.L.W.—in western Pennsylvania and Ohio. He later worked for the Ellen Construction Company building highways and constructing the Clark Valley Dam in Harrisburg in 1937. All of these employments involved accuracy and heavy labor, especially in the case of the Clark Valley Dam, where the work consumed fourteen to fifteen hours a day. In these new environments he met both wildlife and wild people, for example, an extremely well-to-do family who dressed like tramps out of conviction.

His years as an engineer prepared him thoroughly for his second career. As a sergeant in the National Guard, he was called up to active duty in 1940, and, before being sent to the South Pacific, worked for some time as captain in the Corps of Engineers in Washington. His tour of duty in the South Pacific, with its exotic waters, new landscapes, sights, and perils, can be merely sketched rather than detailed. There was the destruction at Hawaii, the Aleutian Islands, the Marshall Islands, and Okinawa, involving both the zest of novelty and an invitation to Japanese assault from the water and the air. The combat engineers were involved in assault waves and were later employed in furnishing the means of transportation—airfields and roads. After the Japanese surrender, Bob served as an engineer in an American-Japanese construction company. During his army career he shook hands with both Eisenhower and MacArthur. A major at the end of the war, he was an instructor for sixteen years in the reserves, from which he retired in 1968.

During the war Bob was defense counsel in two trials for attempted murder, and this legal experience whetted his appetite for a third major career, which he began in 1946. First he was a title searcher in a law office, and then he became an attorney. While working as a title searcher, he entered law school and finished the three-year curriculum in two years by attending evening school after working full days. He passed the New Jersey state bar examination in 1948 and later became senior partner in the law firm of Jeffer, Walter and Tierney, which specialized in real estate and wills.

A lawyer's work often reveals the quirks, selfishness, and even perversity of human beings. After the death of one man, who lived in a ramshackle house illuminated by twenty-watt light bulbs, the firm found over $100,000 in gold pieces hidden underneath beams and stored in cans and cigar boxes that were secreted in unlikely places. In the home of an apparently poverty-stricken woman they found $20,000 in small bills hidden in the oven. Another old lady, who said she could not afford a survivors' home, left $800,000. One old man who made out his own will left certificates worth $50 to each relative who attended his funeral. The firm was, of course, intimately involved in probate law, which some wag has described as "that branch of the law whereby the estate of the deceased is equitably divided amongst the probate attorneys."

During most of these years Bob Walter was pursuing a fourth major career—well-doing. Someone has said, "If you want things done, ask a busy person to do them." Walter was a man of uncommon industry, endurance, and helpfulness. He was both deacon and elder almost continuously in the Madison Avenue Christian Reformed Church; he was on the Eastern Christian High School Board for twenty-five years, and, when the school moved to Oakwood, was heavily involved in raising the necessary funds for that institution, which is a ringing testimony to Christian commitment; he was on the Board of the Holland Home for twenty years; and he was appointed vice consul to the Netherlands for northern New Jersey in 1963, an appointment signed by President John F. Kennedy and Queen Juliana. To all these activities and many others he brought a keen mind that despised fluff, sought out the central issue, and argued cogently for proper implementation. All this was a great deal to do for no pay; in fact, it constituted a fourth career—in service.

In all these activities Bob was heartily supported and abetted by his wife, Ada, a feisty, gifted, and no-nonsense woman. I have known her for years, and if she feared anyone, I don't know who it was. She taught in the Christian school for many years, and I have no doubt that her pupils learned what they had to and much more. Together they have made a memorable contribution to our country, our church, and its institutions, and they leave a legacy of unrestricted well-doing that we should not forget.

Chapter 27

The Cookie Always Crumbles

In the little Iowa towns of my youth I never saw a black person. Paterson, in the years I lived there, had few blacks. As a student at Calvin, I knew a black man by the name of George Washington, but only slightly. The graduate courses I attended at Michigan and Northwestern had no blacks. Over my many years of teaching at Calvin, I had only two black students: Mr. Rambeau, half-French, whom I distinctly remember for his magnificent reading of Shelley's poem "The Cloud," in which he rendered almost perfectly the delicate, airy sounds and rhythms; and Mrs. Hubbard, a charming lady, the wife of Rev. Hubbard, who served a church on Franklin Street.

This was hardly adequate preparation for the next-door arrival of Alice—with her four children, effervescent poodle, and the tumult, tears, and laughter that characterized the family. Our elderly white neighbor across the street had said a few years before, with poignant apprehension, "The Ethiopians are coming." Ironically, he sold his house to a black family who maintained it almost as meticulously as he had. Six years later, when we moved to a more manageable house, the block was integrated and had been enriched by new experiences in human nature, human courage, and adaptability. Those six years revealed an America we had known but superficially—through rumor and the media.

What did it mean to live next door to Alice? It was an experience of two different worlds separated by a fence. On the other side the sense of time was different: there was room for lounging, laughter, and perpetual procrastination. There was less planning, partly because there was so little to plan with. Churches were unentered buildings, except on Easter, when the little children were arrayed in glory in clothes from K-Mart, which were returned the next week. There was sometimes little or no food, and we had to leave bread, milk, and bananas at the door. Things wore out, but repairmen charge $25 to look at them. If my garage roof leaks, I hurry for shingles; but Gene, one temporary husband who was contemplating the leaks in his roof, said: "I don't worry about it. I never seen the rain come down straight. It always come down on a slant."

Ordinary conversations reached the volume one attains only in trying to sing "The Star-Spangled Banner." One day the next-door radio on the porch was pouring out deafening soul rock,; my wife put our radio on the porch and turned up the volume of a radio station that played hymns. Fortunately, it was playing "There Is Power in the Blood" at the time; they turned theirs off.

When Kaylisa Faylynne was about due, I found myself hurtling down Eastern Avenue before dawn and later being told by the policeman at the parking lot at Butterworth Hospital, which was almost empty, to hurry along. When the children came over for breakfast, Anne Marie said, "My mama was crying this morning because none of our people would get out of bed to help her." Later Anne Marie borrowed soap to clean the house and do the laundry. For my wife, it has meant mending, making dresses, and ministering to a forehead bloodied by a drinking glass hurled at a family party. On the other hand, it has meant that Alice, black, poor, and an A.D.C. mother, has given us gifts whenever she could, including an unneeded hot-water bottle, and, once, four purses Gene had apparently appropriated in a department store.

Some years ago, a little after ejecting D. B., Jr., the father of her last child, onto the snowy driveway with appropriate rhetoric and all his belongings, Alice, always interested in and interesting to men, welcomed Gene into the family. Since he had a job and was kind to the children, we urged them to marry. For their honeymoon they went to a Holiday Inn, after packing the children off to Grandma's. At four in the morning Alice came home, and my wife said, "The honeymoon is over already." But Alice had only returned to put a turkey in the oven; she went back to relish to the full the splendors of the motel. Characteristically, they had spent far too much on wedding rings, and for months we got calls from Fox's Jewelry asking us to remind them of their debt. Gene, who had a talent for working in wood, could have supported the family; but he also had a great talent for inertia. Neither one worked, and it was somewhat like children playing at being a family.

Trouble was soon at every door, but instead of meeting it through responsible work, they decided to move to the west side of Chicago. As I looked at the U-Haul loaded with the furniture, the children, and the poodle setting out on this dubious odyssey, I could foresee only bleak disaster. It came within six weeks. Alice phoned me, begging for money to return to Grand Rapids. Her mother-in-law had tried to sell her furniture, had hit her in the face with a hammer, and had threatened to kill her. Fortunately, at the last moment they had left the children with Alice's mother in Grand Rapids.

Alice came home to a house without heat, light, or water. The furniture was still in Chicago, and the children had to sleep on the floor. It was late October, and even the poodle was cold. Since she had left town, there was no welfare check available. Fortunately, the diaconate and the pastor of a nearby church came to her aid, restoring utilities and contributing food. Gradually the furniture returned, some of it partially hacked to pieces by her mother-in-law. Welfare checks were restored. We thought that Gene would now seek a job; but, except for delivering telephone books for a few weeks in January, nobody worked at much of anything. It was a marvel to us that six people, a poodle, and an automobile could exist in such an effortless way.

Idleness, however, has its own perils, and tensions and tempers mounted, reaching a bizarre climax. Gene had a cousin over from Chicago, and, according to Alice, they spent one afternoon popping pills and smoking pot. When Gene and his friend went out for wine, Alice bolted the door. When Gene came home, we were jolted out of sleep by the crash of glass and the splintering of wood. Alice tried to bar him after he kicked down the door, but he beat her about the head. Woody, the little boy, frantically pounded on our door, shouting, "Call the police! Call the police!" We did, and they arrived in three cruisers. Gene and the cousin went galloping down the street, each with a long-barreled gun, one of which had a telescopic sight. Gene was caught, but the cousin merged into the small crowd, and the police at first handcuffed the wrong man.

The police eventually confiscated the guns but let the men go. That was a big mistake, as I tried to point out to them, since I knew Gene would return. He did—about 1 A.M., when we were again awakened by a pitiful screaming. Gene was by this time beating his wife with an immense iron pole used by the city to turn the water off and on at the curb (he had previously stolen it to turn the water back on when the city turned it off). Back to the telephone. More cruisers. Alice in our living room with a bloody towel over her head; three of the petrified children on the floor; and the poodle howling in the night. In the last few hours a man, high on drugs and carrying a formidable, indeed lethal weapon, had smashed a door, hammered his wife twice, and kept the street in an uproar—and he remained free. Irritated beyond measure, I went to the cruiser in pajamas and bare feet and asked the officers, "Would you please tell me what a misdemeanor is?" Later I was told that police officers hesitate to arrest black men involved in domestic violence because their women seldom carry out a complaint. At about two o'clock Alice and her children went to the home of Grandma, that huge, kind lady, only forty-three years old, who once said to me of my wife, "She done got her reward."

By means of the unfathomable adaptation that went on next door, Gene was back in a few days with his pleasant grin, gaudy clothes, and cheerful "How ya doin'?" Alice had taken him back on the condition that he go to work. He obtained work at a first-rate furniture factory and made good money, which he spent largely on himself. Life seemed returning to normalcy, but not for long.

After a night of slamming doors and stormy talk, Alice streaked away with the children in the early morning hours. At seven in the morning, a neighbor's child said that Alice wanted to see me. When I came to the door, she was in a complete daze and had blood on her clothes. The dining room table had a layer of blood on it. I went home and told the Grandma to call the police. When my wife went over with a cup of coffee, she noticed an overwhelming smell of gas. All the jets were on. When Alice had asked me for a cigarette, I had told her that I had only cigars, and I gave her some. Fortunately, she had not lit one of them. When Grandma arrived, dressed like African royalty, she cleaned the table and the house.

The gruesome cause of Alice's attempted suicide need not be clinically described. She had come upon her husband molesting her little daughter. The effect on her was overwhelming: she could not face the horror and disillusionment. This time she pressed charges and honored them: Gene was jailed, and they were later divorced.

*   *   *

Almost ten years ago we moved to a smaller home. Thirty-seven windows, heavy storm windows, ten rooms, and a large basement became difficult to maintain. Furthermore, we were weary of serving as a first-aid station, a fast-food bailout, and a source of telephone calls and supplies ranging from matches to stamps. (Once a relative from Chicago jolted us out of bed at 3 A.M. to fetch Alice to the phone. When I refused, the woman said, "I'll never call you again.") But we were reluctant to leave Alice. At bottom she was a tender-hearted, generous woman fixed in hostile circumstances. One evening, when she knew we were coming home late, she stood in our driveway waiting for us to come safely home. There had been a series of muggings in our neighborhood, and she wasn't going to let it happen to us. We thought she was holding a pistol.

We parted the best of friends. But before we left, I told her as forcefully as I could, "You must leave the dudes alone. They use you and leave you." For a time she did. She had some years of prosperity as a worker at Reynolds' Aluminum; she perked up her house and bought a new car. Then the recession put her out of a job and onto welfare again. The cookie began to crumble. Her friendliness has proved enduring, but so have her troubles. Usually we knew that when Alice called she was in a crisis again; she has the naive idea that we have power to help. In the course of the years, I have written letters to employers, welfare agencies, lawyers, and judges. About three years ago we received a call that Debbie, her second daughter, had been expelled from Ottawa Hills High School because she had drawn a knife on a boy who was threatening her. She was to be expelled just six weeks before graduation. My wife called the principal and told him that Debbie had been carrying the knife for self-defense on her mother's orders. The sentence was mitigated to suspension for six weeks, and she could take her final examinations and graduate.

Early one Sunday morning I was jerked out of bed by a telephone call. It was Debbie, and she said, "My mother stabbed a man and he died!" The circumstance leading up to this newest episode was again her hospitality to a philandering dude. Alice had housed him, but he went out to a boisterous party; at 11 P.M. Alice, in a fury, went to retrieve him. The two of them argued and fought, and, according to Alice, he tried to stab her. Whatever Alice is, she is no patsy. She fought for the knife, which clattered down the stairs, and she retrieved the knife before he did. When he came after her, she stabbed him in the leg, and he stumbled to the floor. Alice panicked. Instead of seeking help for the wounded man, she ran to the car, which held her children, and rushed home. It is characteristic of such a party that no one followed the couple, and the man was not found until he had bled to death. Alice was, of course, discovered as the slayer and jailed.

What help could I give her? I could and did write a letter asserting that Alice would never have stabbed anyone without aggressive attack and enormous provocation. She spent some time in the Kent County Mental Hospital, where my wife and I visited her, and she maintained her innocence with the remarkable resilience that characterized her always. I gave her some money and said, "Go buy yourself some Coke." When everybody started smiling, I realized that the word had different connotations. When the case came to trial, Alice was convicted of unintentional manslaughter and spent six months in jail in Ypsilanti. During that time her son Tom, who had grown up to be a steady, hard-working young man, kept the family intact.

When she returned, she again asked for recommendations for a position. I have never believed in romanticized testimonials, and this task proved to be a challenging assignment in combining integrity with persuasive characterization. I wrote it "To Whom It May Concern," and I hoped it would arouse the concern of someone. Alice never calls to relay good news; she calls to inquire about our well-being and to relate a new dilemma.

The last call came from John (Woody), a most captivating boy when he was little. He had looks, charm, and imagination, and he could have been somebody, but he chose to muddle his life and live by theft instead of work. When he was little, he came to our door one day when he should have been in school. My wife said to him, "Woody, why aren't you in school? You're going to be mayor some day. You hurry up and get there." "Okay," he said and ran off to school. This time he was arrested for armed robbery, and he called me from the Kent County Jail. I asked him whether he had proof that he was elsewhere when the crime was committed, since a witness had testified that he was there. He said, "No," and he complained about his lawyer. I told him it was beyond any lawyer to invent witnesses. He told me he would call to inform me of the results of the trial. He never did, so I presume that he is in prison in

Jackson. He told me not to call his mother, who was "all shook up," and I never did; neither did she mention it when she last called.

I suppose Alice's biography over the last sixteen years is both similar to many others and to a large extent irreparable by human means. The family has been shattered as well as scattered. Anne Marie, her oldest daughter, ran away at fifteen. Our daughter Miriam wrote two poems about her flight and the reaction of her little brother. This is one of them:

Story from the Inside

Woody's eyes, brown on white,
grew like mud stains.
Anne Marie, he whispered,
finger hooked around his ear,
Anne Marie is lost.
Lost.
And she'll get whupped
if she comes home.

When Anne Marie didn't come back
Saturday night
neighbors failed to see the shadow
crying with rain drops
behind the splintered side
of Ferguson's garage.
The black body blurred
by the tongue hanging dark,
crouched close
too cold to care that
the stomach ceased
to growl like a dry mutt's whine,
too empty to grind,
grind.

Eleven years
Anne Marie waits
over old and too tired
no legal slave,
just free labor
bound by blood to
    battered screen
        blistered steps
            gray splotched drapes
                midnight fights.

But the no food meals, no bones, no beans
the cordless phone

the words police
don't understand
slowly lost
Anne Marie
and Woody would never know
where she ran away.

Anne Marie has had two children, one of whom died of crib death. Debbie is in Kalamazoo, John in prison, Tom and Kaylisa Faylynne at home. Alice received a good deal of support—from us, from the Christian Reformed Church, from counselors at Social Services—but her life is still far from secure.

Once, when I showed a little courtesy to a black woman laden with packages trying to emerge from K-Mart, she said—and only a black woman would have said it—"Thank the Lord and thanks to you too." Alice never used these words but expressed the same sentiments. Deep down in her heart remain the residual religious feelings of her youth in Alabama. We pray that the Lord may turn those embers into flame, not only for her present needs but for her eternal salvation and that of her children.

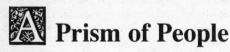 Prism of People

Biographies have become increasingly popular; they rival and sometimes surpass novels in sales. Although the biographer cannot create, he can exercise imagination and art in presenting the character, meaning, and rhythm of a life. Othello, the Moor of Venice, says:

> *Speak of me as I am, nothing extenuate*
> *Nor set down aught in malice.*

Few biographies have achieved this goal. Not until Aubrey's *Lives* in the seventeenth century did the portrayal of sinners rival that of the saints. Aubrey wrote the shortest biography on record: "Abraham Wheelock—a simple man." He also describes a professor who was "pale as the candle he studied by," and tells us about a clergyman who preached for three hours and complained that *he* was tired. Boswell's *Life of Johnson* comes the closest to Othello's request: it portrays one of the greatest of scholars and was written by one of the most curious. Many later biographies have extenuated a great deal and some have set down much in malice.

A good biography flashes a bright light on the oddities of human nature and portrays the failings of genius in little snapshots: Tolstoi standing before a mirror saying, "Well, my dear boy, hurry up. Hurry up. What a handsome boy you are!"; the Borgias, who served with distinction and poisoned with pride; Benvenuto Cellini, the silversmith who plundered a home of two hundred plates to produce a "most perfect liquefaction"; John Calvin, who "only went to Italy that I might have the satisfaction of leaving it." Tolkien, tired of debating in English, turned to Latin and then to Sanskrit, and once gave an impromptu speech in Gothic. When the angelic doctor Thomas Aquinas died, his secretary snipped off a thumb, and his sister the rest of his hand before he was buried. As Daniel Webster lay dying, he said, "Have I said anything unworthy of Daniel Webster?"

Robert Frost is a shining example of a stunning human mix. He was both a great and a popular poet. His popular image as a cracker-barrel philosopher with a gift for rhyme was partly earned and often maligned.

Frost was almost worshiped by some and often detested by others. The wife of a young man who idolized him, when he and Frost came home from a long walk, said, "Well, what did God have to say tonight?" He sparkled on the platform and often sobbed at home. He endured twenty years of obscurity and poverty before *North of Boston* thrust him into the limelight, which he greedily savored for many years. He and his wife had a "lover's quarrel" throughout their long marriage, and when she died, Frost was filled with remorse. He had to bury a little son; and though he tried to save a little daughter by moving "heaven by prayer and earth by money," she also died. His sister went insane and his daughter Irma also spent a large part of her life in an insane asylum. His son Malcolm, whom Frost encumbered and embittered with unwelcome advice, committed suicide. His own violent temper, black moods, bossiness, and self-pity made him play the fool at times. He wrote:

> The saddest thing in life
> Is that the best thing in it should be courage.

Frost did possess courage. Relying on intelligence, courage, and "leaving something to God," he chose "something like a star" and produced many lines lodged in many memories.

The portraits I have rendered in this book are selective and often deal with people who may be called saints. Since I find it difficult "to set down aught in malice," I have largely omitted hypocrites, cheats, exploiters, lovers of selves, bores, the omniscient, the mean-spirited, and the stupid. I have focused on merits rather than demerits; that is one-sided, and I know it.

In one sense, there are no uninteresting people—only uninterested people. Not everybody is wonderful, but everybody is a wonder. From the three-year-old who always asks, "How come?" to the elderly lady who pours salt recklessly on her food because "it is a good preservative," people are fascinating. Even the unrelenting bore can impress one by how good he is at it. One can only wonder what is operating in the mind of a student who, after a lecture on Emily Dickinson's poetry, asks, "What did she die of?" Only a little boy would say, when I brought a pie to his home because his mother was ill, "We *got* pie." It takes a boy-like man to refuse to be considered as deacon because he is "overqualified." One of the brightest persons I knew said, when he was justly accused of stuffing the ballot box, that he did so because he was the best qualified.

* * *

Two months after our marriage, a group of friends organized a literary club that has endured for forty-eight years. At its peak the club had twenty members, but departure and death have diminished our members to eleven. Over the years the club included physicians and teachers, a chemist, an architect, an editor, an artist, and their wives. We began with a list of the hundred best books but ceased when the books became intelligible only to our mathematical wizard. We then read understandable classics and important books by various writers—from Chaucer to Marx's *Das Kapital*. (In the middle of the reading of a paper on *Das Kapital* the cuckoo clock sounded nine times.) And we have reviewed books written by members of the club. For many years we had picnics at the cottages of the affluent members of the club, not an insignificant number. At the beginning some of the papers were inordinately long; but soon they became much shorter, an inconvenience to nappers. After the reading of the paper, we discuss it; and after that we discuss everything. Some of the members have been perennially irenic, and some have had a penchant for dissension; nobody changed anybody's mind. We have not had a great deal of excitement, although one time, when Lake Michigan lapped the fourth step of the stairs leading to the beach, a rather hefty lady slipped into it. We have learned much from books and each other, and we sadly miss the members who have died. But we continue to enjoy good books and good friends as we all face the setting sun.

*   *   *

Some years ago, my wife and I visited an old friend, a lapsed Dutch Calvinist who was celebrating his eighty-fifth birthday with his wife, also eighty-five, a Polish Catholic. According to the health faddists—as well as the U.S. Surgeon General—he should have died long ago because of his inveterate use of tobacco and liquor. As we came in the room, he was watching a spot of sultry soap opera, and his wife was shouting at him in indignation: "Joe, you no wats dat! Dirty! It all dirty! You too old for dat! I tell him no good. Dirty!"

When Joe came to America, he and a friend boarded with my mother-in-law and the three little girls. Though keeping two boarders was an acute inconvenience, it put bread on the table in the days when welfare was nonexistent and life harsh for a widow. Joe remained a friend of the family for life. When I first met him, he was selling Brontë wines. When that company went bankrupt, he supported himself with janitorial work and by marrying a vast Polish woman with legs like tree trunks. Lottie was a kind-hearted, mildly stupid woman who ached all over as long as I knew her. Joe had never got anywhere, but he acted as if he had everything. He was a self-appointed pundit on politics, economics, religion, and morals. You name it, Joe knew it. He was a bright, lively, and interminable talker, and he made preposterous judgments as if they were prophecies. My wife brought him a birthday cake on that eighty-fifth birthday, and Joe said that he fully expected to live to be ninety. But he died in that chair a few months later watching television.

The Reverend Mr. H. V. Hutcherson, a black clergyman, lives a few doors from us. At eighty-five he serves an inner-city congregation, and he told me how happy he was that the bishop had approved him for another year. He is becoming feeble, and as he carries out the trash with bent back and skullcap, talking to himself or singing a hymn in a remarkable voice, one is touched by his waning strength. He is slowing down—but not in his two Cadillacs. Some time ago he was in a wreck with one of them, and he told me, "The other guy just wouldn't get out of my way!" He bought a new Cadillac, and as he sat in the front seat delighting in its appointments, I asked him, "Having a good time, Rev?" He replied, "Yes, we only go this way once. I feel fine on Sunday services, but when they are over I cool off." He uttered the speaker's delight. He formerly led our condominium meetings in prayer, for which he had a gift, extemporaneous and in choice English. He and his attractive wife are an ornament to our community.

Saint Luke tells us about a woman who suffered much from many physicians. Chaucer's Doctor of Medicine was a learned man in his time, skillful in diagnosis, perceptive in the influence of the zodiac, notable in his uncanny knowledge of the right time to apply his potions, indifferent to religion, and a man who "lovede gold in special." But our family has been singularly fortunate in having gifted physicians who were primarily interested in their patients.

Dr. William Vander Ploeg was our family physician until his retirement. When I taught an honors English class in 1934, he was one of the students. He told me later that I had assured the class that no one would get less than a B. I have more sense now, but it was a bright class, and I doubt whether any student deserved less than a B. I did not see him for many years, and then he located his first office a block from our home. He was fortunately immediately available when our little boy ran into the sharp corner of the kitchen counter and I carried him to the office trying to stanch the blood that spurted from his forehead. While we were in the Netherlands, our older daughter became severely ill. He performed a successful operation, and, since we were out of the country and our pastor did not come to visit until her last day at the hospital, he was for a time quite literally serving as her physician, father, and clergyman.

When I was the baseball coach at Christian High, I drank some water from a park fountain that made me violently ill. This illness recurred over many years with dramatic unexpectedness and at the most inconvenient places. It produced high fever, delirium, and a foot so swollen that I could not wear a shoe. Dr. Vander Ploeg discovered the cause of the infection and prescribed medicine that retarded its occurrence and diminished its intensity until it practically disappeared. He was a careful, leisurely doctor who employed psychology as effectively as prescriptions. Informed, unpretentious, but thoroughly knowledgeable, he tranquilized anxiety by his manner and caused cure through insight. Later he performed a long, grueling surgery on our older daughter again and also on our son-in-law. His retirement was a loss to us all.

Doctors' reception rooms differ markedly in atmosphere and tone. I have been to doctor's offices where the receptionist treated me as if I were a draftee, where the whole place reeked of the commercial, where one could not escape the billing department on the way out, and where the service was rendered with impersonal curtness accompanied by lordly objectivity. When my wife and I entered the reception room of Dr. William J. Hanley, we were both delighted by the cheeriness and warmth of the personnel. Marva, Pat, and the others created a relaxed, reassuring atmosphere that mitigated anxiety about prospective surgery for cataracts. My wife and I have been in that office so often over the last decade that someone suggested we move to Muskegon. There was good reason for our being there. Dr. J. Ritsema told me that if I were his father, he would recommend Dr. Hanley for laser treatment. Strangely, both my wife and I had to have lens implants in both eyes, which resulted in remarkable improvement in vision.

We owe a great deal to Dr. Hanley, not only for his great skill but also for his concern and courtesy, which is an authentic expression of personality rather than a professional veneer. He is a man of great personal charm and the willingness to go the extra mile, a man who cares as well as cures. He reminded me instantly of Prof. Faverty of Northwestern University, who directed my dissertation: almost identical in height and build, they looked like they could have been brothers, and they were characterized by the same innate courtesy. We value Dr. Hanley not only as a surgeon who restored our sight when we were on the edge of visual night, but as an uncommon gentleman and friend.

I doubt whether any legacy is more quickly accumulated or more slowly spent than one resulting from an accident. Baseball has bequeathed me four broken fingers, two of which still bulge, six stitches on my upper lip, and a classic black eye. Slippage on a bit of ice when our big dog burst into high gear left an arm with a broken bone in it dangling at my side. Slipping on a soaked carpet plunged me into a water-filled little pit where librarians tell stories to little children, a fall that caused extreme fractures in my shoulder. In both latter cases I owe an immense debt to Dr. Roger Wassink, a son of a valued colleague. He reinserted the dangling arm with meticulous exactitude and set the broken bone. Through uncommon medical expertise he restored the use of my shoulder as far as possible. His notable courtesty, inexhaustible fund of stories, acute insight into human nature, and generosity were therapeutic in themselves. I usually called my wife from the hospital at ten P.M. When she called one evening wondering why I had not called, I told her Dr. Wassink was sitting on my bed chatting with me. His attitude was as distant from that of Chaucer's physician as Chaucer is from us.

When Prof. W. Harry Jellema and his family returned to Calvin after he had taught for fifteen years at Indiana University, we were happy to welcome them back as neighbors. Their two youngest children and our two oldest children were playmates for years. Dr. Jellema was an illustrious man, but his wife had a luster of her own. Like him, Frances was a talented conversationalist. And she was a realist; once I heard her say to her husband, "Now, Harry, tell them something they can understand." She detested snobbery and pretense and was a most kindly lady. On one occasion, when we missed our little son, we finally found him reading stories to her at her sickbed, an example of magnanimous patience on her part.

Although she was a sunny and spirited lady, Frances Jellema lived among the somber shadows of heart disease. She was often ill, and I have seen her husband washing clothes and mending socks. When I came to the door one day, the children were gone to school, the house was cold, and they were both ill. After I finally got the clinkers out and the furnace blazing, I called my wife. Frances was so ill that my wife fanned her to help her breathing. Her husband had a severe case of bronchitis and flu, but I helped him from the couch in his study to be at her bedside. We feared that she was dying. A few days later, my wife saw their little son Jan peering through their bedroom window, and Frances said, "It breaks my heart." She bore her weaknesses nobly, and doubtless her family shared her apprehensions; but we never heard her complain. The words of Emily Dickinson could be applied to her:

> To fight aloud is very brave
> But gallanter I know,
> To fight within the bosom
> The cavalry of woe.

She loved laughter and lived with sorrow. She was a great lady, and life in the family must have been desolate without her.

* * *

The college church my father served in Grundy Center was composed mostly of students, one of whom, William Masselink, taught our catechism class of six or seven, which he motivated through friendliness and occasional ice-cream cones. The Masselink family had moved to town so that their sons could attend the school, and three of them later became prominent ministers in the Christian Reformed Church. They were a kindly family, and William Masselink was one of the kindliest persons I have known. When a tramp came to the manse in Grand Rapids shivering with cold, he went to the closet and gave him an overcoat without noticing that it was the best coat he had. When I came from Paterson to rent a home for my parents, I was a guest for a week at the Masselink home. One of the first things he said to me was, "Now, if you want to have a date, you can use my car." He was our pastor for some years. Sometimes he would wipe tears from his eyes as he preached; this was not out of sentimentalism but profound tenderness. Dr. Masselink had a phenomenal memory. After spending some time at the Free University studying under Dr. Hepp, he preached a series of sermons that struck me as a rerun of the lectures. I was interested in my father's reaction; normally he would have said, "Such material is for the study." But he never said a word. This series of sermons soon ceased, and Masselink returned to the more picturesque and practical.

During those years the followers of Cornelius Van Til championed a militant faith that impaled dissenters. In 1952, Dr. Masselink and Dr. Van Til had a dramatic debate on common and special grace in the old seminary chapel. Masselink may not have been the most profound critic in the phalanx of theological warriors, but he was one of the most courageous. I was prejudiced, I know, but I thought he won the debate; at least, the influence of Van Til waned after the debate.

William Masselink made all the arrangements for my stricken father when mother died, preached a moving sermon, and gave him solace in his loneliness. He also preached at my father's funeral. Later on, when I had a harrowing time trying to prove that I existed in order to get a passport, he was one of several who wrote a letter to the passport office to prove it. My father left over a trunkful of sermons when he died, each written in his beautiful script on specially made booklets—in German, Dutch, and English. What does one do with more than a trunkful of his father's sermons? I was happy when Dr. Masselink asked for them; but after he died his son returned them to me.

Dr. Masselink and his wife were the salt of the earth. His career was her career: she was a pastor too in her effervescent geniality and helpfulness. In my experience he came as close to Chaucer's "persoun of a toun" as I knew:

> But riche he was of hooly thoght and werk. . . .
> This noble ensample to his sheep he yaf,
> That first he wroghte, and afterward he taughte.

* * *

The somber author of Ecclesiastes writes:

> There is no remembrance of men of old,
> And even those who are yet to come
> Will not be remembered
> By those who follow.

In a short time that is true of all but the greatest men and women. For example, I am the only one who remembers my mother's father. It is illusion to believe that we live in the memory of our descendants; we die with their memories. The tiny marks we make on life erode before the letterings on our tombstones do; the wind and the rain beat upon them, and they are gone. In this book I have written about many whom I held in my heart. I have stood beside their open graves when they died at two months, sixteen years, thirty-seven, sixty-one, eighty-two, and ninety-four. Two years ago John De Bie, my friend for over fifty years, died. He was a gifted and beloved teacher, a self-sacrificing servant, immune to jealousy, one of the most unworldly persons I have known. A man of rugged faith and eloquent prayer, he had an ear and a heart for the sick, the sorry, and the suffering. He was a saint with a sense of humor. He is one of many who were good to me and for me, and his name, like those of many others I have mentioned, is written in an infinitely better book than mine.

Index of Persons